# LeeWards
## Complete
## Library of
# Needlecraft

**Times Mirror Books**

New York

# Contributors

**Fuller and Dees**

**PRESIDENT**
James Lueck

**ART DIRECTOR**
George Alexandres

**PRODUCTION DIRECTOR**
William Holmes
George Jenks

**EXECUTIVE EDITOR**
Carter Houck

**PROJECT EDITOR**
Nell McInnish

**EDITORIAL STAFF**
Phyllis Fenn
Carl Richardson
Pat Warner

**LAY-OUT DIRECTOR**
Nancy Crippen
Mary Veitch

**PHOTOGRAPHER**
Myron Miller

**ILLUSTRATORS**
Jacqueline Butler
Marilyn Heard Eubanks
Janice Culbertson
Debbie Benedict
Patrick Gibson
Eleanor Palmer

**CONTRIBUTING AUTHORS**
Jinny Avery
Embroidery, Patchwork, Appliqué
Teacher, Lecturer, Designer

Cecilia Toth
Needlepoint, Rug Making
Needlework Editor for Good Housekeeping Magazine

Sharon Valiant
Macramé
Writer, Teacher, Editor

**CONTRIBUTING EDITOR**
John Bade (Hook Arts)

**CREATIVE STAFF**
Courtney Bede
Kathy Crowe
Martha Ann Crowe
Grace Harding
Joe Ann Helms
Marion Moffat
Sandy Singer

**ACKNOWLEDGEMENTS**
Brunswick Yarn Company
Lily Yarn Company
C.J. Bates & Son

© Fuller & Dees MCMLXXV
Times Mirror Books
380 Madison Avenue, New York, N. Y. 10017
Library of Congress Cataloging in Publication Data
Main entry under title:

A Complete Library of Needlecraft
Includes index.
1. Needlework    2. Fancy work.    3. Textile crafts.
TT705.C75          746          74-32451

Complete Set ISBN 0-87197-085-6
Volume 2 ISBN 0-87197-087-2

# Contents

## Volume 2

A rewarding and expressive kind of stitchery, embroidery can beautifully decorate fabrics by varying basic stitches and using colorful threads and yarns. Embroidery has come a long way from the early disciplined patterns and is now being used in free-form and abstract work to fit contemporary ways of living.

Needlepoint, once referred to as canvas work, is a form of creative needlecraft that has been traced back to Biblical times and is regaining its popularity in America. By applying groups of warp and weft threads to woven fabric, such as linen or canvas, designs can be made for pillows, wall hangings, mantle covers and carpets.

Handmade rugs have been an important part of cultures throughout the world since 2000 B.C. As a craft, rug making produces articles for the home that are both practical and decorative.

A decorative and practical art for centuries, macramé is now more popular than ever. Macramé is easy to learn, and offers limitless possibilities — from the finest of laces to the boldest of wall hangings.

# Introduction

The arts in this volume are in many ways the most free-spirited and imaginative. There are few rules for designing or using any of the four techniques covered; embroidery, needlepoint and bargello, rug making and macramé. There is, however, a basic skill to learn for each art. The variety of stitches and the assortment of materials used is limited only by the imagination. There is a world of material in everyday life from which to choose — nature, hobbies, sports, wildlife, etc.

If you have never tried needle art before, start with one of the less demanding. Taking one technique at the time, work trial samplers to perfect your skill. For instance, very attractive embroidery pieces can be worked with only one or two stitches — the cross stitch is easy enough for a child and the effects are bold and colorful. Only practice can give that smooth feeling of experience in any art form.

After the initial learning and sampler stage, plan a project that is exciting, such as a small rug for a spot that has always seemed dull — a series of embroidered decorations for a jeans suit — a vivid bargello seat for a special chair.

The projects presented in this volume are planned to stimulate the imagination. Some have definite color and stitch schemes, while others have more latitude. Many photographs are presented in full color and full size so that they may be worked with ease. Others will have to be scaled to the proper size. With each project, there is sufficient range for artistic license so that no project must be copied exactly for the total effect to remain the same.

In many of the needlepoint and bargello designs, the large areas of color do not have stitch definitions to prevent confusion. Each square in these projects represents one thread of canvas. The description of the bargello pieces will state the number of threads to be covered by one stitch (every square will still represent one thread). In some smaller designs, it is easier to designate the individual colors with symbols.

There are color keys provided for those projects in which color is especially important to the design or where the designs are suitable for beginners. These may be written out or they may be numbered according to the color chart which follows each chapter. In each section, there are suggestions of ways to estimate the material required for a project. In all cases it is wise to purchase slightly more of each material necessary than is actually required.

# Embroidery

Embroidery is a method of decorating fabric with threads and yarns. As a surface decoration, it gives a wealth of beauty and pleasure in excellent design and color.

The origins of embroidery, one of the oldest of all the arts, are lost in antiquity. Bone needles were found in caves dating to 5000 years before Christ. It is possible that it started in Babylonia and Egypt and then traveled from the East into Europe, reaching its greatest heights in Italy. From there it went to the rest of the world, with each culture developing its own form and discipline. Most of China's embroidery was done in silk; the Japanese used embroidery to embellish printed and painted fabrics; and the Indians incorporated precious metals and jewels into the art.

Throughout the entire sixteenth century, Italy was the undisputed center for embroidery. The Popes collected it, as much of the decoration described in the Bible was reproduced in papal robes and church furnishings. It was heavy with gold and silver thread, and the exquisite work included a diversity of color and form.

From Rome, the popularity of embroidery spread to Paris. It was there that the first guilds were organized. The development of embroidery in England ran almost parallel to that of Italy.

Queen Elizabeth was an accomplished needlewoman who set examples for the rest of the court. Henry VI, the grandson of Elizabeth of York, recorded the first bill of sale for embroidery when he collected twelve samplers done on a Normandy canvas.

After the Reformation, church work began to languish and court embroidery grew in popularity. Patterns, first introduced in the sixteenth century, became more available, refined and graceful in design. Most of the early patterns were for decoration of clothing and costumes such as waistcoats and sleeves.

Long before the arrival of the first settlers, American Indians were doing beautiful embroidery on the whitest and softest of doeskins. White settlers later brought the European patterns and stitches. However, through the years, the form and techniques of embroidery steadily changed in the new country. Old methods and designs were changed to fit a new way of living. Embroidery took on a spontaneity and vibrancy that was unmistakably American.

**Crewel Interpretation of Standard Moon Over The Mountain Quilt Design (first page) planned and created by Judy Avery.**

**Crewel Bedspread Worked On Unbleached Wool (opposite page) from the collection in George Washington's Headquarters, Morristown, New Jersey (a national park site).**

Indian squaws taught the American woman the art of dyeing, using a wide range of colors made from roots, seeds, plants and nuts. Because imported wool for embroidery was scarce and expensive, American women spun wool from their own sheep then dyed it with homemade colors. These homespun wools changed the character of the stitches and created challenge and excitement.

Like the arts of patchwork, appliqué and quilting, embroidery tells the story of a people. Civilization, economic security, contentment or frustration are all stitched into it. Embroidery can express solace or grief; it can express joy and hope; it can denote devotion and patience, indicate simplicity and thrift, or great wealth. In America, embroidery has come a long way from the early disciplined patterns. Although the formal, stylized designs of Jacobean origin are still used, embroidery has been translated into a new level of free-form and abstract work, sometimes called "Stitchery."

The basic stitches of embroidery are few — it is the countless variations of these few that staggers so many would-be embroiderers. However, many effective embroidered pieces use only one stitch, or a combination of two or three. Most Peruvian wool embroidery is done with only a Chain Stitch; Mexican work often employs only Stem and Satin Stitches. It is rewarding to see what can be done by using only one stitch with different colors and weights of threads.

## THE STITCHES OF EMBROIDERY

The stitches described in this section are the most basic embroidery stitches. For convenience, these basic stitches are presented in groups — the Flat group, the Chained group, the Looped group, the Knotted group and a group of Filling and Composite stitches. These, with their many variations, complete the essentials for most embroidery.

There has long been a controversy as to whether threads should be knotted. If the fabric is fine and firmly woven, knots might show through, giving the finished product a bumpy instead of a smooth appearance. If fabric is heavy, nubby or coarse, a few knots on the back will not make a difference. If there is any doubt, do not knot the thread. Bring the needle up from the wrong side

of the fabric leaving a length of a couple of inches; take a tiny Backstitch to secure the thread; then continue with the planned stitch. When the thread is nearly used up, bring the needle out on the wrong side; then weave in and out along the wrong side of the stitches to secure the thread. The "tail" of thread left from the beginning stitch can be secured in the same manner. Also, if embroidery stitches are to continue along the design line or close to the one just completed, the new stitches can catch the thread ends on the wrong side and hold them fast. It takes a little practice to decide the best way to handle this. Keep a scrap of fabric handy for determining the effect of color and thread in new stitches. A few practice sessions often eliminate the need for removing stitches from a project.

Necessary supplies and other suggestions will be covered after the basic stitches.

## FLAT STITCHES

### Running Stitch

The Running Stitch is the most uncomplicated stitch of all. The direction is from right to left. Bring the needle through the fabric from wrong to right side. Keep the thread horizontal, determine the stitch length, then insert needle through fabric from right to wrong side. Running stitches

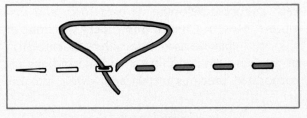

**Running Stitch**

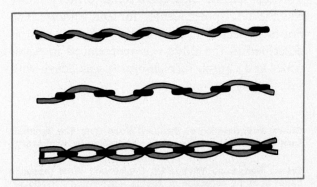

**Running Stitch Variations**

can also be worked vertically; they can be short, long, even or uneven; they can be worked in alternating or parallel rows. The Running Stitch can outline design shapes or, when worked close together, fill the shapes. It can be threaded or whipped in many variations.

## Stem Stitch

The Stem Stitch is also called the "Outline" Stitch, depending on whether the thread is above or below the needle when executing the stitch. The thread should either be to the right or above the needle, for the Outline Stitch; it should either be to the left or below for the Stem Stitch. It does not matter which is used except the stitch will have a more even appearance if the thread is thrown the same way each time. The direction of this stitch is from left to right. The needle enters the fabric at the far left of the design line. Keeping thread above the line for an Outline Stitch or below the line for a Stem Stitch, go down through the fabric then up on design line either

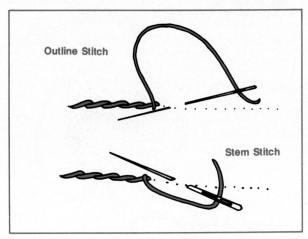

$^1/_2$ or $^1/_3$ the length of the stitch. A Stem Stitch can be whipped, threaded and used as filling. An interesting variation of the Stem Stitch is the Cable Stem. This is worked also from left to right, but the thread alternates so that it lies first above

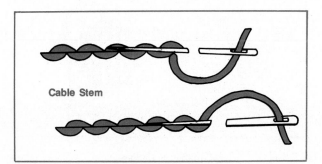

the needle then below, giving an undulating effect.

## Backstitch

The Backstitch is worked from right to left. Bring the needle up one stitch length from the far right end of the design line. The needle goes down at the right end of the design line, then up again one stitch length ahead of the line. Repeat for desired length. The stitches should be evenly spaced. The Backstitch, which gives the effect of an unbroken line, is useful for outlining a design and as a padding or filler.

On even-weave fabric, bring the needle up from the wrong side; take a stitch backward horizontally over four threads. Bring needle up again on same line, but *four threads in front* of point where needle first emerged; repeat.

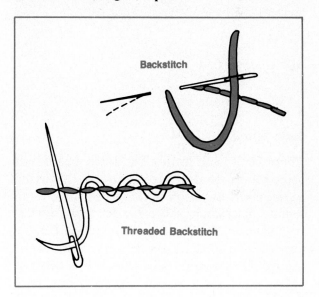

The Pekinese Stitch is worked with a different color thread over a foundation of Backstitches. Work from left to right; bring the needle up below the first Backstitch; without going through the fabric, work a series of loops through succeeding stitches.

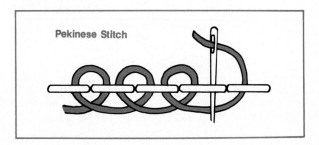

## Split Stitch

The Split Stitch was usually worked with silk floss of graduated shadings in Medieval embroideries. Today it works equally well with any threads or yarns that can easily be split with the needle. The direction is left to right. The needle comes up at left end on line of design. Insert the needle to the right; bring it up to the left splitting the thread so that the needle comes through the middle of the stitch. For fillings and shadings, work the Split Stitch close together in touching rows. It will be more effective if the rows are worked in the same direction.

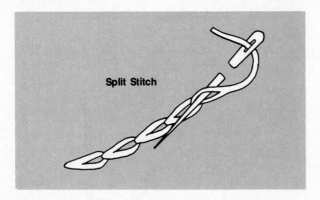

**Split Stitch**

## Satin Stitch

The Satin Stitch is really a Backstitch, but of such importance that it needs to be discussed separately. Instead of working in a line, as in regular Backstitch, the Satin Stitch is worked with stitches side by side to fill a space. Being a very flexible stitch, it can be worked straight or slanted. If used to fill a large area, it is easier to

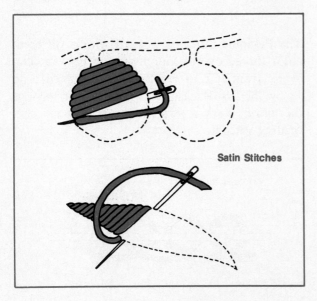

**Satin Stitches**

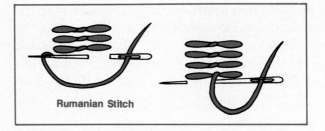

**Rumanian Stitch**

start in the middle and work toward each end. A large space can be broken up into smaller areas for filling; this keeps the stitches from being too long. However, if long surface stitches are essential to the design, Satin Stitches can be "tied down" with a tiny slanting stitch, called a Rumanian Stitch. An area filled with Satin Stitches can

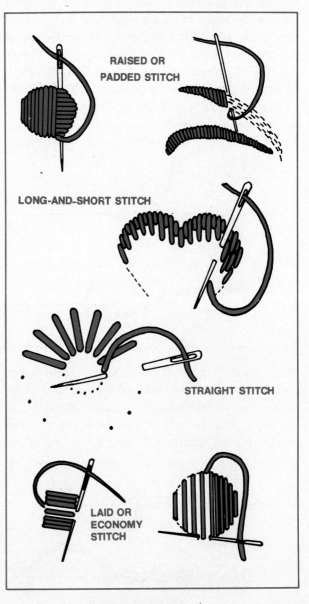

**RAISED OR PADDED STITCH**

**LONG-AND-SHORT STITCH**

**STRAIGHT STITCH**

**LAID OR ECONOMY STITCH**

**Satin Stitch Variations**

be graduated from wide filling stitches into a narrow Stem or Outline Stitch.

A Satin Stitched area can also be raised or padded. Outline the space with Stem or Chain Stitches; fill the inside area with tiny Running or Seed Stitches. Work the Satin Stitch *over* the space outline; this gives an even, rounded look, and keeps the outside edge smooth.

Satin Stitches are effective when used as a Long-and-Short Stitch, especially for shaded work. A single Satin Stitch is called a Straight Stitch. An economical version of the Satin Stitch was devised by the early colonists in America. Because it saved thread, this stitch was called "Economy" or New England Laid. It looks like Satin Stitch but is a little flatter. Take the thread across the area to be filled, as in Satin Stitch, but leave the width of a stitch between each two threads. Instead of going over and under, as in Satin, take a tiny stitch through fabric at edge of design outline, then fill the open spaces with stitches. The back, or wrong side of this stitch, looks like an outline in Backstitches; the filling is not visible.

## Cross Stitch

Almost any weight of thread or yarn can be used for the Cross Stitch, depending upon the purpose of the finished project and the background fabric. It is easier to work on an even weave fabric or on mesh where the threads can be counted. On Penelope canvas, made especially for Cross Stitch, every fifth line is blue. Cross Stitch is easily worked on checked fabric, such as gingham. In working Cross Stitch on felt, terry cloth or any tightly woven fabric, baste a piece of Penelope canvas over the design area. Work the stitches through this; when the design is finished,

carefully pull out the mesh threads one by one. When using mesh in this way, keep the Cross Stitches tight. Then when the canvas threads are removed, the Cross Stitches will lie flat against the base fabric. Cross Stitch borders are very effective, although the stitch is adaptable to almost any design. It can be worked in rows, patterns or as a separate stitch. In working a row, make a line of slanting stitches from left to right; make the Cross Stitches from right to left. This stitch is more effective when crosses are all in the same direction. The Cross Stitch can be used as a filling stitch, for couching, or in any combination with other stitches.

The reverse of Cross Stitch is Assisi work. In this, the *background* is filled in with Cross Stitches, but the design is left blank.

## Herringbone Stitch

The Herringbone Stitch can be worked open or closed, in parallel lines or irregular lines; it can be tied down, threaded, interlaced, used for fillings and couching. It can also be used as a disciplined, geometric border. Interesting examples of this are shown in many of the paintings of Giotto, a famous 14th century painter.

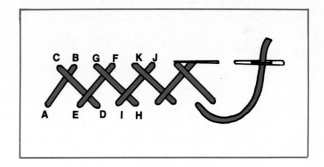

The direction for all Herringbone Stitches is from left to right. While learning the stitch, work over canvas or draw two parallel lines $1/2$ inch apart. On each line, mark off $1/2$-inch intervals to make imaginary squares. Bring needle up at A, down at B, up at C, down at D, up at E, down at F; repeat. This gives a diagonal or slanting stitch much like a Cross Stitch, with a small *x* at the top and at the bottom. A different effect can be created by placing CB and ED closer together. Try this stitch in curving lines; space it from close together to wide apart. Try it with different weights of threads. To close the Herringbone

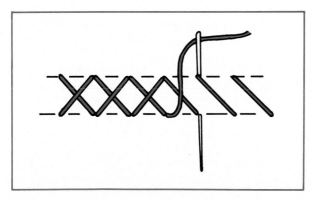

**Cross Stitch**

Stitch, bring the needle out slightly to the right of the previous stitch. Thus, AB and EF are closely parallel.

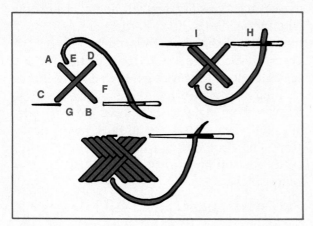

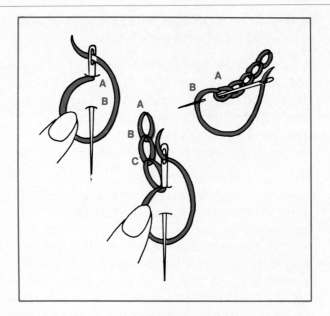

**Closed Herringbone Stitch**

**Chain Stitch**

For interlacing or threading, use a different color and weight of yarn; gold or silver threads are also effective. Start at the top, with thread pulled through the fabric — if possible. If not, using two or three tiny stitches, tack it in place on the surface with mercerized or silk thread. Slip the needle with interlacing thread under the long slanting stitch; over the crossed threads at the bottom; under the slanted thread going upward; over the cross at the top; continue in this manner.

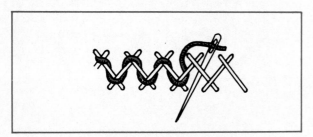

**Threaded Herringbone Stitch**

To "tie down" or tack the Herringbone Stitch, take a Vertical Stitch over each cross at top and bottom. This Vertical Stitch can be a Straight Stitch or a small Detached Chain Stitch.

## CHAINED STITCHES

### Basic Chain Stitch

The basic Chain Stitch is easy to learn, simple and fast to do. It has countless variations and effects and can be used singly or in combination with other stitches. Its direction is vertical, from top to bottom. Bring the needle out at A, and use thumb to hold the thread below the needle. Take needle down either in the same hole as A or right next to it. Bring needle out at B, directly below A, with thread *under* the needle. This is the first chain. Now, holding thread below chain with thumb, take needle down at the same hole as B or right next to it, *inside* the loop, and continue in this manner.

Chain Stitches make a wonderful outline as well as filler, and many Peruvian wool embroiderers use this stitch alone. It has different effects depending upon the threads or yarns used. In fact, a Beauvais Stitch is nothing more than a Chain Stitch worked with heavy yarn.

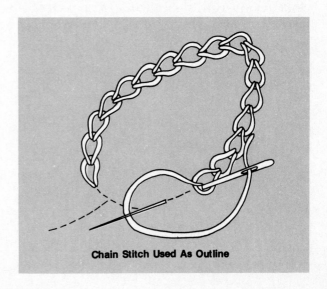

**Chain Stitch Used As Outline**

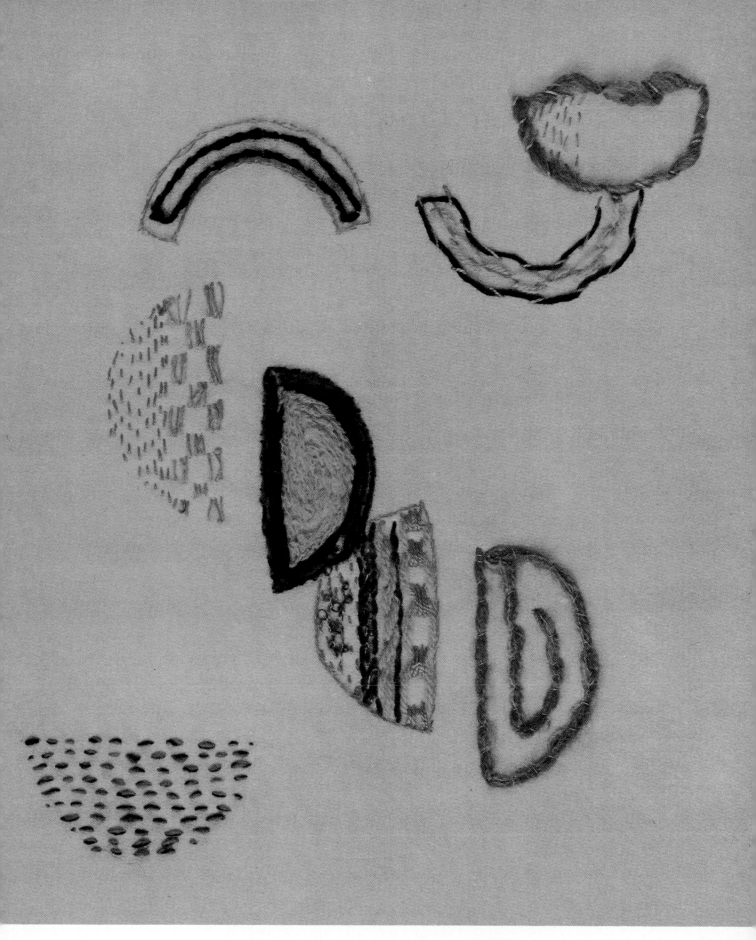

**Flat Stitch Sampler Worked In Geometric Shapes**

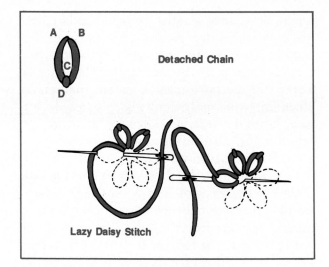

variety of threads, and overlapping, create interesting texture on fabric. In experimenting, make several rows of Chain Stitches; the first with even stitches, and the rest of varying length and size. Make some rows close together, others a space or so apart, then a row of Zigzag Chain. Do a series of Detached Chain Stitches; use tiny, even rows of Chain Stitches to fill spaces.

A single or detached Chain Stitch is also called a "Petal" or "Lazy Daisy" Stitch and is used often for simple flower designs. For the Detached Chain Stitch, the needle is brought up through the fabric at A. Hold the thread down with thumb, and take the needle down at B. C is just inside the loop, with thread under the needle. To secure the stitch, needle goes down at D, over the looped thread and directly under C. Many interesting variations can be created by varying the anchoring stitch C to D. The Detached Chain Stitch also can be used as couching. Open Chain Stitch looks almost like a ladder. It is worked the same way as regular Chain Stitch, except that AB and CD are not close together but a stitch-length apart. Direction is still top to bottom. Work within imaginary parallel lines, or vary the width and length at will. Several rows of Open Chain worked in a

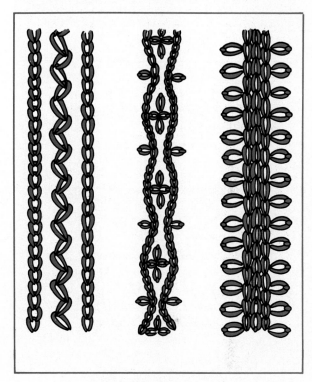

**Chain Stitch Border   Variations**

## LOOPED STITCHES

### Buttonhole Stitch

The Buttonhole Stitch is often called Blanket Stitch for it was used originally as a decorative edge for blankets. The stitches are the same, except that a Buttonhole Stitch is worked very close together while a Blanket Stitch has a space between each stitch. For embroidery purposes, this stitch is usually called Buttonhole.

Stitch direction is left to right. Bring the needle up at A. Hold the thread down with thumb, and take the needle down at B, up at C (directly under B) with thread *under* needle; repeat. Imaginary parallel lines might help in learning this stitch too. Try a few straight lines, then some curved ones.

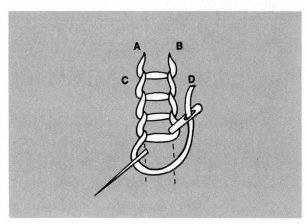

**Open Chain Stitch**

**Detached Chain Stitch Sampler: Green worked from center out, purple from edge to center.**

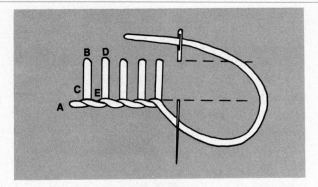

**Buttonhole Stitch**

begin, draw two parallel lines ½ inch apart. Mark ½-inch intervals along the bottom line; mark intervals on the top line too, but space them halfway between the bottom marks. This stitch is worked in the same manner as the Buttonhole Stitch only with a different angle. To produce a lacy, knitted effect, use Detached Buttonhole Stitches. Make a heading row of Backstitches or Stem Stitches; then work a row of Buttonhole Stitches through the heading *only* and *not* through the fabric. At the end of the row, turn the fabric upside down and work a second row of Buttonhole Stitches into the preceding one — again without going through the fabric. To finish off, either anchor both ends with a stitch through the fabric, or work the last row of stitches through the fabric. (See section on Filling Stitches.)

### Featherstitch

The Featherstitch is similar to the Buttonhole Stitch, but the angle is different. Stitch direction is vertical instead of horizontal. Bring the needle out at A, and hold thread down with thumb. The needle goes down at B and up at C, which is vertically below A. From now on, alternate stitches from left to right.

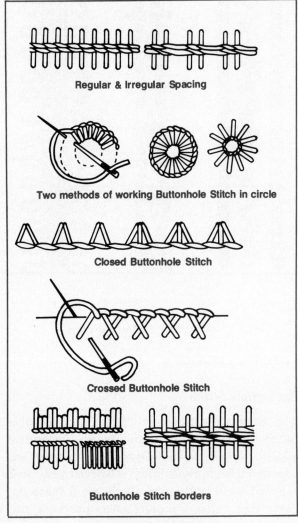

Regular & Irregular Spacing

Two methods of working Buttonhole Stitch in circle

Closed Buttonhole Stitch

Crossed Buttonhole Stitch

Buttonhole Stitch Borders

**Buttonhole Stitch Variations**

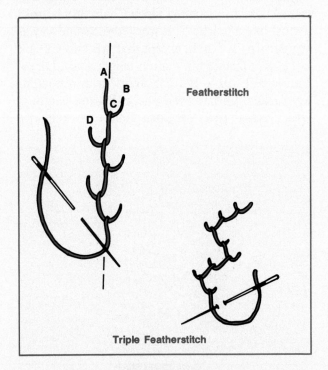

**Featherstitch**

**Triple Featherstitch**

Try this stitch with regular as well as irregular spacings. Experiment with circles — start one on the outside so that spokes go into a common hole in the center; then do another, starting from the center and working spokes outward. Closed Buttonhole Stitches look like a row of triangles. To

For a Double Featherstitch, work two stitches to a side before alternating; for a triple stitch, work three to a side before alternating.

The Fly or Y Stitch is another variation of the Featherstitch. Worked in the same manner, it can be held down with small stitches (A and C), long stitches (B) or Detached Chains (D). Variations of the Fly Stitch make very attractive borders and fillers.

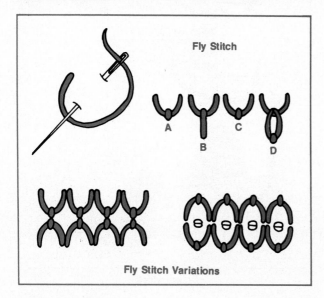

**Fly Stitch**

**Fly Stitch Variations**

## Van Dyke Stitch

The Van Dyke Stitch is another versatile stitch. If worked evenly, it makes a good border or outline. It can also be used as a filler since the stitches can be shaped and graduated. This is a Vertical Stitch, worked from top to bottom. To begin, bring the needle up at A, down at B, up at C, down at D, up at E. Now, without catching the fabric, take the needle under BC threads, making a loop, and go down at F. Continue in this manner. If this stitch is worked between parallel lines, the "arms" of the stitch will be regular, down the middle. If the parallel lines are very close together, the finished stitch gives the effect of a thick, raised braid.

The Van Dyke, Ladder and Ceylon stitches are all similar. The Van Dyke has one loop, the Ladder has a loop on each side and the Ceylon has three or more loops. The base of the Ladder Stitch is two flat stitches, one under the other, and the Ladder is worked with a loop at each side. The base of the Ceylon Stitch is one short Straight Stitch. Work a loop through it without catching the fabric; then work a loop through each side of the preceding loop and continue to increase to the desired width.

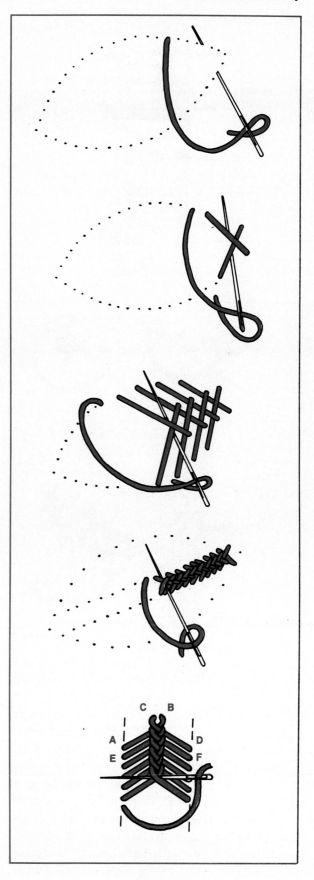

**Van Dyke Stitch**

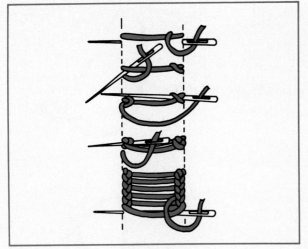

**Ladder Stitch**

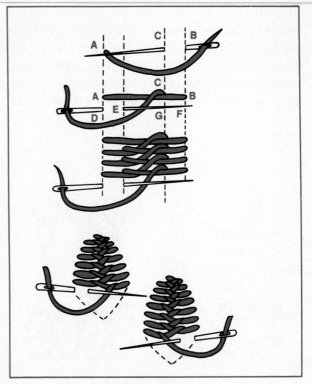

**Cretan Stitch**

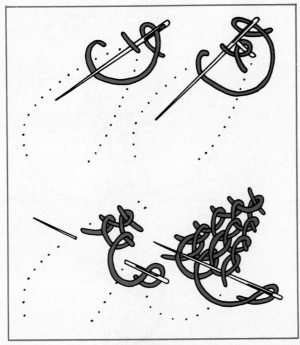

**Ceylon Stitch**

## Cretan Stitch

The Cretan Stitch came originally from the island of Crete where it was used in bright colors to decorate skirts and vests. Although the direction of this stitch is vertical, it can be worked horizontally or in a circle. Bring the needle up at A, down at B, up at C, keeping thread *under* the needle and held down with thumb. With thread still below the needle, go down at D, up at E, always pointing the needle back toward the center. This stitch is really in the Featherstitch family, but it is flatter, wider and worked horizontally.

## KNOTTED STITCHES

### French Knot

The French Knot is possibly the best known of the knotted group of stitches and can be used singly or in groups. Begin by bringing the needle up through the fabric; keep the needle horizontal and close to the fabric. Hold thread between thumb and forefinger and wind thread around the end of the needle once or twice. Keeping the thread taut, insert point of needle down through the fabric right next to the place it emerged. The weight of thread used will vary the size of the knot. A round eye needle is best to use for this

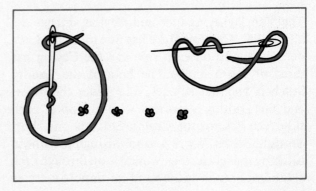

**French Knot**

stitch since it keeps the coils even. This is especially true for the Bullion Knot.

### Bullion Knot

To begin a Bullion Knot, bring the needle out at A, and go down at B as though you were starting a Backstitch. Bring the needle out again at A — the distance AB will be the finished length of coils — but do not pull the needle all the way through. Wind the thread several times around the needle (as many times as needed to fill length of stitch), then slip needle between fingers, holding coils securely with thumb and forefinger. Pull the needle through all the coils, keeping the thread taut, until the coils rest securely against the fabric; then take the needle down through the fabric and continue with next stitch.

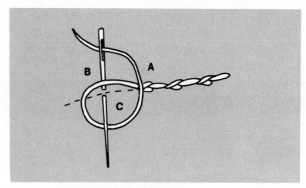

**Coral Knot**

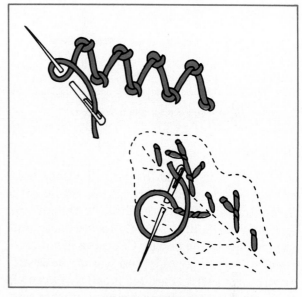

**Coral Knot Variations**

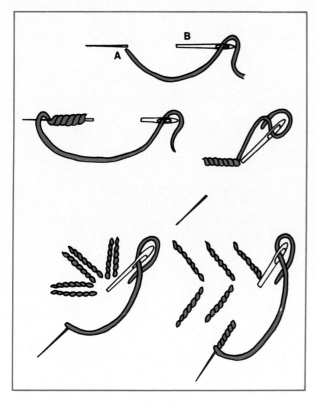

**Bullion Knot**

### Coral Knot

The Coral Knot Stitch can be worked in any direction, but it might be easier in the beginning to work from right to left. Bring the needle out at A; hold thread along line of design with thumb. Insert needle at B, come up at C with thread *under* the needle; repeat. This makes a knot at intervals along the thread.

### Four-Legged Knot

Visualize this stitch as a cross, either regular or irregular. Come up at A, down at B and up at C. Before completing the C to D stitch, slip needle under the center of the cross to make a knot; do

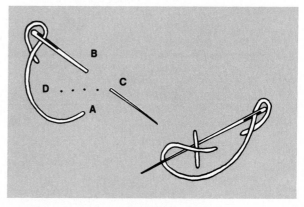

**Four-Legged Knot Stitch**

not pick up fabric in this movement. When knot is formed, the needle goes down at D completing the cross. The arms of this stitch can be any length. These Detached Four-Legged Knot Stitches can be used as fillers for space or background. They make pretty stars in a night sky.

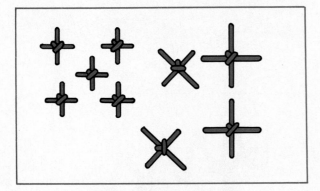

**Four-Legged Knot Stitch Variations**

## Couching

In working with thread or yarn too uneven or too heavy to be pulled through the fabric, it is often necessary to "tie it down," "tack it" or "couch it" to hold it securely to the fabric and become part of the design. Couching is not confined solely to threads and yarns, however. Ropes, cords, wire, twigs, beads and shells can all be couched with different types of stitches and often a combination of stitches. For practice, ar-

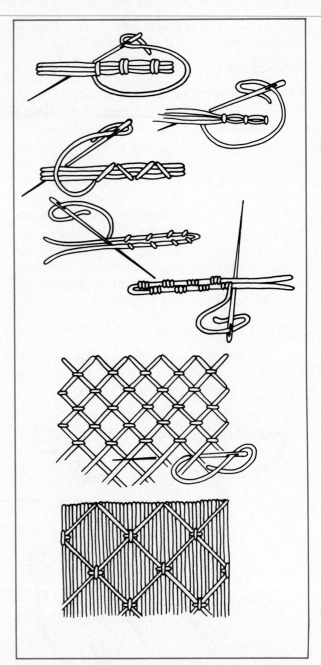

**Fancy Couching Stitches**

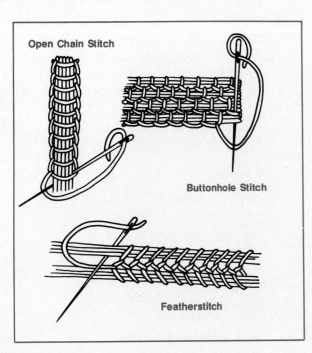

Open Chain Stitch

Buttonhole Stitch

Featherstitch

range several strands of yarn along lines to be covered on the fabric. Hold the yarn in place with pins placed at right angles. With thread or floss, take a tiny stitch across the yarn at regular intervals into the fabric. The tacking thread can be matching or contrasting in color, depending upon the effect desired. Practice couching with a regular Chain Stitch, an Open Stitch, a Featherstitch or Herringbone. Experiment with different groupings, colors and weights of yarn.

**Chain Stitch Sampler Worked As A Tree Trunk**

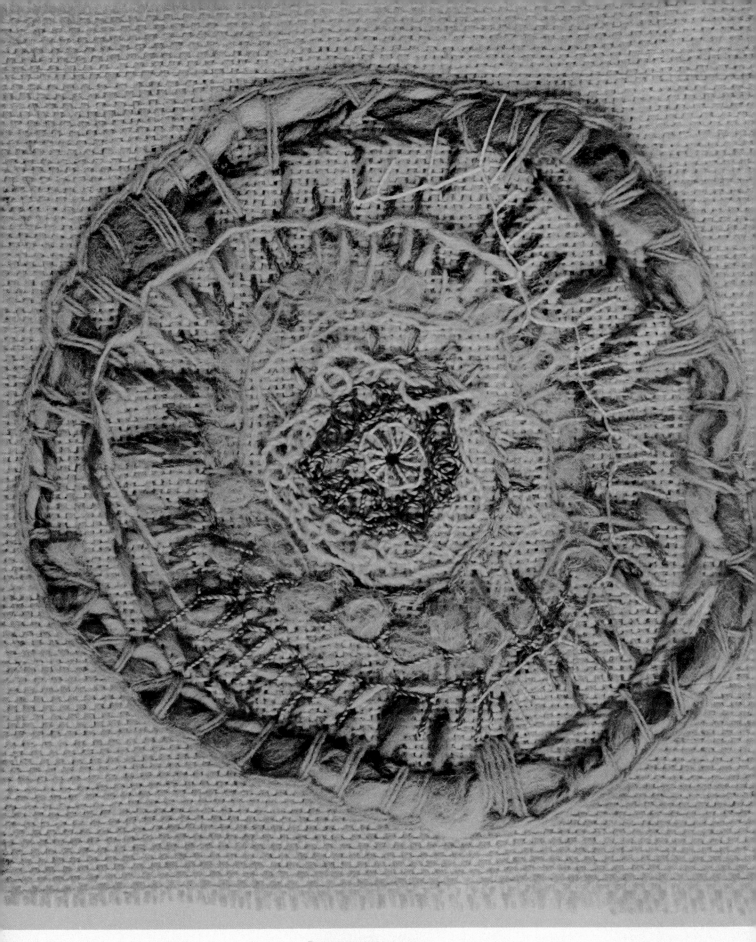

**Buttonhole Stitch Sampler**

## FILLING STITCHES

### Seed Stitches

Seed Stitches are tiny Straight Stitches or Backstitches (usually of equal length) repeated at random to fill in a specified area. Seeding is often worked with two stitches very close together.

**Seed Stitches**

### Sheaf Filling

Make three vertical Straight Stitches the same length and close together. Bring needle up through fabric in center of the three stitches, but slip needle under the stitches so that it emerges on the left side.

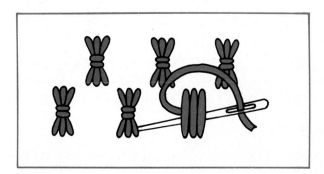

**Sheaf Filling**

Without picking up any fabric, wrap thread around the three stitches twice, then take needle back down through fabric in same place it emerged.

### Star Filling

Make a Cross Stitch; then make a Horizontal Stitch so that there are six spokes. Now, in the center, work a very small Cross Stitch over the intersection of threads.

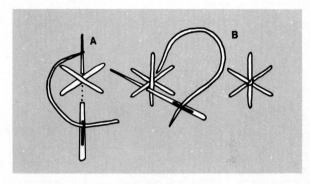

**Star Filling**

### Wave Filling

Working from left to right, make a foundation row of vertical stitches. This foundation row can be straight, radiating or undulating. The last two will give an airier effect. For the second row, bring the needle up through fabric diagonally below and to the right of the last foundation stitch. Slip needle in back of the foundation stitch without taking any fabric. Insert needle diagonally below next foundation stitch and take a tiny horizontal stitch through the fabric. Continue across the row of Straight Stitches, then turn work upside down and go back across with another row of wave stitches. This gives a loopy effect when the stitch is about $1/2$ inch long. If stitches are small, it looks like knitting.

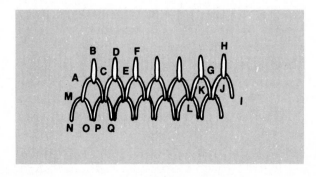

**Wave Filling**

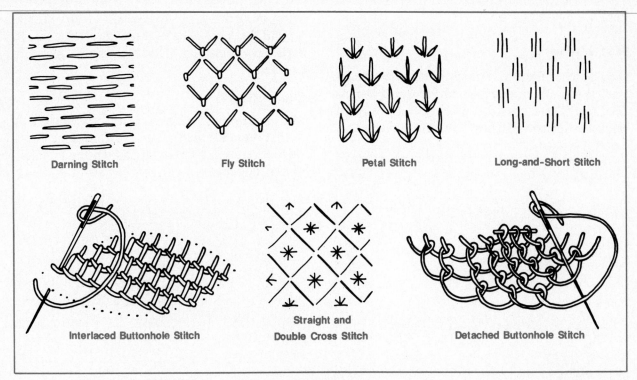

Darning Stitch    Fly Stitch    Petal Stitch    Long-and-Short Stitch

Interlaced Buttonhole Stitch    Straight and Double Cross Stitch    Detached Buttonhole Stitch

**Filling Stitch Variations**

## COMPOSITE STITCHES

Composite Stitches are simply a combination of two or more stitches. They are rich in texture, exciting to explore, and the variations are endless.

### Whipping

Add a line of Whipping Stitches to a line of single Running Stitches, double or multiple Running Stitches, Chain Stitches or Backstitches. The Whipping Stitch is right to left. Bring the needle up through the fabric below the foundation line. Go *over* the worked line in a slanting direction; then go down *under* the foundation stitches but not through the fabric. This is repeated the length of the line.

### Threading or Lacing

Instead of whipping over and over a line of embroidery, bring the needle up through the fabric at right end of design line; then weave thread in and out of the foundation stitches. This is single threading. For double threading, make a second line in reverse. Almost all stitches used for design outlines can be threaded. Two foundation lines fairly close together can be interlaced — thread through the top line then the bottom, then back to the top and so on. A tapestry needle is easy to use for this, because the blunt end slides easily under the stitches.

## ABBREVIATIONS OF COMMON EMBROIDERY STITCHES

| | |
|---|---|
| Ru | Running Stitch |
| Spl | Split Stitch |
| Ou | Outline Stitch |
| SS | Stem Stitch |
| CrS | Cross Stitch |
| WR | Whipped Running Stitch |
| Se | Seed Stitch |
| WB | Whipped Backstitch |
| But | Buttonhole Stitch |
| CS | Couched Square Flling |
| Fl | Fly Stitch |
| Ch | Chain Stitch |
| LD | Lazy Daisy Stitch |
| FK | French Knot |
| Fe | Featherstitch |
| Fsh | Fishbone Stitch |
| Her | Herringbone Stitch |
| Sa | Satin Stitch |
| L&S | Long-and-Short Stitch |
| Bul | Bullion Knot |
| VaD | Van Dyke Stitch |
| Cr | Cretan Stitch |
| Co | Coral Knot |
| FiW | Filled With |

## THE FABRICS FOR EMBROIDERY

Fabrics for embroidery cover such a wide range it is almost impossible to list them all. The fact is that any fabric which can take a needle can be embroidered, including leather and suede. Natural fibers perhaps wear better and are easier to work on — wools, linens, cottons, medium to heavy silk. Other acceptable fabrics include everything from loose to closely woven materials, from sheerest weights to upholstery weights, nubby and tweedy to plain and smooth. Add to this some patterned fabrics too — plaids, stripes or checks. Some of the synthetics handle very well, as does a close-pile velvet; the design will often dictate the choice of fabric.

Texture is created by fraying or raveling the edges of certain fabrics — burlap or wools, some linens. Separate or pull out the threads in a loosely woven fabric leaving spaces to incorporate into the design. Sheers such as chiffon, organdy, net or lace, can be enhanced with delicate tracery; also, a layer of net or a sheer fabric laid over embroidery gives it a muted color and texture.

Select firmly woven fabrics for articles which will get hard wear. Although they may be washed, most embroidered articles are better off with dry cleaning. Do not always start from "scratch" in embroidery; many ordinary ready-made things can be made to look special with the addition of a little embroidery.

Try designs or monograms on towels, sheets, pillowcases, place mats or other table linen. Use quilted fabric for a vest, skirt or pillow and decorate it with embroidery. Work a design on a sweater or cover a wool blanket with embroidery.

In experimenting, start with the easier fabrics — felt, burlap, medium-weight wools, monk's cloth, ticking or denim. Pin little practice pieces in a notebook, along with an explanation of the stitch or stitches used.

## THE THREADS OF EMBROIDERY

There is a wide range of threads in embroidery. As the decoration of a fabric, embroidery creates texture and adds color as well as a play of light and shadow. Embroidery threads must be suitable for the design and fabric too; a delicate silk floss might be lost on a nubby background, and a heavy yarn would not be suitable for a delicate fabric. The thread should always pull through fabric without fraying.

A well-rounded collection of embroidery threads could include mercerized sewing threads, silk thread (both regular and twist), 6-strand embroidery floss, pearl cottons in various sizes, crochet cottons, raffia, metallic threads and yarns and knitting wool in all weights and textures. Small quantities of bouclé, mohair and chenille, although expensive, are useful. Leftover yarns and "thrums" may also be used and many interesting threads and colors obtained by raveling various fabrics. Save the Lurex and colored cords from gift wraps, and common string — fuzzy to smooth, thin or thick, all weights, all textures.

Many of the heavy, uneven yarns cannot be pulled through the fabric but can be couched or tied down with a variety of embroidery stitches.

## OTHER NECESSITIES FOR EMBROIDERY

Along with fabrics, threads and yarns, there are other items necessary for embroidery. A good assortment of needles includes regular sewing needles, both sharps and long-eyes, and embroidery or crewel needles in various sizes. These needles are long and sharp, have a larger eye for ease in threading and are suitable for closely woven fabrics. Several sizes of tapestry needles which are heavier, with blunt ends and large eyes may be used for heavier yarn and string, raffia, etc. Use them too, in embroidering burlaps, some wools, and loosely woven linen and cotton. The blunt end will go between the fabric threads rather than pierce them. A rug needle, similar to a tapestry needle but larger, is needed occasionally.

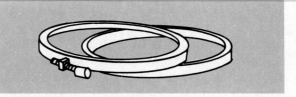

**Hoop Frame**

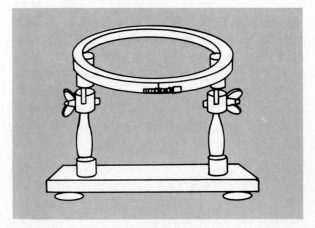

**Lap Frame**

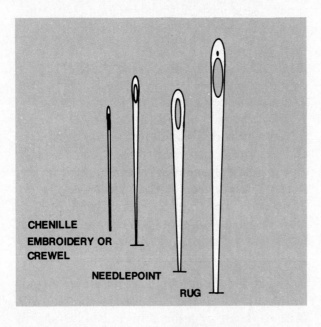

CHENILLE

EMBROIDERY OR CREWEL

NEEDLEPOINT

RUG

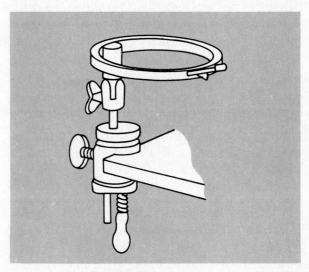

**Table Tambour Frame**

Good sharp scissors are needed for fabric, and smaller embroidery scissors for clipping threads. Keep a thimble for your middle finger. Hoops and frames are useful too. Many times they keep puckers from forming, and it is also easier to work some types of embroidery when fabric is stretched tightly. Hoops come in several sizes. They are made of two rings of wood which fit inside each other. There is a spring or screw on the outer ring which permits you to tighten or loosen the work. Canvas stretchers, obtainable from an art supply store, help with larger pieces; many times an old picture frame will do as well. Rein-

force the sides and ends of your fabric with folded strips of muslin basted on securely. Then, with needle and heavy thread, lace through the muslin strips around the frame or stretcher.

A tracing wheel, carbon paper, sharpened chalk pencils and ordinary pencils are necessary for transferring a design. A ruler with a metal edge is helpful as well as a notebook or file for designs and ideas and perhaps a magnifier to wear around your neck.

**Simple Shapes and Designs of Embroidery**

## THE DESIGNS OF EMBROIDERY

The designs of embroidery overlap the designs of appliqué and other needlecrafts, with nature the most abundant supplier. Vegetables and flowers, birds and animals, trees and plants, the sun, moon and stars, seaweed and seashells are all good sources. A small detail or cross section of one of these will often serve for an interesting study in stitches.

Many household and kitchen items have interesting shapes — bottles, cups, pitchers, bowls, and various other utensils.

Architecture — a row of houses, a steeple, a bridge, a cityscape can also be translated into embroidery. The general impression is more interesting and more personal than a detailed copy. Look at ads in newspapers and magazines; study photographs, poems and stories, children's books. Letters and numbers make stunning graphic designs.

There are several ways to transfer a design to fabric, and the type of fabric will largely determine the method. If fabric is firm and closely woven, try the tracing wheel or stylus with dressmaker carbon. Typewriter carbon will smudge, so do not confuse the two. Bear down rather heavily so that the design will show up. Another method of transferring a design is to use transfer pencils. These are available in some needlework or art supply stores or from some mail order houses. Place tracing (not carbon) paper over the design, then copy the design with the transfer pencil. Now put the tracing paper, design side down, against the right side of the fabric, with design centered in place. Use a fairly hot iron (not steam) against the paper; the heat will transfer the marked design from paper to fabric.

For nubby or tweedy weaves of fabric or some knits, use tissue paper to transfer the design. Draw the design on tissue, then baste in place on fabric. Thread a needle with contrasting sewing thread, go over the design with small Running Stitches, sewing through both paper and fabric. Tear the paper away carefully when finished. Often the embroidery will cover the Running Stitches completely; if not, they are easily removed later.

**Design drawn on batiste. Batiste basted to wrong side of sweater.**

**Design transferred to sweater with small running stitches on outline.**

To transfer a design to a sweater or other stretchable fabrics, draw or trace the design on batiste, organdy or organza; then baste this, with design side *up,* in place against *wrong* side of sweater or knit. With contrasting thread, transfer the design with small Running Stitches which will show on the right side of the sweater. When working the embroidery — from the right side — work through the knit *and* backing both, to stabilize the embroidery and keep it from stretch-

ing. When finished, trim the excess backing close to the design outline. Embroidered sweaters have a more professional look if they are lined.

For embroidery on pile fabric, such as terry cloth, velvet or corduroy, use Penelope or other canvas, as explained in the section on the Cross Stitch. Be careful in working this so that the threads of the canvas can be pulled out later.

In experimenting, you may devise a method of transferring an acceptable design that is not mentioned here. If you decide to draw the design directly on fabric, mark just the guide points of the design, or keep the lines as light as possible. Dark pencil lines will not come out and often embroidery stitches will not cover them completely.

Embroidery kits are available everywhere, with designs already stamped, fabric and yarns and colors chosen. These may help in learning the craft, but they rob you of creativity and could dull enthusiasm for future work. It is important to try stitches first on a practice piece — this helps in learning them and determines the effect of the stitch and color on the fabric. Many years ago, it was customary to make a sampler with variations of the stitches learned. Instead of the old-fashioned kind, try a modern sampler — embroider a pocket, a belt, a purse, gloves, a pair of socks or other small article with a variety of stitches.

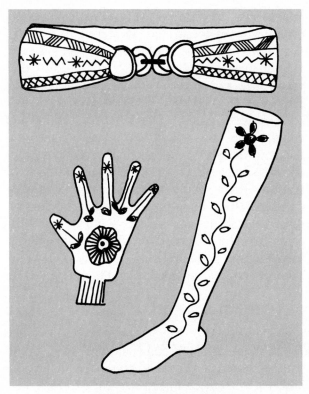

**Modern Embroidered Samplers**

## KINDS OF EMBROIDERY

Although there are many types of embroidery work, we will only explore the most popular ones used today.

### CREWEL

Crewel, or Jacobean Embroidery, comes to us from England. The word crewel comes from the word *krua* which means wool, and crewel embroidery actually means wool embroidery. The term crewel, so often misunderstood, now really applies to the design. Threads used can be linen, cotton or silk as well as wool and almost any background fabric. The first crewel or Jacobean designs came from the *palampores,* the East India Company painted or printed and sent to England. The Tree of Life was the standard design; it rose from mounds of *terra firma* in graduated shading. These trees were exotic; foliage was lush with leaves and intricately embroidered flowers; excited birds were caught in flight or rested nervously on branches too small to hold them. These designs were all big and bold, for they decorated wall hangings and bed curtains and were made primarily to keep out cold winds.

These designs arrived in the New World with the colonists, but changed in concept to fit the new patterns of living. The American woman began to substitute and initiate. Imported wool yarns were difficult to get, and often too expensive to buy when they were available. Hand-spun and hand-dyed wool and linen threads were used instead of the fine English and French wool yarns, and a new look was born. Some of the big designs were scaled down, and a spontaneity and freedom, typical of America, was added. In Colonial times, the first dye that women learned to make was indigo, and some of the earliest crewel designs were embroidered solely in shades of blue. From this beginning came an offshoot of crewel known as Deerfield Embroidery, also known as "Blue and White." The thread is linen as well as wool, but the designs are the same.

The basic stitches of crewel work are few, but many variations can be created with them. The common stitches are Chain, Stem, Long-and-Short, Straight and Satin, French Knot, Running, Feather and Herringbone, with some composite stitches used as filler.

**A Jacobean Design**

## FREE EXPRESSION OR FREE-FORM EMBROIDERY

This type of embroidery is often called *Stitchery,* since it exceeds the boundaries of traditional embroidery. It has a contemporary and abstract quality; it is more than just decoration of fabric because it sometimes creates textures of its own.

**Abstract Design for Variety of Stitches**

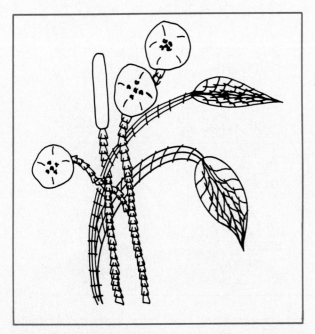

**Design using Open Chain Stitches, Featherstitches and Small Couching Stitches.**

A good way to start is to drop several pieces of different types of yarn on the fabric and study them. Often they assume shapes of their own or suggest ideas to follow. Couch or tie down the yarns, then add texture with layers of stitches in certain areas. Add a few beads or sequins, shells, seeds, pieces of cork or pasta, wood shavings or twigs. Couch down a length of wire — copper, or the colored plastic telephone cords. Mass the stitches, exaggerate them, and play light against shadow. Try a simple design — an apple, a tree or a bird. Break or soften the edges of the design, distort the shape and balance the textures. This type of stitchery is mostly used in wall hangings, for screens or room dividers or pictures; it is not suitable for wearing apparel or pillows.

## BLACK WORK

Black Work is black embroidery worked on a white ground. It probably originated in Persia, and was introduced in Spain by the Moors in the 8th century. It is often called Spanish Work. Catherine of Aragon took it to England when she became the wife of Henry VIII; she made shirts and vests for Henry in Black Work. The early designs were basically geometric, composed of squares, curves, arches and spirals, with much couching and filling.

In Spain, embroidery wool from native black sheep is used more often than anything else. In England, black silk was often used, and sometimes highlighted with the addition of a gold thread. Black Work today is increasingly popular, possibly because the sharp contrast of black and white gives the work a very contemporary look.

Although any type of design is acceptable, a scaled-down Jacobean or geometric design is most popular. The Backstitch, Buttonhole, Chain, Coral, Stem and Outline Stitches are commonly used, with many filling variations. Since there are no distracting colors in this work, the design depends entirely on the stitches, and thus is good for beginning projects. More disciplined geometric patterns or designs are easily worked on even-weave or counted-thread fabrics. A small design worked on a pocket or the corner of a luncheon mat is effective; a large design worked on draperies or a skirt could be dramatic.

**Black Work**

## WHITE WORK

White Work is very similar to Black Work except the designs are embroidered with white threads on white ground, making a far more delicate appearance. The thin muslin or cotton dresses both women and children once wore were often embroidered in this way. A simple floral or leaf spray was sufficient to enhance the fine fabric; Satin, Lazy Daisy and Stem Stitches were often the only ones needed.

One such baby dress, handmade of fine cotton balloon cloth, had pin tucks, lace insertions and rolled hems. Delicate sprays of flowers were embroidered on the white fabric with two strands of white embroidery floss. Only two stitches were used — the Satin Stitch and Stem Stitch. The little flowers could be done with the Lazy Daisy Stitch as an alternative. A few French Knots set off the delicate design.

## SHADOW EMBROIDERY

Shadow Embroidery is thought to have 18th century origins. It is worked with white thread on white transparent fabrics such as organdy, lawn

**Child's Christening Gown, Embroidered and Hand Sewn by Carter Houck (White Work).**

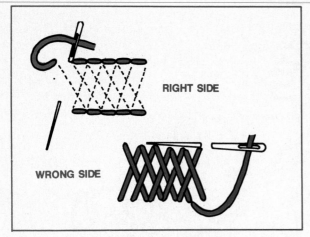

**Stitch Used For Shadow Work**

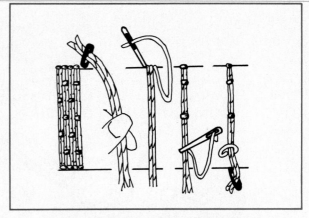

**Starting and Finishing Flat Gold Embroidery**

or batiste, and perhaps some of the newer synthetic fabrics. The technique is to work mainly from the wrong side of the fabric. Large spaces or areas of design, such as leaves or flower petals, are worked in a *closed* Herringbone Stitch on wrong side. Six-strand embroidery floss is a good choice of thread for this work. When starting, leave several inches of thread before beginning to stitch. When finished, thread the "tail" through a needle and weave it through several stitches without catching the fabric, then clip the thread close. From the right side of the fabric, the closed Herringbone Stitch appears to be a Backstitch outlining the design; the crosses of the Herringbone provide a shadowy filling of the space. Single stems or lines are worked on the *right side* of the fabric, with Stem or Outline Stitch. Shadow work is very effective on room dividers or curtains, or sheer place mats.

A modern effect can be achieved by using color instead of the white embroidery threads. Select colors of deeper intensity than the desired effect. When the embroidery is finished, the color will show through muted and almost opalescent. Outlining from the right side of the fabric should be done with white. For a different effect, try a colored translucent fabric instead of the white. Embroidery can be worked in deeper shades, or in white; the final outlining from the right side should be done in threads matching the fabric.

## GOLD WORK

Gold Work, as the name implies, is luxury work. Its origins go back to Biblical times, and during past centuries, it was lavishly used, not only for ecclesiastical garb, but for court dress, royal robes and formal attire. Today, it is mostly used for Church embroidery, but a small evening bag, eyeglass case or belt would provide elegant accents for evening wear. Japanese gold threads are the most available and easiest to handle for traditional work. All of these metal threads need a special technique because they are springy. They cannot be pulled through the fabric, but must be couched down or laid on the material. In working with these threads, use two strands at a time. The gold is easily damaged and also tarnishes easily, so handle it as little as possible. Instead of unwinding a skein, gently pull the two loose threads from either end of the skein, keeping the unused part of the skein wrapped in tissue or a soft cloth. Use only short lengths of the gold — just enough to cover the outline or working row; leave a tiny bit extra at each end to work through to the wrong side of the fabric.

A firmly woven fabric is the best to use — a heavy silk, satin or linen. However, velvet, leather, kid and suede can also be embroidered with gold. These last-mentioned materials, when used, should be backed with a firm fabric, preferably a medium-weight linen. It is also necessary to use a frame or hoop for this work, since it must be taut at all times.

Designs should be simple and basic, with extra "frills" eliminated. A good design source for this work can be found in heavy silk brocaded fabric. The brocade patterns provide the design to be covered with gold threads, and this eliminates the step of transferring a design to fabric. When using Gold Work on velvet, it is easiest to work the gold on a piece of linen first. When finished, cut around the edge carefully leaving a tiny bit to turn under, then appliqué this to the velvet. If you plan a line of couching around the outline of the design, it is not necessary to turn under the linen edge. Just trim it closely and tack it to the velvet. The couching will cover the raw edge of the design.

For couching traditional Gold Work, use a strong twisted silk thread in a gold color. The couching will be almost invisible. However, it is possible to use a colored thread as a couching thread and incorporate the stitches as part of the design. Be sure all the stitches slant in the same direction and are regularly spaced. When gold threads are laid together to fill a design area, it is important that no space shows between the threads. To achieve this, use two movements for the couching stitches. First, bring needle up to the *right* of the gold thread, and second, take needle down on the *left*. Bring the needle up and take it down a tiny bit *under* the gold threads to help them lie closely together without space showing. When starting

and finishing work, use a needle with a wide eye to pull the ends through. Insert the unthreaded needle from the right side of the fabric until only the eye is visible; thread the eye with about ½ inch of the double gold threads, and finish pulling needle through cloth. Anchor the gold from the right side with a few close couching stitches at the point where the needle went down.

Gold embroidery can be worked effectively by using substitutions for the traditional and expensive gold threads. There are several types of Lurex threads available, as well as tiny round or flat gold-colored threads or braids and cords. These Lurex or other threads do not tarnish and are not easily damaged.

They have a further advantage in that they are inexpensive and readily accessible. They can be couched with linen or cotton floss, or either weight of silk thread — the regular A size, or the buttonhole twist, depending on the desired effect. Look in mail order catalogues from needlework houses, and check the gift-wrap departments of stores as well as notions-and-trim departments of fabric shops. Since this area has not been explored fully, it is challenging and exciting to look for suitable materials for original design techniques.

## SHISHA EMBROIDERY

Shisha embroidery or mirror embroidery, originated in India around the same time as the Taj Mahal. The mirrors for this type of work were actually hand-cut pieces of mica, said to keep away evil spirits. These mica pieces are quite difficult to find today. However, there are easily acquired substitutes that work just as well. Small round mirrors of various sizes and thickness are sold at bead supply stores. *Paillettes,* which are large, flat sequins, can also be used. A product called Mylar, available at most art supply stores, makes a very good substitute. Cardboard circles covered with heavy-duty aluminum foil also might do. Keep in mind that none of these can be washed. Regardless of what is used, the technique is the same. First, the mirror must be attached or anchored to the fabric with a kind of thread frame. This is a little like tying a package. Bring the needle up at A, close to mirror edge; take thread vertically over mirror and go down at B;

**Decorative Couching Variations Suitable For Gold Or Lurex Threads**

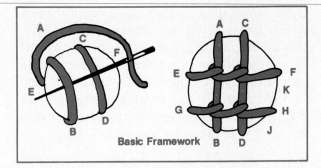

Basic Framework

repeat for C and D. Bring the needle up at E for horizontal row; then, with thread up, go over and under AB, also CD, and down at F. Repeat for G and H (see diagrams). This is the basic frame. There is a choice of Cretan or Buttonhole Stitch worked through the thread frame and into the fabric to complete the design. The Cretan Stitch is worked in a circular fashion. Thread the needle with pearl cotton or stranded embroidery floss. The thread goes *over* the CDGH crossing, then under it, down at J and up at K. Pull the thread tight. As the frame is worked, the inside stitches will be close together and the outer ones farther apart to complete the circle.

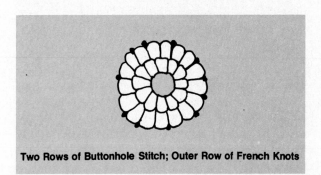

Two Rows of Buttonhole Stitch; Outer Row of French Knots

For the Buttonhole Stitch border, bring needle up at I, cross over then *under* CDGH. The needle goes down at J, very close to mirror edge, and up at K. With thread to the right, continue the stitch, always going over, then under the framework. Both Cretan and Buttonhole Stitches may be single or double at the outline; they also may be finished off with an edging of French Knots or Lazy Daisy or Detached Chain Stitches. Mirror embroidery can be worked on almost any firmly woven fabric; it would also be an exciting addition to ready-made articles of clothing — skirts, vest or shirts. Depending upon the fabric or the article, strong cotton thread, heavy silk thread or wool yarns (thin) can be used.

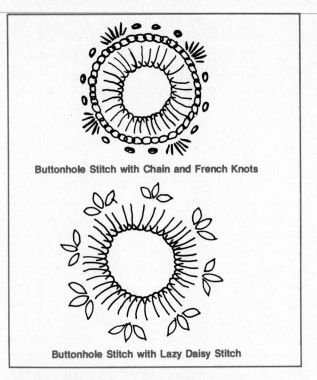

Buttonhole Stitch with Chain and French Knots

Buttonhole Stitch with Lazy Daisy Stitch

## BEAD AND SEQUIN WORK

Adding beads and/or sequins to work is simply an elaborate extension of embroidery and is suitable for pictures, wall hangings, evening clothes and accessories. Such work should be dry cleaned. Most notion or hobbycraft stores or mail order catalogues have small plastic envelopes containing an amazing assortment of beads and sequins.

There are tiny round seed beads, mostly opaque or "chalky." There are glass beads lined with dye which are more formal in feeling and have a rather fragile coloring. There are transparent glass beads where the color is in the glass, and the effect comes from light hitting the beads at various angles. Long slender bugle beads look rather like tiny pieces of spaghetti. There are all kinds and sizes of imitation pearls and wooden

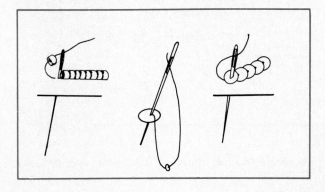

and cork beads. The best type of bead to use depends upon the project. Most of these beads have a hole centered through them while some of the bead-like "jewels" are flat on the back side, with tiny holes in each end so they can be sewed on like buttons. Beading needles are long and very slender in order to slide through the holes in the smaller beads. Strong thread, often doubled, is used.

If you wish to use beads just to outline a design, string the beads on a thread and lay the thread along the line of design as in couching. With a second needle and thread, tie or tack down the string of beads with a tiny stitch into the fabric between each bead; keep the beads close together so the line appears unbroken. For a different effect, sew the beads on separately with a small Backstitch. Loops or a fringe of beads are good decorations for the neckline or sleeve edge of garments. However, in any design where beads hang free of the fabric, they must be anchored securely. Bring the needle up through the fabric and secure with a tiny stitch; thread through the desired number and color of beads, including an anchor or end bead. Now take beading needle *around* the end bead, not through it; then insert needle through all of the remaining beads back to the starting point.

Sequins are as varied in size, shape and color as beads. They are flat or cupped. For either style, a regular needle can be used since the hole in the middle of the sequin is large enough to accommodate it. If a design line is to be covered with sequins, sew them on with a Backstitch so that they overlap each other like fish scales. If sequins are scattered throughout the design, use a seed bead or other bead to secure them. Bring the needle up through the fabric, through the hole in the sequin and then through the bead. Take the thread *around* the bead, then back through the bead, then back through the hole in the sequin and fabric, and end off. Large sequins, or paillettes, have a hole on the edge. These can be attached with one or two tiny over-and-over Whipping Stitches.

Transfer the design to the fabric using one of the methods described earlier. If the fabric is a sweater or other stretchy material, it might be easiest to work the design through tissue paper. Draw the design on the paper with a ball point pen. Baste it in position on the right side of the sweater or article, then work the bead and/or sequin embroidery through the tissue paper. Use a backing or underlining to stabilize the work, and use hoops if needed. When the design is finished, tear the paper away carefully. Strong, transparent nylon thread works well with this type of embroidery, but keep the thread lengths short to avoid tangling.

To make a garment with bead decoration, do the embroidery on the fabric before the garment is cut out. Baste around the pattern piece on the fabric; work the embroidery, then cut out the garment piece following paper pattern lines. If the beading is close to an edge — such as a neckline — use a zipper foot on the machine when assembling the pieces.

## HEMSTITCH (ITALIAN OPENWORK)

Table linens, sheets, handkerchiefs and any article with a straight edge can be hemmed with a lacy embroidery often called Hemstitch. When the same techniques and stitches are used to make intricate designs in the center of fabric, it is called Italian Openwork. This type of embroidery is used on clothing as well as on table linens and household items.

*Types of Fabric:* Openwork can only be worked on an even-weave fabric in which threads can be counted easily. Test to see that threads can also be pulled easily and will leave an attractive opening. Most linens, many woolens and some cottons are appropriate.

*Preparing Work:* Decide on the design; measure and mark for corners, hems, etc. Pull as many threads as necessary for the stitch that will be used. The more elaborate stitches usually require a wider band of pulled threads. With fine embroidery scissors, cut the threads at corners and at the ends of designs.

If the piece is to be hemmed with the embroidery, decide between a mitered corner or an overlapped corner, as shown. The thicker the fabric, the harder it is to work an overlap — thus mitered corners become necessary in heavy fabrics. In a hemmed piece, after the threads are pulled, the turned edge of the hem must be basted very close to the band of pulled threads so that each stitch will catch the edge of the hem and hold it in place.

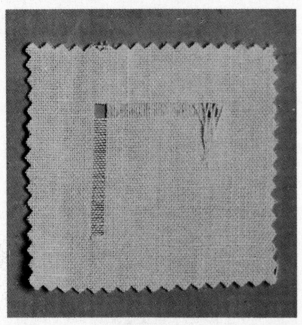

Pulling threads.

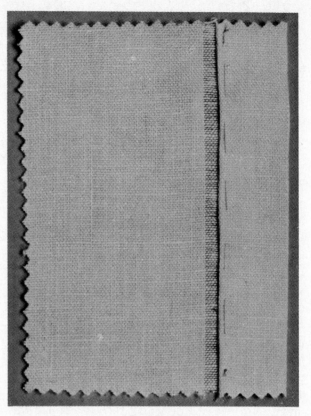

Basting hem.

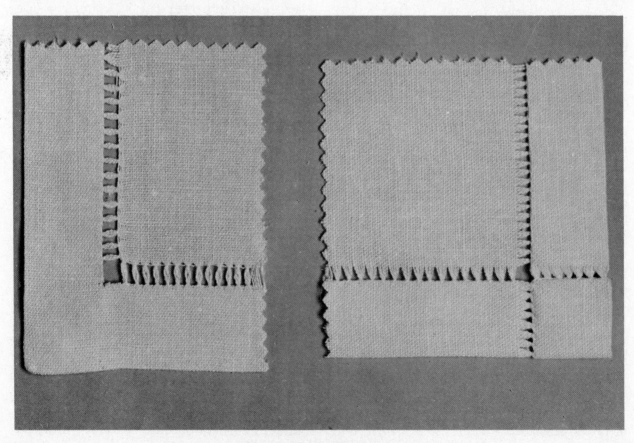

The two treatments of corners

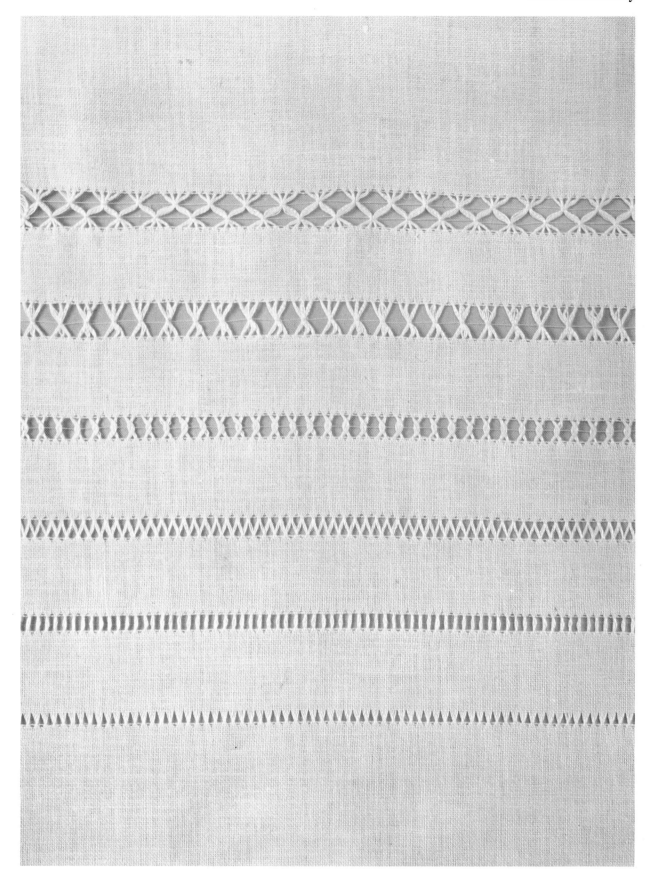

**Hemstitch Sampler**

*The Stitches:* There is one basic stitch for hemstitching. In simple one-sided hemstitching, that stitch is used along the edge that holds the hem. In the more intricate patterns it is used on both edges. Start by taking a stitch in the edge of the first row of thread above the opening; bring the needle up through the wrong side of the fabric. Pass the needle under a group of four to six threads and up again to the right side (not catching any fabric threads with the needle). Pass the needle back again around the same group of threads but this time up through the edge of the first row of thread above the opening. Pull the stitch tight, making a little bundle of the wrapped fabric threads. It often helps to push the encircling thread up against the top edge of the opening with the thumbnail as the stitch is pulled. Pass the needle under the next group of four to six threads, up to the right side and back around the same group and through the edge as before. Continue until all the threads are taken up in bundles.

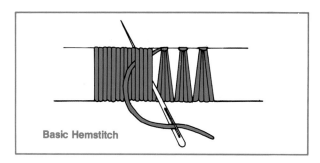

**Basic Hemstitch**

Ladder hemstitching is worked with the same stitch; then the same groups of threads are worked in the same way back along the other edge of the opening. Serpentine hemstitching must be worked in even-numbered groups, four,

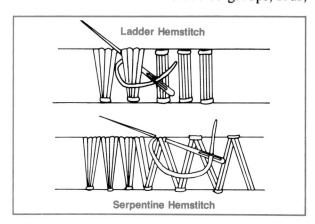

**Ladder Hemstitch**

**Serpentine Hemstitch**

**Three Types Of Smocking — Top to Bottom: Honeycomb, English (worked over shirring threads) and Cable and Wave.**

six or eight threads in each bundle. The opposite side is worked back by picking up alternating groups, half of the threads from one group and half from the adjoining group.

Interlaced hemstitching has many variations, depending on how wide an opening is desired and how many groups are pulled together. Make the groups of bundles rather slim and in ladder form. For the simplest interlaced stitch, tie the stitching thread around the center of one bundle at the right end of the row. Bring the needle over the face of the work, around behind the third bundle and up over the second bundle. Flip the needle so that it is now pointing from right to left and pull the thread tight. This will make the third and second bundles crisscross. Pick up the fourth and fifth bundles in the same way. Though the stitch is never wrapped or tied until the needle reaches the left end of the work, the thread will lie in place along the center of the row and hold the crisscross pattern in place. In other interlaced designs where the bundles are grouped together in threes and fours or in double alternating lines, it is necessary to wrap the thread around each group. For some interesting variations see the Hemstitch sampler.

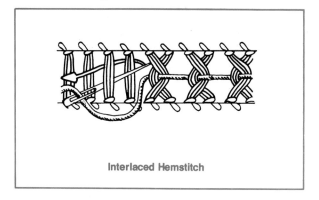

**Interlaced Hemstitch**

## SMOCKING

Children's clothes, aprons and informal wear, as well as articles for the home, are enhanced with smocking. Not only does this simple embroidery decorate the fabric but it also shirrs it evenly and smoothly. The proportion of the shirring is two or three to one so that it is best done on light-to-medium-weight fabrics.

There are three types of smocking and very few stitches to learn. The most common type for clothing is the cable and wave which can be done either by thread count on squared fabrics such as gingham and dimity or from a printed pattern. These two simple stitches — the Cable and the Wave, are both variations of the Outline or Stem Stitch.

English smocking employs the same two stitches, but the fabric is shirred with threads run evenly by hand before the embroidery is started. In this way, the fullness is more exactly controlled and an entire area can also be filled with a small solidly worked design. This is the best method to use when making up new designs on fabrics which are not squared.

**Beginning Step For English Smocking**

If the gathering stitches are run evenly (as shown) for English smocking, it is then a simple matter to pick up the fabric in each ridge made by the pulling up of the thread. You may then work in Cable or Wave or in conventional Outline Stitch. The latter is used for filling in solid areas.

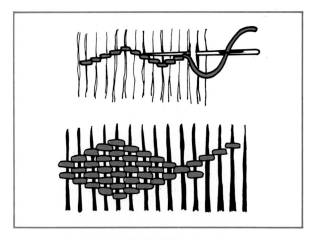

**Completed English Smocking Pattern**

Honeycomb is worked over squares by picking up a small stitch at one corner of the square and then, moving to the right, picking up a small stitch at the second corner. Run back through the first stitch and *down only* again at the second, pulling up tightly. Two threads will now pass over the outside of the pleat that has been pulled

together. Pass the thread under the next square and be sure to let it lie flat. Repeat the stitching between the third and fourth corner to pull up another pleat. On the next row alternate the position of the pleat. Continue so that the pleats form a zigzag arrangement.

Honeycomb smocking is generally done on a slightly larger scale and therefore is suitable for slightly heavier fabrics. The one stitch used is almost entirely concealed behind the fabric, only a small pick showing on the surface. It can be done on thread count, squared fabric or from a printed pattern.

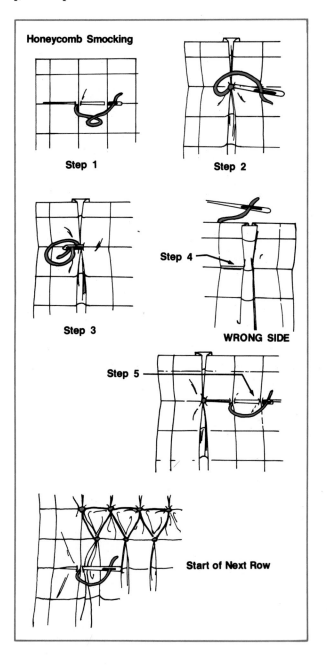

Honeycomb Smocking

Step 1

Step 2

Step 3

Step 4

WRONG SIDE

Step 5

Start of Next Row

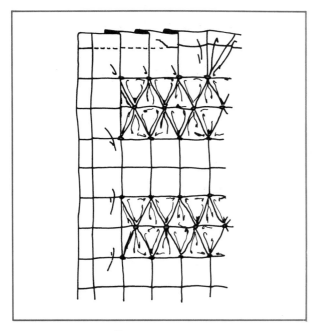

**Honeycomb Smocking**

The Cable Stitch is worked like Outline, from left to right on the row, with the needle picking up the fabric from right to left. Using dots or the edges of squares as evenly marked points, bring the needle up through one dot; down half way between the second and third dot; then up in the second dot, with thread below the needle. Pull the thread up away from line stitching. Put the needle down between the third and fourth dot; then up in the third dot, with thread above the needle. Pull the thread down away from the line of stitching. Continue along the line, alternating the thread, up, down, up, down.

In a one-step Wave, the thread is held below the needle at the bottom of each Wave; then below

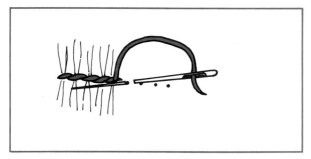

**Outline or Stem Stitch**

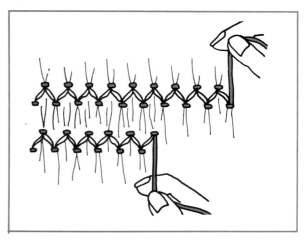

**Wave Stitch**

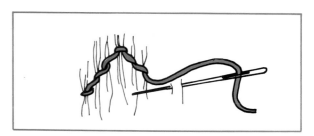

**Trellis Stitch, a variation of Wave Stitch**

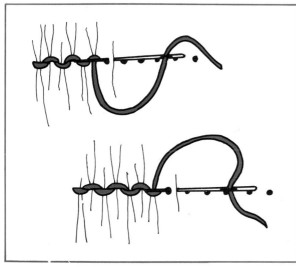

**Cable Stitch**

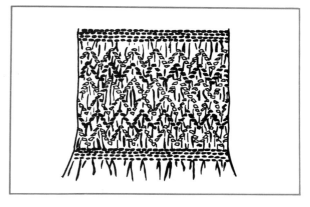

**Midriff smocking worked with Wave Stitch**

again as the next stitch is taken higher up. Then the thread is thrown above the needle as the stitch is taken across the top and held above as the next stitch is taken down. In a two-step or more Wave, the same system is used with the thread always held down as you go up, and up as you go down.

## TENERIFE

Tenerife embroidery comes from Tenerife, the largest island in the Canary group. It is sometimes called *darning* and sometimes *needle-weaving*. It is lace-like in appearance, with the stitch being worked over a wheel or frame of supporting long Straight Stitches. Work from the right side and from the center out (like a spider web). The finished effect is almost woven in appearance. Pearl cotton is perhaps the best choice of thread.

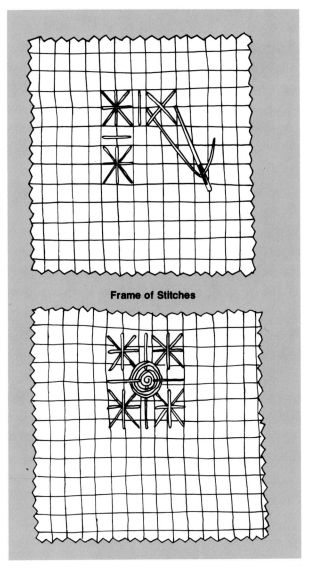

**Frame of Stitches**

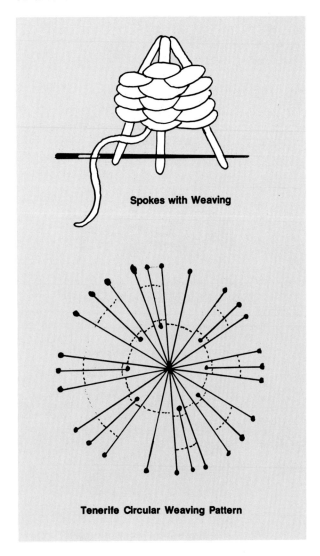

**Spokes with Weaving**

**Tenerife Circular Weaving Pattern**

Tenerife embroidery can also be worked on checked fabric, such as gingham. This has the appearance of drawn work, except that it is worked completely on top of the fabric and the threads are not actually drawn.

The easiest way to transfer a design is to make a perforated pattern. Center it in place on the fabric; then with a pencil, lightly mark dots through the perforations. Make a wheel-like structure with any number of spokes; sections of the spokes will be covered later. The part of the spoke not covered will be an integral part of the design, so consider this when choosing the color and texture of the thread to be used. Additional spokes can be added to an outer ring of the wheel, alternating the weaving design. Practice several variations of this before starting the design on your project.

When the foundation wheel is laid, bring the needle up at center, to the left of any spoke. Work from left to right. Go over and under a spoke then on to the next, and so on. The design can be varied by going over three spokes and under two. In the weaving, the needle never goes through the fabric. This permits the use of various sizes of yarn and a blunt needle.

## MACHINE EMBROIDERY

Machine embroidery is relatively new in America. It is somewhat faster than handwork, but as it is not portable, and there is not the wide selection of stitches available as in handwork. The overall effect is interesting and unusual, however, and it is an exciting medium to explore. A sewing machine with a zigzag attachment is very helpful but not absolutely essential. There is no need for an automatic machine with a wide range of set decorative stitches either. Many machines come with a special darning foot. Practice will help master this technique of embroidery. The manual of directions for the machine will be helpful also.

To use the machine for embroidery if there is no darning foot, remove the presser foot entirely and drop the feed. This means lowering the teeth so they will not engage while the machine is running. Ring hoops are essential too, as the fabric must be taut, and you will need both hands free to manipulate the frames.

Be sure the machine is threaded properly before starting. If there is doubt about the sharpness of the needle, put in a new one. Place the fabric over the *outer* ring of the hoops, right side up; then place the smaller hoop inside, and tighten the frames so that fabric is smooth and stretched. The fabric in the hoop will lie flat on the machine bed.

Mercerized cotton thread, both in solid and ombre shades, is best and easiest to use. It is a little heavier and feeds more evenly than polyester threads, which tend to break and tangle in the work.

First efforts in machine embroidery should be strictly practice sessions, for it takes a while to learn how to control the machine. In the beginning, use the same thread in both needle and bob-

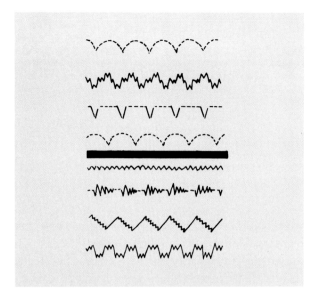

**A Sample of Machine Decorative Stitches**

bin and keep the tensions even. Later on, experiment with one or both tensions changed — for instance, a loose bobbin tension and tight top tension will give the stitching a very loopy, shaggy effect. Try hand-winding the bobbin with heavy-weight threads or floss.

Lower the presser bar in starting. Since the feed has been dropped, the teeth do not control the fabric — you do. If the machine has a reduction gear, use it, this slows it down and gives you more control. Move the hoops by hand; the stitch size depends upon the speed of the machine. For a small stitch, run the machine fast but move the hoops slowly. For longer stitches, move the hoops quickly with the machine at moderate speed. Create texture by piling up stitches; hold the hoops so that the fabric cannot "travel," and let the stitches pile up on each other. Try curves and circles, close and spaced rows; then overlap the stitches to see the effect.

If the machine will not switch from straight stitching to zigzag while working, stop the machine to switch over but be sure the needle is up or it may bend and break.

Try zigzag stitching close and open, wide and narrow. Drop one or more pieces of yarn on the fabric and zigzag over it. You can enclose it entirely within the width of the stitch, or catch part of it and finish the machine couching with random straight stitching. Learn to work in a reverse as well as a forward direction; let stitching lines radiate, cross each other and follow angles as

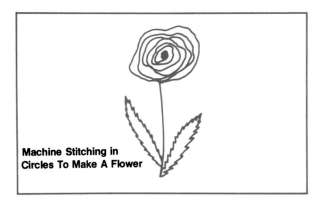

**Machine Stitching in Circles To Make A Flower**

well as curves. After practicing for a while, try drawing a simple design with a pencil directly on the fabric. Put in only the main lines and not the details. It is impossible to copy a design exactly using the machine; the embroidery will be more interesting if the drawing is used just as a guide. Going round and round in increasing circles gives a flower shape; this can also be used to fill in spaces or background. Experiment with different effects; these alone may suggest a design.

Machine embroidery combines beautifully with other forms, such as machine appliqué, which is covered in the Appliqué chapter. For another experiment, baste two pieces of fabric together, one on top of the other. Place the double fabric in the hoops, then stitch some simple shapes — circles, ovals, triangles etc. Remove the hoops from the machine, cut the top layer away from the shapes, as you would in reverse appliqué, then continue stitching until the design is complete.

Some hand embroidery added to machine work helps to emphasize certain parts of the design. It is the individual and personal experimentation that gives this work its novelty and excitement.

## THE FINISHING TOUCHES

Most embroidery projects need to be finished off for a professional look. Some suggestions have been covered in the sections on quilts and pillow and wall hangings; ready-made articles of clothing usually need no additional work.

Sometimes, however, it is difficult to keep appliqué or embroidery clean while you work on it. If the project is washable, swish it gently through tepid-to-cold suds made with cold-water soap. Do not wring or squeeze, but rinse thoroughly

until water is clear. Lay embroidery on or roll it up in a clean towel to absorb excess moisture, then block and press while damp. When you press, be sure to protect the work. Spread a clean turkish towel on the ironing board and lay embroidery face down on it. Use a press cloth against the wrong side, and press with a lifting motion with a medium to hot iron. The toweling will act as a cushion to protect raised embroidery or appliqué and small beads or found objects.

If the work needs to be blocked rather than pressed after washing or cleaning, put it in hoops, stretchers or frames of proper size. You can also use a board covered with muslin. Lay the dampened work on this, straightening sides and corners; then stretch in place using push pins around the edges to secure. Lay a clean wet cloth over the work, whether on the board or in hoops; keep it there until the cloth is dry. The fabric will respond beautifully to this and come out unwrinkled and fresh looking.

To frame needlework, be sure there is sufficient border around the design to turn under. Cut heavy cardboard to fit the rabbet at back of frame, then trim the cardboard *very slightly* according to the thickness of the fabric. Place cardboard in correct position over *wrong* side of embroidery; stick a few pins along the edges to hold it in place. With needle and thread, lace from side to side and end to end to secure the embroidery over the cardboard. If the folds at the corners are too bulky, cut away the under part. If the background fabric is not too heavy, masking

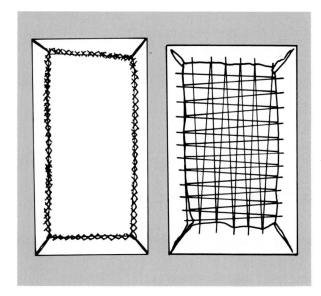

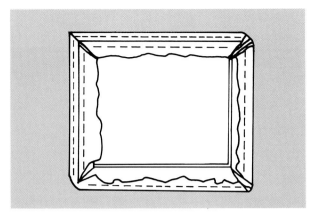

tape may hold it in place on the cardboard, eliminating the thread lacing.

Wall-hangings and banners are not framed. If they need extra weight to hang evenly, interline them with sail cloth, canvas, Pellon® or felt. Turn the edges of the hanging over the interlining and baste in place along the edges. A felt lining can be whipped or blind stitched to the basted edge; a buttonhole or blanket stitch, or a heavy couched yarn can finish off the edges. If edges of a wall hanging or banner are to be bound, simply baste the hanging, the interlining and lining together; then sew binding through all three layers.

Some banners can be finished with machine or hand-sewn hems along the sides and bottom

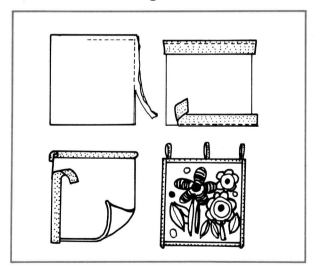

(perhaps with fringe along the bottom end). For extra weight, sew a casing on the wrong side, by hand, just above the fringe, and insert a flat strip of wood — window shades are weighted this way.

A wooden dowel or metal drapery rod slipped through a casing at the top is an effective and easy

way to hang projects. However, tabs or loops may be preferred. For loops, cut rectangles from fabric twice the finished length and width, with seam allowances. Fold the rectangles in center lengthwise, *right sides together,* and stitch along the edge, leaving the ends open. Turn to right side, work seam either to the back or to one edge, and press. Fold loops crosswise and measure to be

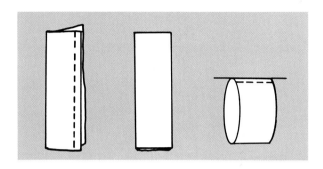

sure there is room for the rod or pole to slide through. Baste across the ends of the loops, then line them up evenly along the top edge of the hanging or banner. Be sure the first and last loop are even with the sides of the banner. Baste these loops in place against the right side of the banner, loops down. Now place lining against banner, right sides together; pin securely, then baste. The loops will be concealed between the banner and the lining. Turn banner to wrong side; the basting stitches holding the loops in place are now visible and are a guide for stitching. Stitch up one side, across the top, catching the loops securely; then stitch down the other side. Leave the bottom open for turning. When banner is turned and pressed, finish off the bottom edge in any of several ways — close it with hand or machine embroidery stitches, use fringe or a border or decorative braid.

# *ABBREVIATIONS of EMBROIDERY STITCHES AND COLOR CHART*

Ru . . . . . . . . . . . . . . . . . . . . . Running Stitch
Spl . . . . . . . . . . . . . . . . . . . . . . . . Split Stitch
Ou . . . . . . . . . . . . . . . . . . . . Outline Stitch
SS . . . . . . . . . . . . . . . . . . . . . Stem Stitch
CrS . . . . . . . . . . . . . . . . . . . . Cross Stitch
WR . . . . . . . . . . . . . Whipped Running Stitch
Se . . . . . . . . . . . . . . . . . . . . . . Seed Stitch
WB . . . . . . . . . . . . . . . . Whipped Backstitch
But . . . . . . . . . . . . . . . . . . Buttonhole Stitch
CS . . . . . . . . . . . . . Couched Square Flling
Fl . . . . . . . . . . . . . . . . . . . . . . . . . Fly Stitch
Ch . . . . . . . . . . . . . . . . . . . . . Chain Stitch
LD . . . . . . . . . . . . . . . . . Lazy Daisy Stitch
FK . . . . . . . . . . . . . . . . . . French Knot
Fe . . . . . . . . . . . . . . . . . . . . . Featherstitch
Fsh . . . . . . . . . . . . . . . . . . Fishbone Stitch
Her . . . . . . . . . . . . . . . . Herringbone Stitch
Sa . . . . . . . . . . . . . . . . . . . . Satin Stitch
L&S . . . . . . . . . . . . . . Long-and-Short Stitch
Bul . . . . . . . . . . . . . . . . . . Bullion Knot
VaD . . . . . . . . . . . . . . . . . Van Dyke Stitch
Cr . . . . . . . . . . . . . . . . . . . . Cretan Stitch
Co . . . . . . . . . . . . . . . . . . . . Coral Knot
FiW . . . . . . . . . . . . . . . . . Filled With

1. Pale Pink
2. Medium Pink
3. Dark Pink
4. Light Red
5. True Red
6. Dark Red
7. Maroon
8. Red-Violet
9. Purple
10. Lavender
11. Blue-Violet
12. Dark Blue
13. Medium Blue
14. Light Blue
15. Turquoise
16. Light Aqua
17. Dark Green
18. Medium Green
19. Bright Green
20. Leaf Green
21. Pale Green
22. Chartreuse
23. Olive Green

24. Chrome Yellow
25. Bright Yellow
26. Gold-Yellow
27. Medium Yellow
28. Pale Yellow
29. Light Orange
30. Medium Orange
31. Red-Orange
32. Beige
33. Sand
34. Light Brown
35. Medium Brown
36. Dark Brown
37. Black
38. Dark Gray
39. Medium Gray
40. Pearl Gray
41. White
42. Ivory
43. Coral
44. Gold
45. Brown-Gold
46. Burnt Orange

# *EMBROIDERY PROJECTS*

# EMBROIDERY PROJECTS

## WILD STRAWBERRY BOUQUET

This design can be worked on a pillow or as a picture. Use crewel yarn on wool or linen, or four strands of six-strand embroidery floss on linen. Work all leaves, flowers and berries in Long-and-Short Stitches; all stems and veins in Outline Stitch; and flower center and berry seeds in French Knots.

Full Size Motif

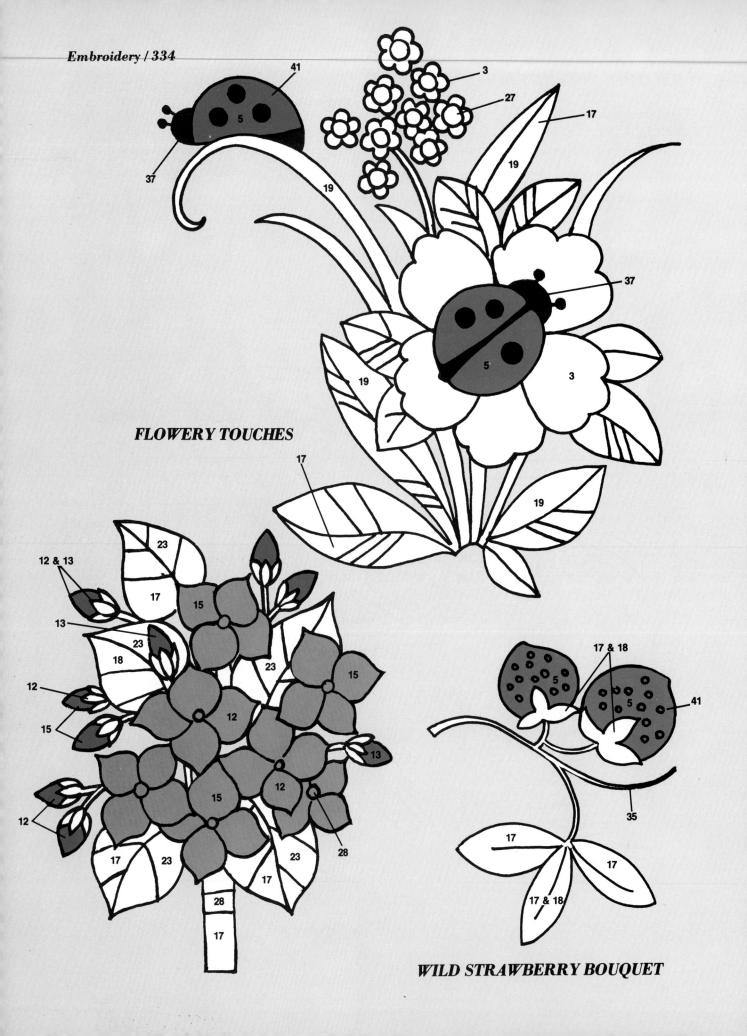

**FLOWERY TOUCHES**

**WILD STRAWBERRY BOUQUET**

## FLOWERY TOUCHES

These motifs may be used singly or in groups on clothing or in home decorating. Use crewel yarn on wool or linen, or four strands of six-strand embroidery floss on linen or other lightweight fabrics. Work all large areas in Long-and-Short Stitch or Satin Stitch; all stems and veins in Outline Stitch; and small centers, dots and seeds in French Knots. Mix shades of green in leaves and at the base of buds to add depth and texture.

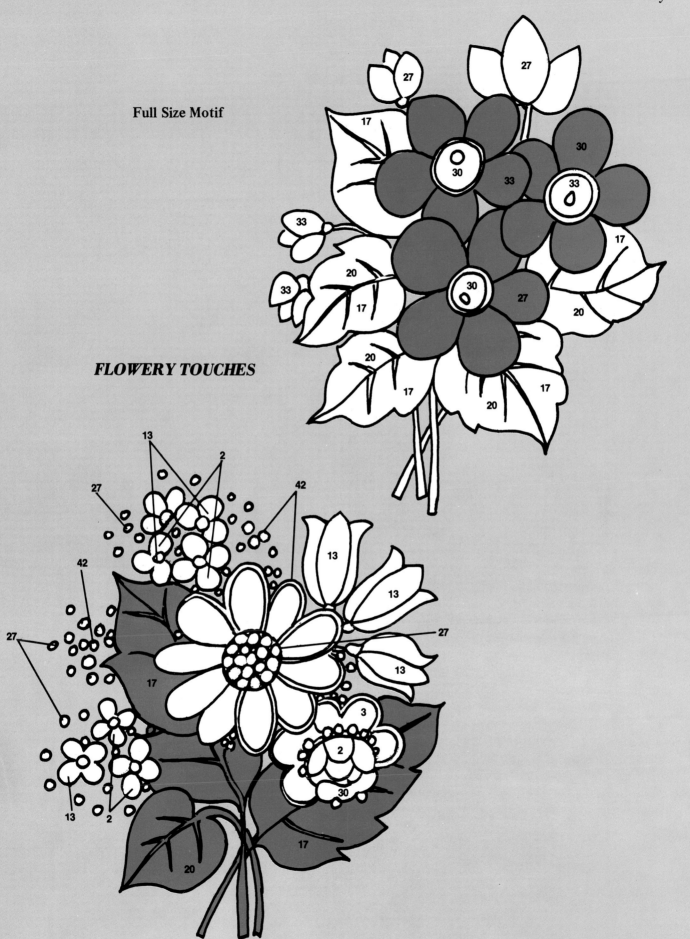

Full Size Motif

**FLOWERY TOUCHES**

**Full Size Motif**

## MONOGRAMS WITH FLOWERS

Household linens, jeans and a host of other items may be decorated and personally identified with easily embroidered monograms. They may be worked in two colors or in several colors and shades. The letters may be used alone or cut from fabric and appliquéd. Work the leaves and flowers in the Chain Stitch, filling from the outline in to the center; or use the Satin Stitch. When working names into a piece of stitchery, use a variety of stitches such as Couched Square filling to achieve variation and a stitched sampler effect. Enlarged letters may be used as a central motif for a Trapunto or White Work bedspread, or reduced, as a signature to a large piece of needlework.

Full Size Motif

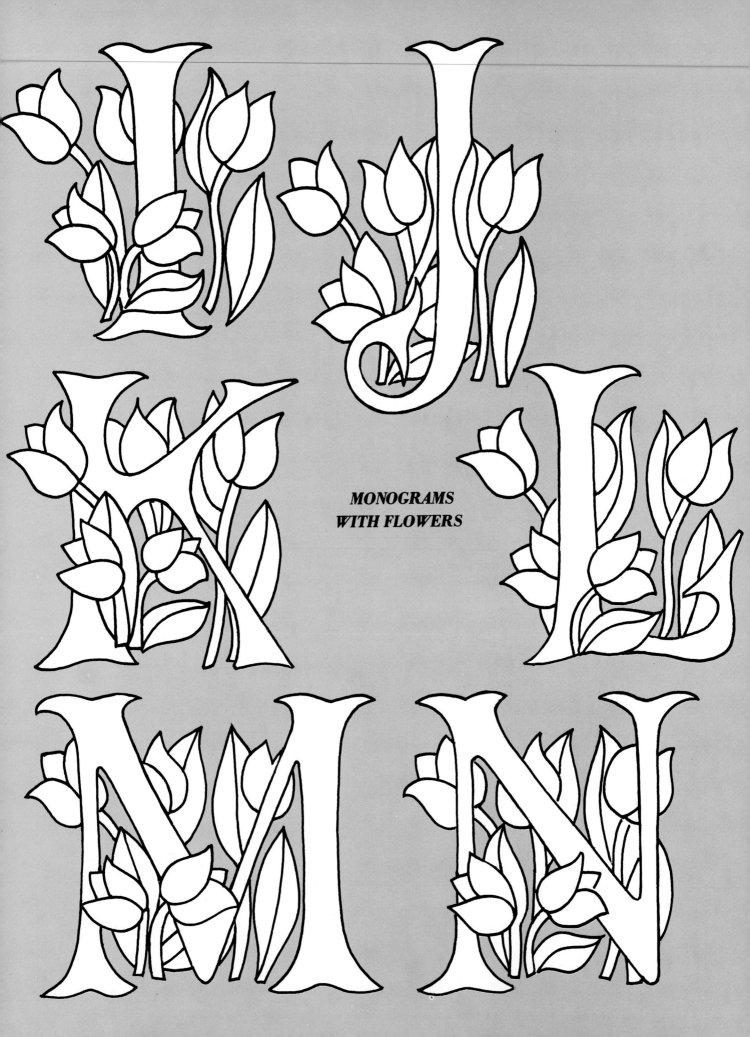

MONOGRAMS
WITH FLOWERS

MONOGRAMS WITH FLOWERS

**MONOGRAMS WITH FLOWERS**

**Full Size Motif**

## GLASSES CASE WITH CREWEL FLOWERS

Another small project using the basic crewel stitches is this charming glasses case. It is worked here in four shades of green, lavender, pink, coral, yellow and pale blue. After completion of embroidery, each side is mounted on stiffening, such as crinoline, and whipped together around the edge with matching thread and using small stitches. Slip stitch a lining to the back of each piece before joining the edges or make a complete lining to drop inside and slip stitch it around the open edge only.

**Full Size Motif**

## CREWEL PICTURE FRAME

This very personal picture frame is simple to make and is also a good project for a beginner. The sampler is done in the most basic crewel stitches. We have used eight colors and shades; but choose your own color combinations. Outline the frame and cutout in main color using the Chain Stitch; also do the name and connecting stems in the Chain Stitch. Work the leaves and flower petals in the Lazy Daisy Stitch; seeds and flower centers in French Knots; and flower buds in Satin Stitch outlined with Stem Stitch.

Cut two pieces of stiff cardboard to match inner and outer lines of our embroidery pattern. Glue felt or cotton padding to one side of one cardboard. Cover this with embroidered piece, fitting evenly around the inner line, clipping corners as necessary. Fit excess fabric around cardboard and glue back in place. Let dry, then glue second cardboard over raw fabric on back. Let this dry and glue onto plastic frame.

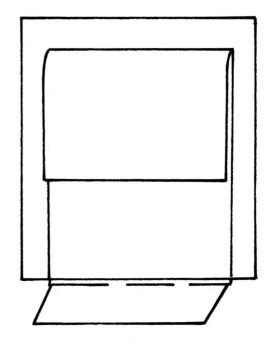

**FANCIFUL FLOWERS FOR DECORATIONS**

## FANCIFUL FLOWERS FOR DECORATIONS

The Backstitch and Satin Stitch are used for these bright flowers to decorate jeans or a denim skirt and bolero. Create variety by using the Lazy Daisy Stitch, French Knots and the Chain Stitch. Use washable yarn or six-strand floss in several colors. Three of these flowers will also just fit along the left edge of a table mat and one similar flower on a napkin. Make a colorful ribbon bookmark with one flower, using Lurex thread.

Full Size Motif

## ANNA THANKFUL AND THE BIRD IN THE TREE CREWEL

### Designed and created by Jinny Avery

Here are two designs to work in crewel yarn on linen or in wool for pictures, pillows, knitting bags or whatever you wish. Use the colors from the picture or ones of your own selection.

# THE BIRD IN THE CREWEL TREE

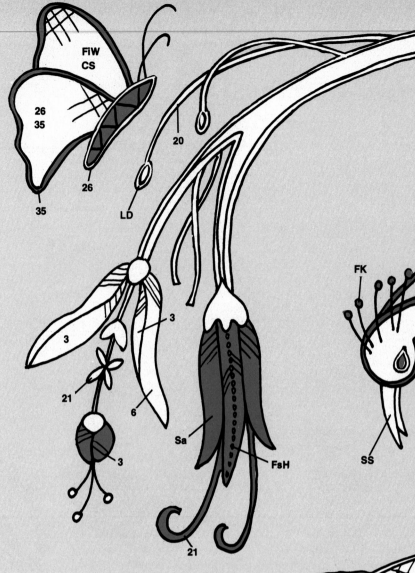

**Full Size Motif**

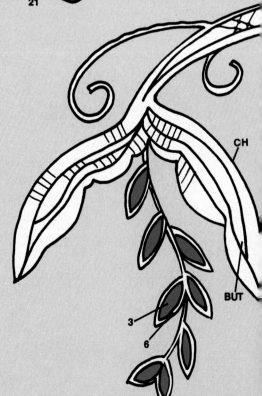

## JACOBEAN PILLOW

*Designed and created by Carter Houck courtesy of Lady's Circle Needlework*

A fine piece of crewel for the person ready to try lots of stitches! Though colors are suggested, you may plan your own, using blues or purples or colors to fit your decorating scheme. This design fits a 14-inch square pillow. It can be enlarged for the lower edge of drapery panels or used in variations and repeats around a window or bed valance.

26
CO
FsH
BUT
L&S
FsH
17
6
33
20
21
17
FEA
20
36
33
36
WR
21
33
FlW
CS
20
22

ANNA THANKFUL

# BUTTERFLY BUNTING

### Designed and created by Sandy Singer

A bunting is a perfect gift for a new baby. You can make your own pattern from the diagrams and dimensions given here, or use the embroidery patterns on a bunting made from commercial patterns.

For the pattern given (size infant to 6 months), 1½ yards of 45-inch fabric, 1¾ yards of 36-inch fabric and the same amount of lining material will be needed. Use a 20, 22 or 24-inch zipper. The embroidery is worked in six-strand, two strands doubled in the needle, in five colors. Sug-gestions for color arrangement are given on large butterfly only. Shades of pink, blue and lavender on pale pink or white would be as effective as the gold tones.

After embroidery is completed, sew zipper in front of bunting; seam front to back bunting. Leave opening in shoulder seam at neck, 3½ inches each side of center (total opening 14 inches to correspond to lower edge of hood). Fold hood; seam one edge from fold to raw edge for back of hood. Sew hood to neckline. Assemble lining in same way, leaving center front seam open. Turn in all raw edges on both pieces and Blind Stitch lining into bunting, around face, bottom of sleeves and along zipper.

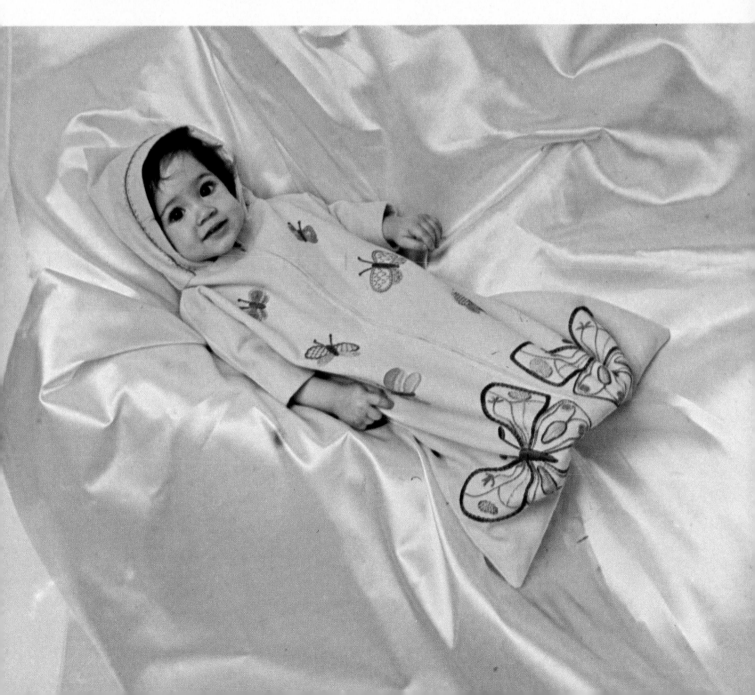

## CROSS STITCH BANDS AND BORDERS

Only two or three colors will make charming borders and edges in Cross Stitch. These can be used (as shown) on clothes or on table linens. On a very large scale, these borders can be stitched in yarn on draperies and valances.

## CROSS STITCH BUTTERFLIES AND FLOWERS

Use these lovely, quick and easy designs to add color to table mats, napkins or the neckline of a peasant blouse. They may be worked over cross stitch canvas or by thread count. Don't forget the possibility of using the same design for needle-point.

Combine these patterns with personalized monograms or use them singly on towels and sheets. The size of the designs can be altered to fit any size monogram by simply changing the size of the cross stitch canvas used.

### Colors

| | | |
|---|---|---|
| 1. | ) | **Medium Green (18)** |
| 2. | X | **Leaf Green (20)** |
| 3. | = | **Bright Yellow (25)** |
| 4. | \ | **Gold Yellow (26)** |
| 5. | / | **Pale Yellow (28)** |

| | | |
|---|---|---|
| 6. | ‖ | **Pale Pink (1)** |
| 7. | · | **Dark Pink (3)** |
| 8. | — | **Dark Blue (12)** |
| 9. | 0 | **Medium Blue (13)** |
| 10. | + | **Light Blue (14)** |

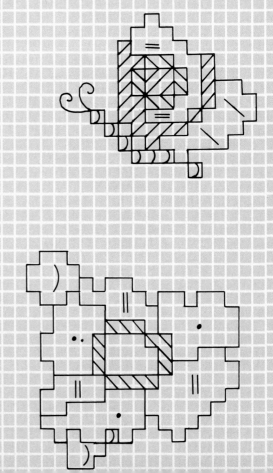

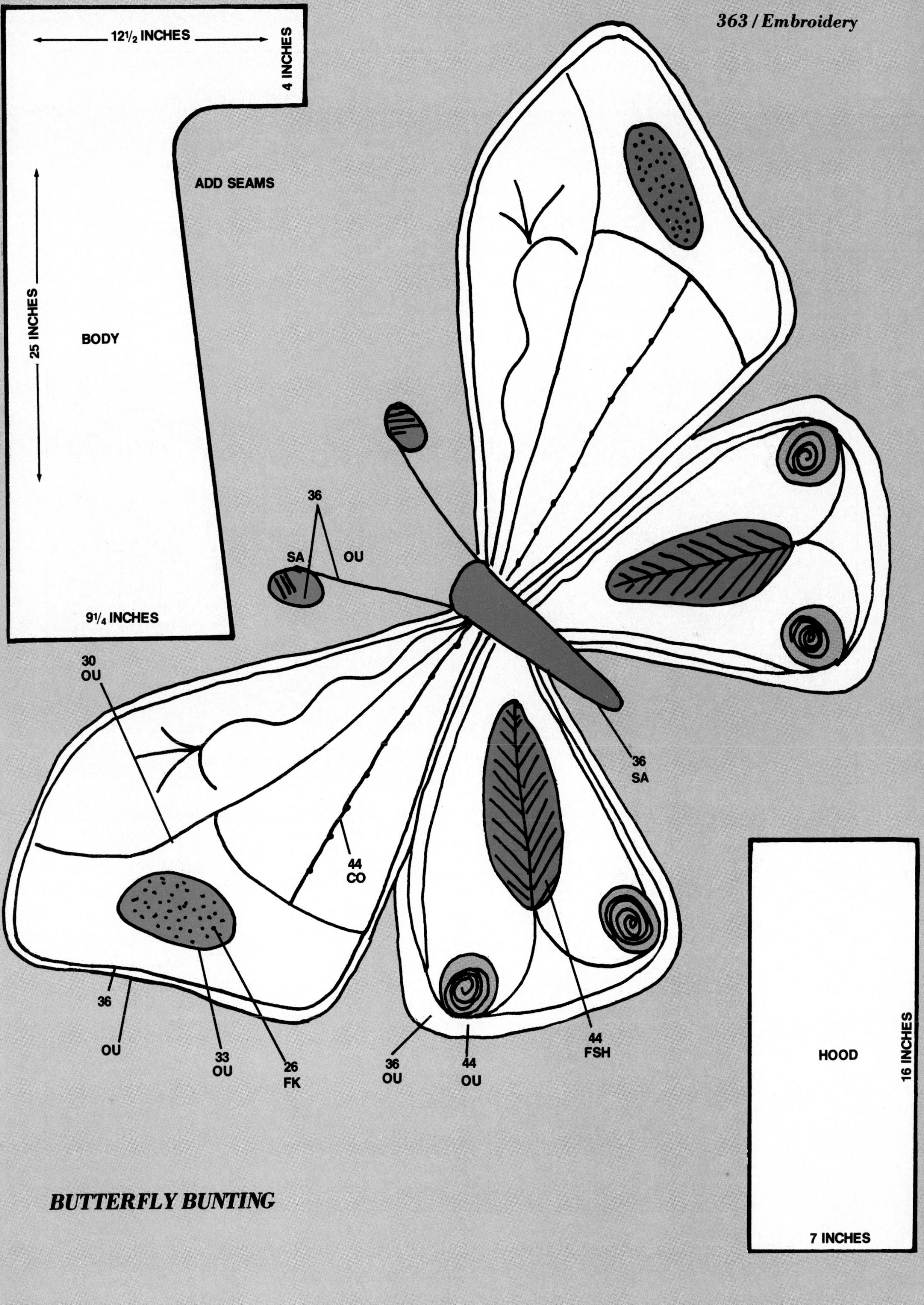

PLACE FRONT WITH SEAM

12½ INCHES

4 INCHES

ADD SEAMS

25 INCHES

CUT BACK ON FOLD

BODY

9¼ INCHES

36

SA

OU

30
OU

44
CO

36
SA

36

OU

33
OU

26
FK

36
OU

44
OU

44
FSH

HOOD

16 INCHES

7 INCHES

*BUTTERFLY BUNTING*

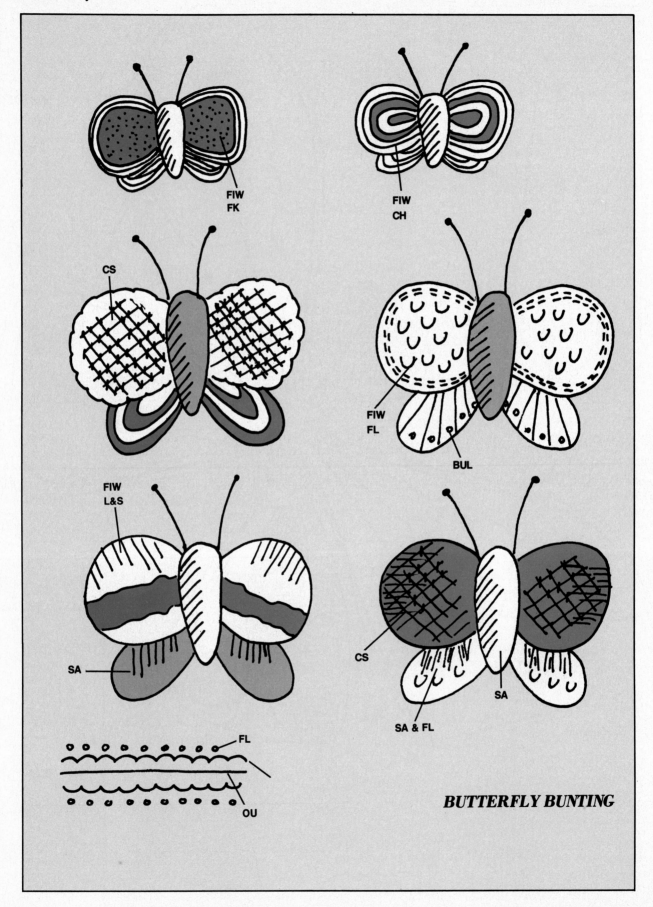

FIW
FK

FIW
CH

CS

FIW
FL

BUL

FIW
L&S

SA

CS

SA

SA & FL

FL

OU

*BUTTERFLY BUNTING*

## ABSTRACT STITCHERY

### *"And Tears Flowed Like Wine"*

### *Designed and Created by Jinny Avery*

This stitchery is a "yarn adventure," executed with a few basic embroidery stitches, a variety of yarns and textures on a length of fairly heavy hand-woven cotton. The design itself is from a conventional paisley. The shapes are cut in varying sizes from paper and moved around on the fabric until a pleasing balance of shape and form are achieved. Because this is a very personal thing, such design arrangement will vary greatly with each person. Rather than distract with color, we have confined the design to neutrals. Thus, the textures and stitches convey the design image. Many of the yarns used are hand spun, and cannot be pulled through a fabric. Consequently, they must be couched. In one or two sections, unique effects are achieved through the use of mohair yarns, which imparts a muted and delicate feeling. The pearls were added as an afterthought; the contrast of the sheen with the dull yarns is an exciting blend; the eye tends to follow the line of pearls and paisleys as though they were teardrops.

In planning or working on any stitcheries, it is a good idea to thread-baste the finished outline on the fabric, so there will be sufficient border left for finishing.

Stitches used are Cretan, Open Buttonhole, Double Buttonhole, Feather, Herringbone, Chain, Detached Chain and French Knot. Some of the couching is plain, other couching is done with a variety of stitches. All of the stitches used, however, are part of a basic group and uncomplicated in execution. This stitchery is a study in neutrals; it would be equally as exciting and challenging to plan one in blacks.

## BEADED BOAT

### *Designed and Created by Courtney Bede*

A cotton T-shirt can become a thing of beauty embroidered with a beaded sailboat. Opaque tiny beads are worked evenly round and round inside the sailboat outlines. First it is necessary to stretch the cotton knit on a hoop, then baste white woven fabric with the design drawn on it to the back to give extra body to the beaded design.

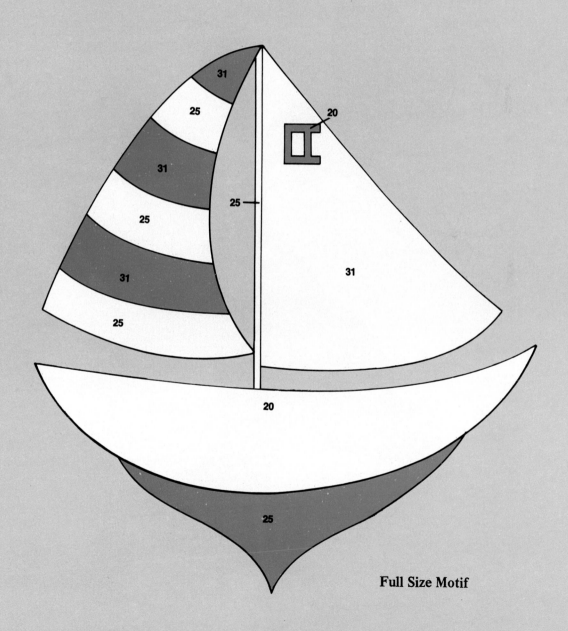

Full Size Motif

**BLOUSE DESIGN IN BLACK WORK
AND WHITE WORK**

**Full Size Motif**

## BLOUSE DESIGNS IN BLACK WORK AND WHITE WORK

### Designed and Created by Sandy Singer

The classic peasant blouse is always around in pattern books and always perfect for large or small spots of embroidery. The effect is quite different in White Work and Black Work.

A. An easy White Work design is done entirely in Chain Stitch in three strands of six-strand embroidery floss. The design on the sleeves is a repeat of the smaller bird and some flowers.

B. Black Work is done on an even-weave fabric, this one a fine wool, so that the straight geometric designs can be worked evenly by thread count. This one is worked in Backstitch, Running Stitch and Cross Stitch in three strands of six-strand embroidery floss. The sleeve motif is a repeat of the center of the front design.

**Full Size Motif**

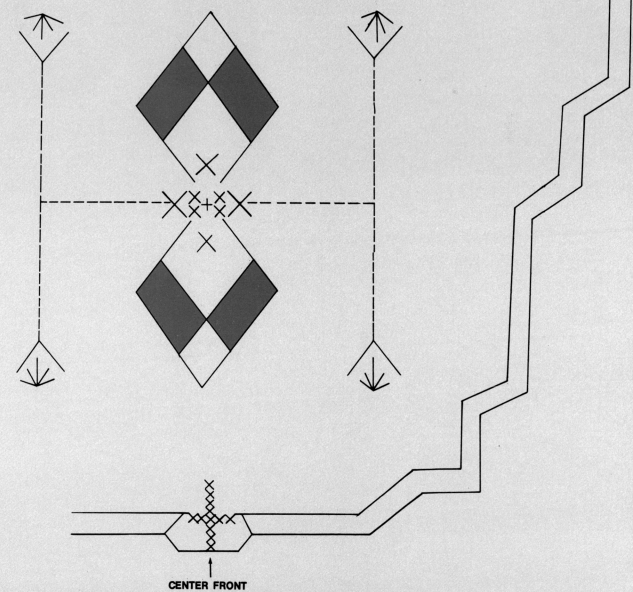

**CENTER FRONT**

## SHISHA IN CREWEL YARN

### Designed and created by Sandy Singer

A border design is worked entirely in Chain Stitch with mica mirrors accented with Buttonhole Stitch. Red, orange and yellow are used on the dark brown wool bolero.

**Full Size Motif**
**A. Tropical Flower**

**BOTTOM**

## THREE FLORAL PILLOWS

All of the following designs may be worked as shown in a minimum variety of stitches, (Satin, Long-and-Short, and Outline) used to fill in the entire areas. They can be worked lightly but with a greater variety of stitches, if you choose.

**A. Tropical Flower:** Five shades of green and five shades of yellow and orange plus a dark red-violet are used for this design for a 12-inch square pillow.

**B. Poppies:** Dark red, four shades of pink, two shades of green and medium-orange are used for this 12 x 14-inch pillow.

**C. Butterfly:** White, black, gray, red, orange, two shades of yellow, two shades of blue, two shades of green and three shades of brown are used for this 12 x 14-inch pillow.

# FLORAL PILLOW

**B. Poppies**

TOP



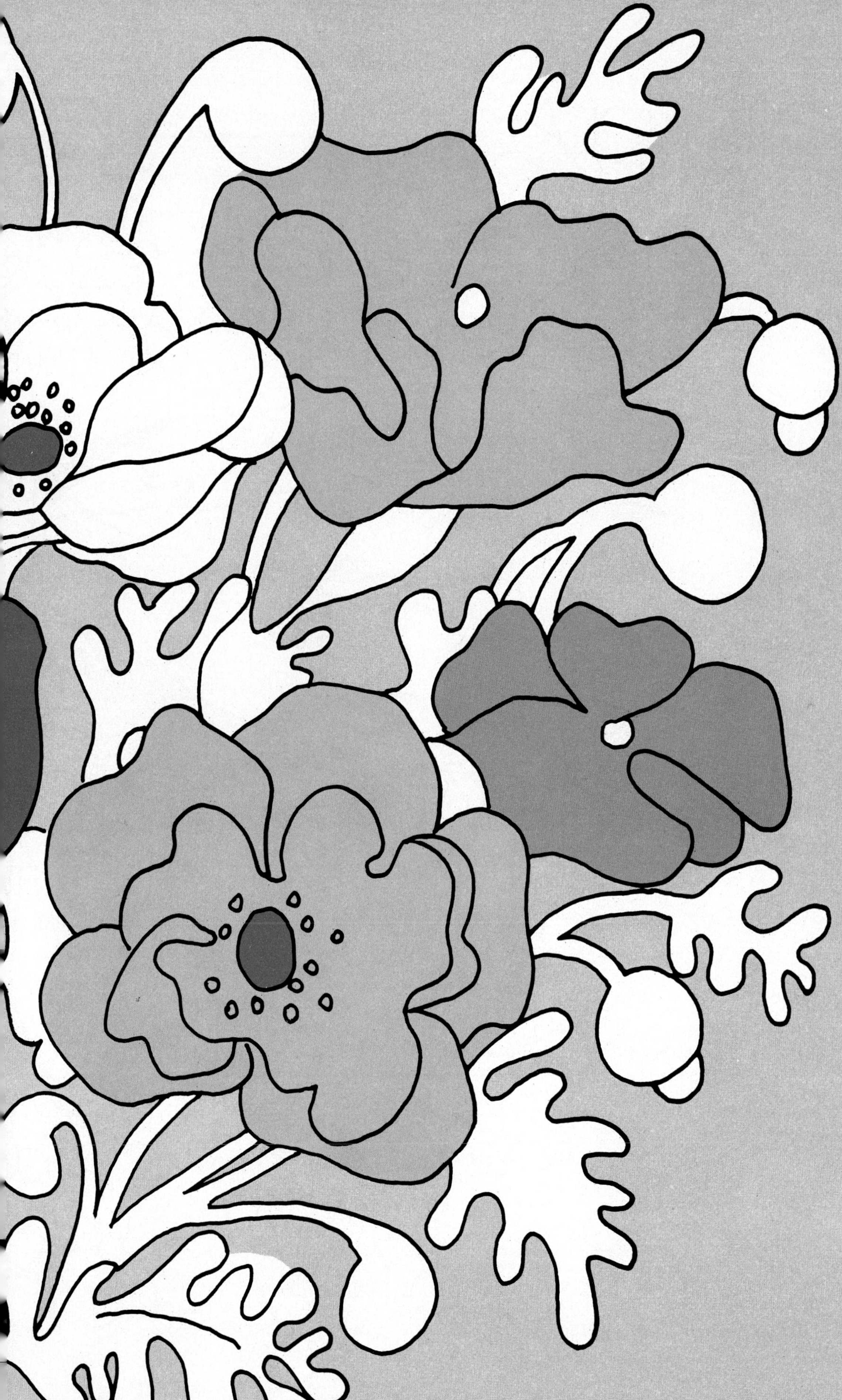

**FLORAL PILLOW**

C. Butterfly

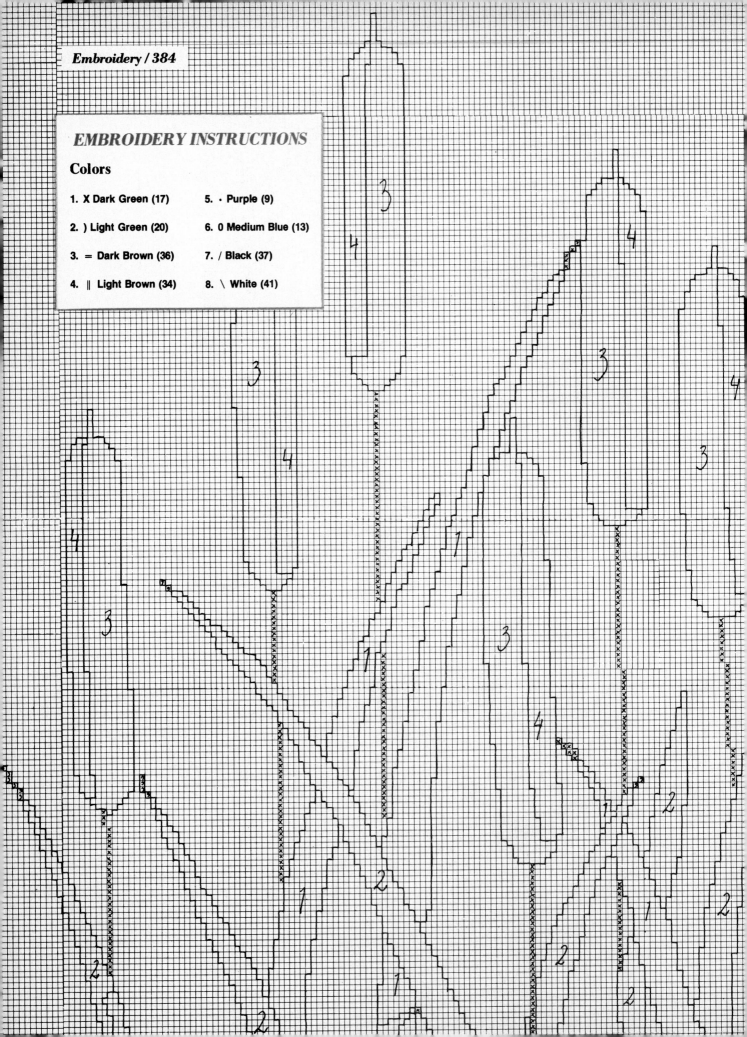

**EMBROIDERY INSTRUCTIONS**

**Colors**

1. X Dark Green (17)        5. · Purple (9)

2. ) Light Green (20)       6. 0 Medium Blue (13)

3. = Dark Brown (36)        7. / Black (37)

4. ‖ Light Brown (34)       8. \ White (41)

## BUTTERFLY CROSS STITCH

Use this graceful and interesting design for wall-hanging, screen or pillow. Coarse decorator linen is best for thread-count Cross Stitch. The size of the design can be increased or decreased as you desire, depending on the stitch size.

## TENERIFE POCKETS

### Designed and Created by Grace Harding

Use this design or any of many that can be worked by the same system, on pockets of skirts and aprons, on blouse fronts, curtains and pillows. Follow the close-up for arrangement of this design and work in pearl cotton.

## PICTURE OR PILLOW DESIGNS

A. The stitches used here are Satin, Outline, Long-and-Short and for a solid filler in some sections alternating rows of Chain and Outline. Copy the colors in the picture or choose your own. There are four greens, three oranges, two yellows, three blues, three pinks, red and black in the original.

B. Using only Outline and Long-and-Short Stitches, this flowering tree can be worked in two shades of pink and three of green.

**Full Size Motif**

## PICTURE OR PILLOW DESIGNS
Full Size Motif

# Needlepoint

The art of ornamental needlework has existed since the earliest civilizations. It was mentioned in the Bible, examples were unearthed from Egyptian tombs and it was practiced by American Indians. Some type of needlework, usually used to enrich garments and other personal possessions, has been found in every civilization.

Canvas work or needlepoint, as it is now most frequently called, is stitchery of varying sizes worked on woven fabric, canvas or linen. Applied with a needle to a group of warp and weft threads, needlepoint usually covers the complete surface of the material. It is not to be confused with real tapestry which is woven on a loom.

In early centuries, needlework was most often used pictorially to reflect the social mores and culture of the time. Dating from the fourth century, Coptic pieces still in existence depict rather primitive renditions of birds and animals. These motifs were the same as those used to decorate utensils and shelters.

The art of canvas work and embroidery reached

**Wall Hanging from American Indian Motifs, designed and created by Marion Moffat.**

its maximum heights during the thirteenth and fourteenth centuries. Particularly notable, both in design and technique, was ecclesiastical embroidery which was usually worked in gold or silk thread on fine even-weave linen. Many craftsmen died in the Black Death of the fourteenth century without passing on their craft. Thus, by the end of the fifteenth century, fine canvas work design had practically disappeared and a coarser style developed.

Due largely to the Reformation, embroidery in the sixteenth century placed emphasis on domestic and ceremonial rather than ecclesiastical articles. Needlework guilds produced cushions and table carpets of excellent quality for royal and wealthy estates. Led by Mary Queen of Scots, needlewomen of the day found stitching a useful means of occupying their hands while enriching and decorating their large homes. Many examples of the work of this period are contained in museums today.

The seventeenth century brought some notable changes. Stitchery was used for clothes and household purposes. Needlework pictures were produced purely for decoration and to show the worker's skill. Samplers originated as a method of teaching and as a permanent record of stitches.

The American colonies utilized needlework as a major method of recording the scenes of the new land. This personal approach to the subject produced a fresh feeling in the depiction of fruits, flowers, birds and animals. It also created a style that continues in great favor in present day needlework. The needlewomen of the colonies found it necessary to produce their own plant dyes for wools and achieved some very distinctive colors.

The eighteenth century brought further changes to needlework. Large carpets of Georgian style were produced in canvas work. Canvas embroidery was also found on shoes and upholstery. Chair seats worked by Martha Washington can be seen at Mt. Vernon. Many reproductions of the Old Masters and naturalistic representations of animals and flowers were stitched for curtain tiebacks, mantel pieces, etc. A technique which developed fully in the Colonies was Bargello, sometimes called the Flame Stitch. This form of needlepoint is one of those frequently used in modern day creative designs.

Most of the pieces of the nineteenth century were worked on painted canvases printed in Berlin. The yarn was a harsh, analine-dyed wool imported from Berlin to England and America. Because of the availability of these painted canvases or charted designs in needlework shops, little effort was given to creative interpretation for a number of years.

In the years since World War II, needlework has reemerged as a creative art incorporating a new awareness of color and texture. There is also a strong penchant for experimentation similar to that of earlier centuries. Needlework in the twentieth century can be an exciting experience for the craftsman with a skillful hand and a creative mind. Imagination and a fresh approach have combined with the advances in machinery and technology to make exciting dye colors and well-made canvases and yarns. This great revival of needlework is the result of the desire to bring individuality and beauty to creations of the machine age. Old patterns and techniques worked with new materials present an entirely different appearance. Textured wall hangings and colorful canvases have become important in softening the harsh textures and straight lines of contemporary buildings.

## NEEDLEPOINT

As you begin to work with needlepoint you will be confronted by a number of unfamiliar terms. The following descriptions will be most often encountered.

Needlepoint is a general term for working with thread and canvas. The basis of needlepoint technique is the commonly termed Text Stitch, worked in one of three basic methods: Basketweave, a stitch that keeps canvas shape best; Half Cross Stitch, the stitch which requires the least amount of yarn; and, the Continental Stitch, a sturdy stitch that can take much wear (See Basic Stitches, pg. 401). These stitches are used on canvas in all mesh sizes.

**Petit Point:** This is needlepoint worked on mono mesh or double mesh canvas with eighteen or more meshes to the inch. This fine canvas work, meaning "little stitch," is found where great detail is needed and is frequently worked in combination with Gros Point (big stitch) on double mesh.

**Gros Point:** This is the most commonly used stitch today. It is worked either on mono mesh or double mesh with eight to sixteen meshes to the inch. inch.

**Large Gros Point Or Quickpoint:** Once used mostly for rugs, this stitch size is now being used for everything from belts and pillows to giant wall hangings. Stitch size varies from three to seven meshes to the inch on mono mesh or double mesh canvas.

## TYPES OF CANVAS

Early needlepoint was worked on loosely woven material such as coarse linen until the advent of

**Full Size Needlepoint and Bargello Canvas: 22 to the inch mono for petit point; 16 to the inch mono for petit point and petit bargello; 12 to the inch and 10 to the inch mono for gros point and bargello; 10 to the inch double mesh (Penelope) for gros point, mixed gros point and petit point; 5 to the inch double mesh (Penelope) for rugs and quickpoint.**

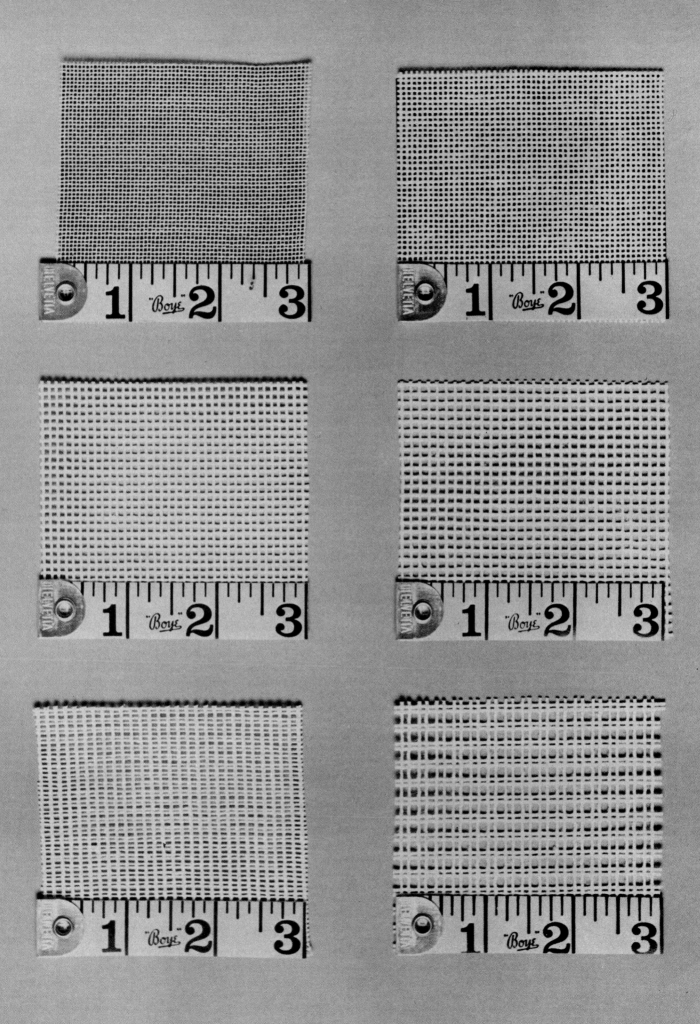

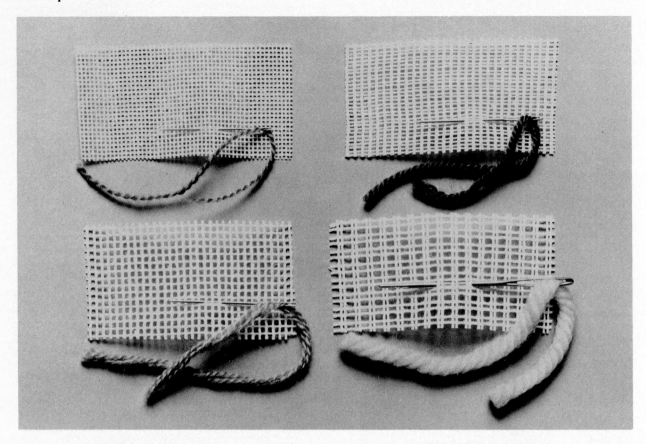

Needlepoint Yarns: Top Left, Crewel; Top Right, Persian; Bottom Left, Tapestry; Bottom Right, Rug.

single thread canvases. Modern canvas, invented by the French in the 1860s, is a woven fabric with evenly spaced meshes used as a base for needlepoint stitches. Canvases differ according to the number of holes per square inch. The fewer the number of holes per inch, the thicker the thread or yarn required; the greater the number of holes per inch, the thinner the thread or yarn. There are twenty or more holes to the inch for very fine work and as few as three or four holes to the inch for rug or quickpoint canvas.

The range in canvas width will vary from 24 to 36 inches in small meshes to from 36 to 54 inches for rug or quickpoint canvas. When buying canvas, look for the best quality available. It is important that the mesh be regular with no weak threads or knots. Whenever possible, make sure that the canvas is wide enough for the finished project. This will prevent the piecing together of strips of canvas, either before needlepointing or after the work is completed.

**Single Thread Or Mono Mesh:** This canvas has single, evenly spaced threads running in both

directions: crosswise and lengthwise. Any stitch method with the exception of the Half Cross Stitch may be used on single thread canvas.

**Double Mesh Or Penelope:** This canvas is woven with double threads instead of single, leaving evenly spaced square meshes for the needle. Gros point and petit point can be combined in one piece by splitting double threads apart to form single holes for the smaller stitches. This is helpful when more detail is necessary in certain sections of a design.

## YARN FOR NEEDLEPOINT

Needlepoint yarn must contain long staple fibers. Other types of yarn may be used only if they have a tight, firm twist. Knitting yarns are not suitable for most needlepoint. Since the twist is not firm enough, knitting yarn wears thin from pulling through the canvas. The traditional, finest and most lasting yarns are those made of 100% wool.

**Crewel Yarn:** This yarn, normally used for crewel embroidery, makes a good petit point yarn.

It is fine, springy two-ply yarn usually sold in 20-yard skeins. It can be used on Double Mesh canvas with ten meshes to the inch when the canvas is split, or on petit point canvas with twenty meshes to the inch.

**Persian Yarn:** Also a two-ply yarn, Persian Yarn is not as springy as crewel yarn. It is usually sold by the ounce in needlework shops and comes in lengths made up of three strands of wool. This is a versatile yarn that can be used on a large number of canvas sizes. Generally one strand would be split off to work on eighteen to twenty mesh; two strands on twelve, fourteen and sixteen mesh; and, all three together on eight and ten mesh.

**Tapestry Yarn:** The best brands of this yarn are usually sold by the skein in mothproofed, matched dye lots. It is four-ply and comes in 40-yard skeins. Tapestry wool can be used on twelve and fourteen mesh Mono Mesh and on ten-mesh Double Mesh. It can also be used for petit point when split down to two of its four ply.

**Rug Yarn:** Often called Quickpoint yarn, rug yarn is four ply and usually more rough and wiry in texture than the others. Available in cotton, synthetics and wool, it is sold either by the pound or in skeins. Rug yarn is used on canvas which is eight mesh or lower to the inch. It is presently used extensively for Quickpoint pillows and pictures as well as rugs.

## ESTIMATING AMOUNTS OF YARN

Decide on the canvas mesh size and the type of yarn best suited to that mesh. Using the stitch of your choice, make a 1-inch square and note the amount of yarn used. Multiply the amount used to work the 1-inch square by the number of *square* inches to be covered by that color. This gives the approximate yardage for one color. Do this for each color.

To figure the number of skeins needed, divide the yardage by the number of yards in a skein.

*Amount of yarn used multiplied by number of square inches = yardage needed.*
*Number of yards needed divided by yards in skein = number of skeins needed.*

## TYPES OF NEEDLES

Use tapestry or rug needles for all needlepoint projects. These needles have a blunt point and an elongated eye. The blunt point is designed to prevent the needle from splitting the canvas threads. Also, since the needle goes through the open mesh of the canvas, there is no need for a needle with a sharp point. The longer eye is necessary to accommodate the relatively large size of the yarns used in needlepoint.

## THREADING THE NEEDLE

Fold a strand of yarn over the sharp edge of the head of the needle and pull it down tightly over the needle. Pinch the yarn between thumb and forefinger as you withdraw the needle. Keeping the strand of yarn pinched in one hand, feed the doubled yarn into the long eye of the needle. Pull the doubled strand through the eye and then release one end of the strand so that you have a short doubled strand near the head. A strand of yarn should be no longer than 18 inches because it will fray during the repeated pulling through the canvas.

**Threading the Needle: Hold yarn between thumb and forefinger; feed yarn into eye; pull through.**

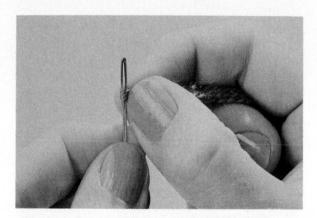

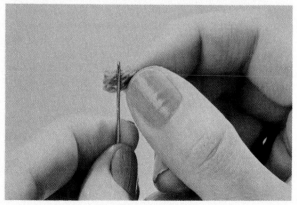

## STARTING THE CANVAS

Before working on the canvas, make sure to allow margins on all sides. These margins will be necessary for the blocking and mounting of the finished design. For small projects, allow 1 to 1 1/2-inch margins. Larger projects need at least 2 inches on all sides beyond the area to be worked.

If it is necessary to join pieces of canvas in order to reach the desired size, it is best to do so before the project is started unless the size of the project is a factor. Overlay the two pieces of canvas by several meshes and align the threads of the canvas so that the meshes match. Baste them together every several inches before working the stitches. The needlepoint is worked through both layers. For large projects, join the pieces together before completing that portion of the design.

To prevent fraying at canvas edge, bind all the raw edges with masking tape or baste on twill tape or wide bias binding. On quickpoint pieces such as rugs, be certain that the masking tape is wide enough to hold firmly. The edges may also be turned under 1/4 to 1/2 inch and stitched in place by hand or by machine. This also keeps the yarn from catching the edges of the canvas as work progresses.

**Top Left, Masking Tape; Top Center, Turned Under and Basted; Bottom Left, Cotton Twill Tape Binding; Bottom Center, Cotton Bias Quilt Binding; Right, Pieced and Stitched.**

## STITCHING HINTS

**Starting Work:** Pull the needle through leaving a 1-inch end. Do not make a knot. Fasten the end into the work by working over it during the first few stitches.

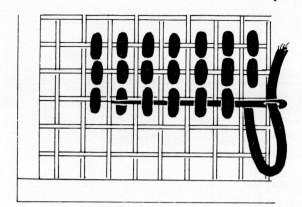

**Ending Work — Back of Work**

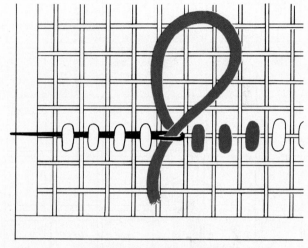

**Yarn carried under worked stitches**

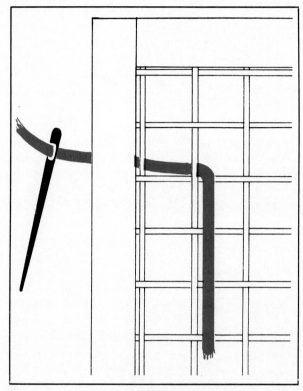

**BACK OF WORK**

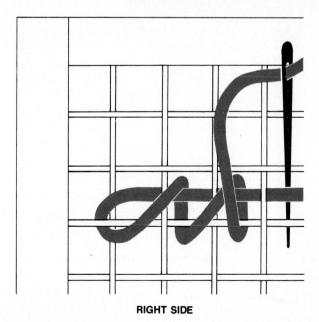

**RIGHT SIDE**

**Ending Work:** Draw yarn to back of canvas through last mesh (stitch). Run the yarn under a

few stitches at the back of the work. Cut yarn off very close to work.

**Meeting a Worked Area:** When you come to a worked area while doing background or to another portion of the design, loosely carry yarn under the worked stitches and continue across the row. If the worked area is more than five stitches or so, fasten off yarn and begin again at opposite side to continue row.

## BASIC STITCHES

### Half Cross Stitch

The most commonly known needlepoint stitch is the Half Cross Stitch. It can be done only on double mesh canvas because it will slide without the double threads of the mesh to hold it in place. Since the Half Cross Stitch does not provide much backing on the reverse side of the canvas, it

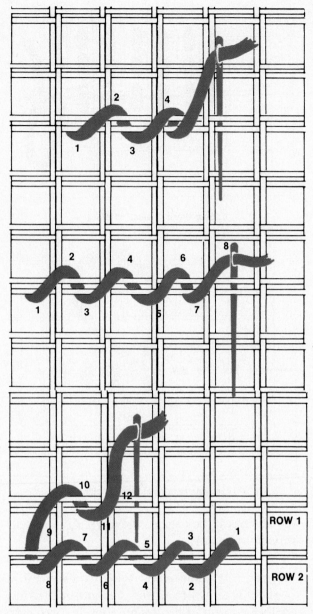

**Half Cross Stitch**

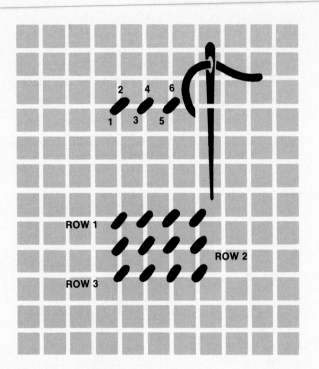

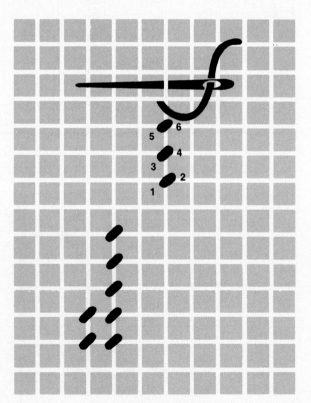

**Vertical Half Cross Stitch**

has a tendency to wear out quickly. This stitch will also stretch the canvas out of shape. However, it is often used because it takes less yarn and is easy to work.

Always work from *left to right*. Start at the bottom of a stitch. Cross over one mesh of the canvas (diagonally from 1 to 2) and insert needle for next stitch (bring needle up at 3 and then diagonally to 4). The needle is always inserted in the vertical position. When the row of stitches is completed, turn work upside down so that the next row can be worked again from left to right (9 to 10).

## Continental Stitch

The Continental Stitch, preferred by many needlepointers, works equally well on either mono or double mesh canvas. It provides a good backing on the reverse side of the canvas which means it will withstand a lot of wear. This stitch, when worked over a large area, has a tendency to pull the canvas out of shape quite a bit and therefore requires more blocking than other stitches. Requiring more yarn than the Half Cross Stitch, the Continental is frequently used for a sturdy background for pillows or chair seats.

The Continental looks like the Half Cross Stitch on the surface but it is always worked from *right to left.* Bring needle out at bottom left corner of a stitch, (up at 1) and then diagonally to upper right corner.

Insert needle (down at 2) and cross behind stitch just completed to new stitch (3) on left. When one row is completed, turn work upside down so that

next row can again be worked from right to left (9 to 10).

### Basketweave Stitch

The Basketweave Stitch is preferred as a background filler stitch. It does not pull the canvas out of shape and can be worked without turning the canvas around. This stitch has a firm backing that takes a lot of wear. It can be worked on either mono mesh or double mesh canvas.

The Basketweave Stitch is actually woven into the canvas, forming a durable web. The needle is brought up and over one mesh to the right (1 to 2 on sketch). Note that the needle is inserted *horizontally* and brought up again (3). These steps are repeated on the diagonal across space being worked. On the next row, also worked on the diagonal one mesh below, the needle is inserted *vertically* (8 to 9). Each succeeding row has one more stitch than the row before.

These three basic types of stitches can be mixed in one needlework piece if desired. For example, it

**Continental Stitch**

**Basketweave Stitch**

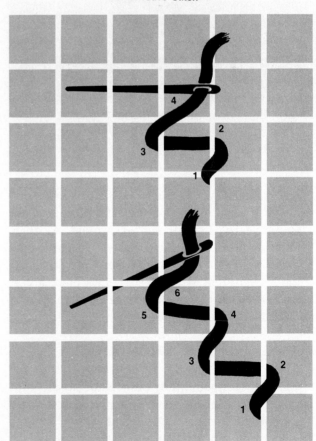

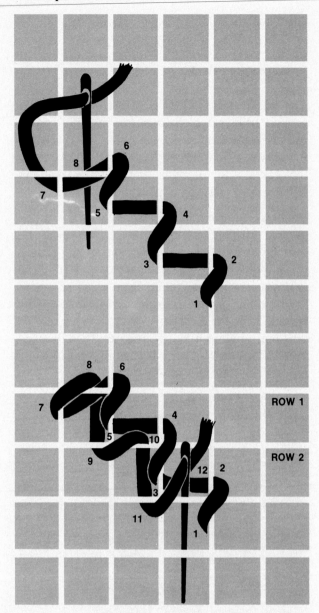

**Basketweave Stitch**

is sometimes easier to work Half Cross or Continental stitches in one portion of a piece and use Basketweave stitch for the background. At other times a more complicated and varied motif may make it difficult to use the Basketweave Stitch for the background. If color areas in a piece are at least 1 inch in size, Basketweave Stitch can be used throughout the piece.

## TYPES OF NEEDLEPOINT DESIGNS

**Charted Designs:** Many designs for needlepoint pieces are available in the form of charts. With the use of a chart or graph, a design can be worked on any size canvas. Each square on the chart represents a corresponding stitch to be taken in the canvas.

**Painted or Tinted Pieces:** Designs are painted directly on the canvas in colors like those yarn colors to be used in working the needlepoint.

**Preworked Designs:** Imported needlework pieces often have the design already preworked by hand with only the background left to be filled in. Once very formal, these designs have now become brighter and more modern. Novelty stitches used for background or borders relieves the tedium of these pieces.

**Tramé:** Yarns in the colors to be worked are laid in long stitches across the canvas in the exact pattern. The needlepoint stitch, usually Continental or Basketweave, is worked over the long laid stitches, following the color indications. Tramé is often combined with a pre-worked design where the background will be done in a pattern instead of a single color.

## EQUIPMENT

In addition to proper needles and yarn, it is important to have good tools. Very few items are needed; but those mentioned here will make the needlework neater and stitching faster.

**Scissors:** An important tool is a good pair of embroidery scissors. They should be small with narrow, pointed blades and must be kept sharp. Protect the blade points by keeping them in a holder.

**Thimbles:** Although this might seem like an unnecessary encumbrance, the use of a thimble can save fingers from constant needle pressure. Metal thimbles are generally better than plastic or bone. Thimbles come in different sizes so correct fit is important.

**Frames:** In these days of high mobility, almost every needlepointer prefers to carry her work with her for enjoyment at odd moments. This makes the frame an optional piece of equipment. Frames are most important when working a large and heavy piece, or, when using complicated stitches that require the use of the hand under the canvas. The round frame or hoop used for embroidery or crewel stretches needlepoint out of shape and is therefore not desirable. A rec-

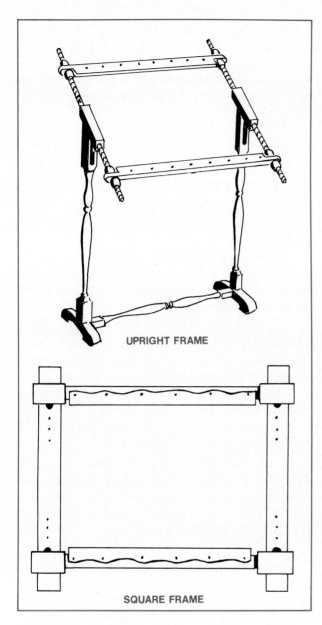

UPRIGHT FRAME

SQUARE FRAME

tangular frame with two roller pieces at the top and bottom is preferable. The canvas piece is tacked onto the strips of fabric on the roller pieces. It is then laced onto the ends to hold it taut. Specific instructions for mounting the canvas on these frames are included with each frame. Rectangular frames may be mounted on a stand or held in the hand.

## FINISHING

**Washing or Cleaning:** If the needlework piece is just slightly soiled, brush over the surface with a clean cloth dipped in cleaning fluid. If the piece is badly soiled, cold water soap or a mild liquid soap is the best washing solution.

Dip the piece into the solution but do not wring or squeeze it. Thoroughly rinse in cool water. Lay flat on several clean dry towels and carefully roll to soak up the excess water. Unroll and block.

**Blocking:** Needlepoint must be blocked when it has been completed. No matter what size stitches are used or what the finished size of the piece, some distortion is inevitable.

Place the needlepoint face down on a board (plywood works well). The board should be marked with perfectly straight lines horizontally and vertically. One-inch squares premarked with a T-square for accuracy are helpful. Before marking, cover the board with an old sheet or cloth. If the needlepoint is not wet from washing, dampen it on the wrong side using a sponge and cold water. It should be wet but not saturated. Wetting the canvas softens the glue sizing so that when it dries the canvas piece resets and holds its shape.

Using rustproof tacks ($^1/_2$ to 1 inch apart), fasten the top side down along the edge of the canvas on the straight line of the board. Continue, tacking the top, then the two sides and the bottom. Straighten and stretch to meet the premeasured outlines.

The needlepoint should remain on the board until thoroughly dry, even if it takes several days. If the needlepoint piece is badly warped out of shape, restretch, wet and let dry again. When it is dry, remove from the board. Spray starch or fabric finish can be used on the back to hold the shape more securely. Place a slightly damp cloth over the right side and steam very gently. This will fluff the yarn and give a finished look. Needlepoint can be blocked by a professional dry cleaner but the accuracy achieved by the above method is superior.

## GETTING DESIGN IDEAS

Just about any subject can be translated into needlepoint designs as long as the possibilities and limitations of this art are understood.

The basic thing to keep in mind is the grid-like structure of the canvas. Straight lines will be translated exactly. Curves and undulating lines become a progression of steps, with the eye completing the shape. Larger, gentler sloping curves are more successful than small tight circles. Finer mesh canvas will reproduce more detail and translate a complicated design more faithfully than a coarser canvas. Stylized designs and simplified forms are more successful than realistic drawings.

## FINDING DESIGNS

It is a simple matter to reproduce a pattern from drapery fabric, upholstery, wallpaper or china. Garden flowers offer numerous suggestions. Individual hobbies are excellent sources of design.

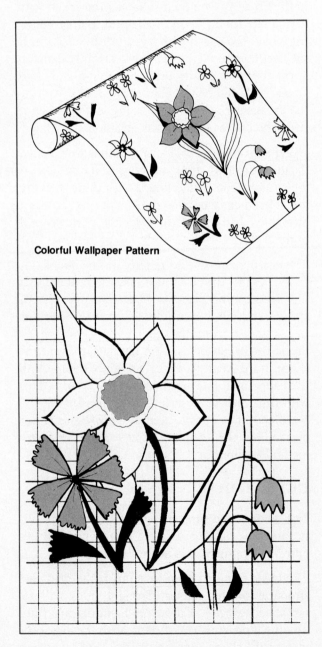

**Colorful Wallpaper Pattern**

**Needlepoint Motif**

Shells, sports symbols, birds, etc. offer multiple opportunities for translation into needlepoint. Motifs such as monograms, family crests and school emblems lend themselves perfectly. Fabric swatches, art books and posters are excellent inspiration.

The following guidelines will aid you in planning a needlepoint piece.

**A.** The proportions of the design should relate to the dimensions of the canvas. Leave enough area surrounding the major motif for background.

**B.** Select a large mesh canvas (3 to 5 meshes per inch) for bold, simplified designs and a smaller mesh (10 to 14 meshes per inch) for more detailed work and shading.

**C.** Use basic stitches (Continental, Half Cross or Basketweave) for intricate shapes, shading and detail. Fancy stitches look better on simple designs or background.

**D.** Use color effectively. Gradual shading requires very close tones of the same color. Use widely separated tones to contrast two shades in the same color family. Shade with two or three tones of the same color for depth, using the darkest at the front or base and the lightest at the rear or top.

## DESIGN PLACEMENT

Finding a design to fit the exact space requirements is rarely possible. Usually a design must be composed from a number of elements to attain the right size or shape and the correct proportions.

To combine design elements in one composition, first draw the outlines of the project on a large piece of paper. Then copy each of the separate components on small pieces of tracing paper. Motifs may be taken from several compositions in a catalog or floral print.

When you have traced all the portions of the design on separate pieces of paper, lay them out on a large paper and experiment with various arrangements of the designs. To reverse a design simply turn the tracing over. To add more components, just trace additional ones. After arranging the composition, use a large sheet of tracing paper to copy the final arrangement.

**Square Method of Enlarging a Design**

## ENLARGING OR REDUCING DESIGNS

There are two simple methods frequently used to enlarge or reduce designs to the proper proportions.

**Photostat Method:** This is an easy method for changing dimensions of a design. Take the design to a photocopy shop where it can be photostatically enlarged or reduced to the proper dimensions. Ask the shop to make a positive image because the negative is difficult to see. Several photostats can be pieced together for a large design. Photostating costs very little and is the most efficient and accurate way of changing design dimensions.

**Square Method:** Divide the design into 1-inch squares; outline the desired size of the project on a piece of paper; then divide the paper into exactly the same number of squares as in the design. When this has been done, although the number of squares is the same, their comparative size will be different. In a larger design each square will be larger; in a smaller design each square will be smaller. Now, working square by square from this design, make a freehand copy in the matching squares on your project. A fairly accurate reproduction of the original is possible without any special art skills.

## TRANSFERRING DESIGNS TO CANVAS

Using a waterproof or indelible marker, trace the design onto the canvas. A grey or other neutral color should be used because a dark marker will show through light-colored yarn. Felt tip markers are best.

Once the design is outlined on the canvas, color can be indicated by coloring entire areas with indelible markers. Acrylic paints or indelible markers can also be used to indicate color. Thin the acrylic paints with water and use sparingly. If the paint is too thin, it will soak and distort the canvas. Too much thick paint will clog the meshes but not saturate them. Acrylic paints dry quickly and do not run or bleed when the canvas is dampened for blocking or dry cleaning.

## DESIGNS FROM GRAPHS

While working from a graph is a slower stitching process, it is more accurate because each stitch is placed in a designated mesh.

No outlines are drawn on the canvas, however, close reference lines can be provided by marking both the graph and the canvas in equivalent sections. Stitches can be counted and located from these smaller areas.

First draw vertical and horizontal center lines across the graphed design. Then draw heavy lines at 1-inch intervals. Mark the center of the canvas by folding it in quarters. Duplicate the 1-inch squares of the graph on the canvas by marking at 1-inch intervals, using an indelible marker or straight pins.

## NOVELTY STITCHES

**Mosaic Stitch:** Consists of long and short stitches taken alternately in diagonal rows. Insert the needle one mesh to the right going up one mesh for a short stitch (1 to 2) and two meshes (3 to 4) for a long stitch. In each succeeding row, a short stitch is worked into the end of a long stitch and a long stitch into the end of a short stitch. Work from bottom of canvas toward top.

**Checkerboard Stitch:** Starting in upper left corner, work diagonal stitches from left to right over first mesh (1 and 2). Bring needle out in mesh below in line with completed stitch (3 and 4). This will form a longer diagonal stitch. Working in same manner as last stitch, work longer diagonal stitch (5 and 6). To complete the square, decrease length of stitches to two meshes (7 and 8) and then to one mesh (9 and 10): this forms a square. Make three more squares in the same manner, alternating direction of stitches and making ends of stitches of adjoining squares in same meshes of canvas.

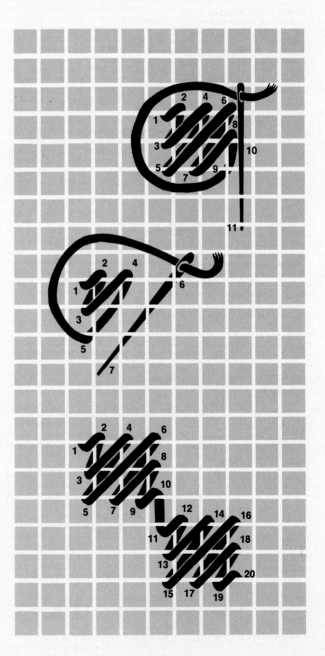

**Mosaic Stitch**

**Star Stitch:** Each star consists of eight stitches all meeting in the center. Make each star in the same way. Work over two meshes of canvas for each stitch of the star, bringing the needle up (1) and down (2) through the center mesh each time. Work around to complete the star.

**Stem Stitch:** Work diagonal stitches from the top of canvas to bottom over two meshes of canvas each way; make each stitch one mesh below last (1 through 8). Work the second row in diagonal stitches in the opposite direction (9 through **16**), with the lower end of stitches in same meshes as first row. When the diagonal stitches are completed, work Backstitch in between diagonal rows (17 through 23), using a second color if desired.

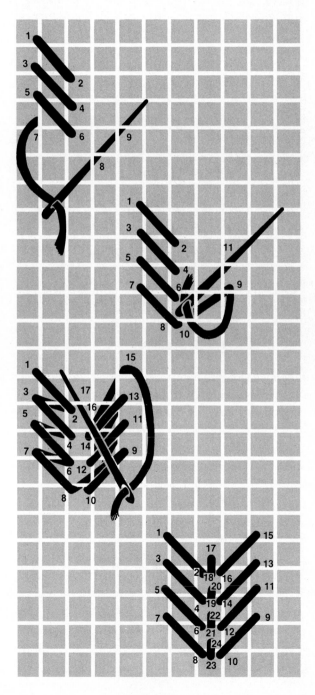

**Star Stitch**

**Stem Stitch**

**Scotch Stitch:** Work first stitch over one mesh (1 and 2). The next stitch is worked over two meshes (3 and 4), then over three (5 and 6). To complete square, decrease length of stitches to two meshes (7 and 8), then to one mesh (9 and 10) to form a square.

To do Alternate Scotch Stitch, work every other block, checkerboard fashion, in Scotch Stitch. Work basic Needlepoint Stitch in alternating squares. Use Basketweave Stitch (see pg. 403) to eliminate the warping effect of diagonal stitches on the canvas.

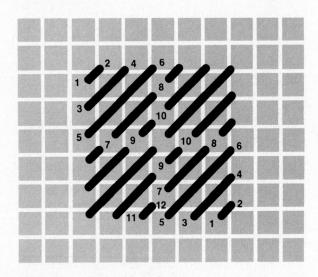

**Scotch Stitch**

**Jacquard Stitch:** Starting at upper left, work diagonal stitches over two horizontal and two vertical meshes, bringing needle out in mesh below preceeding stitch. Make six stitches (1-12).

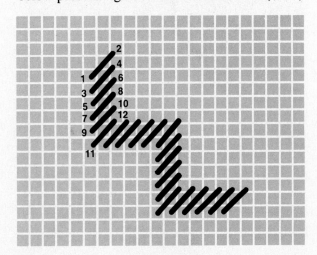

**Jacquard Stitch**

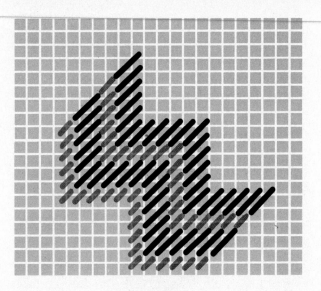

**Jacquard Stitch**

Then, work five stitches to the right keeping them parallel. Continue to work five stitches alternately down then to the right for desired depth. This forms a zigzag effect. For the next row to the right of the original row, work diagonal stitches over one mesh of canvas, making the same number of stitches down and across. Repeat these two rows alternately.

**Knotted Stitch:** Make a slanted stitch up over three rows, inserting needle one mesh over (1 and 2). Bring needle up for next stitch two meshes lower in same row (3) and cross first stitch inserting needle one mesh up (4). Repeat the above for next stitch. To work next row, repeat with stitches meeting in the meshes between slanted stitches.

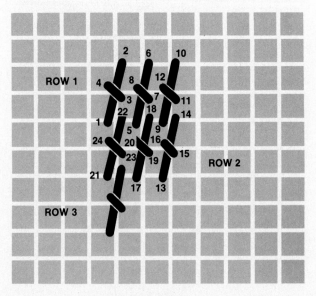

**Knotted Stitch**

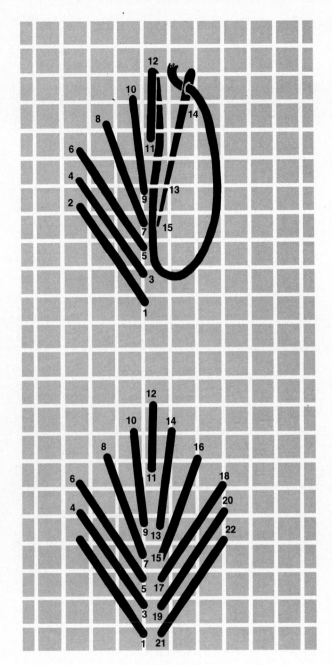

**Leaf Stitch**

**Leaf Stitch:** Starting at the bottom center of leaf, make a diagonal stitch three meshes to left and four meshes up (1 and 2). Bring the needle out one mesh up at center (3) and make two more stitches parallel (3 through 6). Make next stitch one mesh up at center then over two and up four meshes; make another stitch in same way (7 through 10). For top center stitch, bring needle out two meshes up at the center (11) and make a vertical stitch up over two meshes (12). Complete the other side of leaf to correspond. Make sides of adjoining leaves in the same meshes.

## BARGELLO

Bargello, a form of needlepoint, has some basic characteristics that are very easy to recognize.

The stitches are upright on the canvas or parallel to the threads of the canvas. Most needlepoint stitches are worked diagonally and cover both the warp and woof of the canvas. Bargello stitches cover *only* the warp or *only* the woof threads of the canvas. The remaining canvas threads are covered by the thickness of the yarn. Stitches are usually worked in a repeated pattern throughout the piece.

Colors are usually, although not always, worked in progressions of shadings and related colors which are repeated over and over until the entire canvas is filled.

Most familiar patterns are built upon one row of stitches. After the first row has been counted out, the following rows follow the same pattern (stitch). The canvas is then usually filled in with rows each following the preceding row.

Adjoining stitches frequently overlap the second stitch two threads above or below the previous stitch. This overlapping of adjoining stitches produces many of the familiar basic geometrics, diamond and serrated patterns.

### CANVAS AND YARNS

The canvas most commonly used is mono or single thread canvas. Double thread or Penelope canvas can be used but it tends to push stitches too far apart. This allows the canvas itself to show through. (See Photo of Canvases, page 397.)

The canvas used for Bargello is of the same type as that used for other needlepoint projects. It is extremely important, however, to obtain canvas that is woven evenly. If the canvas is uneven, there is no way to make the finished stitches even. This also applies to canvas which has been stretched out of shape.

A mesh size should be selected that is compatible with the yarn. The yarn must cover the canvas without distorting the mesh. Since no yarns cross diagonally over the mesh, it is sometimes difficult to obtain good coverage. A beginner must be careful not to pull the yarn too tightly. It must relax and "fluff out" to cover the canvas. When

working with up and down stitches it may be necessary to add another yarn ply to attain the proper coverage. (See Chart of Needlepoint Yarns, page 398.)

Canvas comes in several colors of which white and tan are the most popular. Both are satisfactory and may be used for the same purpose. When working with white or very light yarns, white canvas may be more desirable. However, when working with very dark or black yarns, the white canvas will show through so a tan canvas is recommended. Because dark canvas is of firmer texture it will not show through white yarn. Thus, when it is necessary to use both light and dark yarns, it is best to choose the darker canvas.

## COLOR

Bargello patterns not only allow for color experimentation but also make this experimentation extremely important. Work up small samples in two colors. Then reverse the colors on another sample and watch what happens. Work a patchwork design using the same pattern in every possible color combination, or, use a number of different patterns and textures all in the same color. Some colors darken, others turn grey, others assume a vibrant glow like stained glass. Don't be afraid to use new colors or colors in new combinations. Sometimes a seemingly strange shade will have a wonderful effect in a most unexpected way.

### TYPES OF STITCHES

Following are a selection of Bargello stitches and variations. The Bargello stitches are differentiated from needlepoint stitches in that they are worked parallel to the canvas threads, and usually worked in a given sequence of colors and stitches.

**Laid Stitch With Backstitch:** Bring needle out at bottom (1) for the first row. Insert needle in fourth mesh directly above (2) and bring out between strands of the first mesh to the left (3) of the first stitch and into the fourth mesh directly above (4). Insert needle between strands of first mesh to left at bottom (5) and bring out in the fourth mesh above mesh (6). Continue in this manner making each row with the bottom of stitches in same mesh as top of last row. Make backstitches between rows and over one mesh (7 and 8).

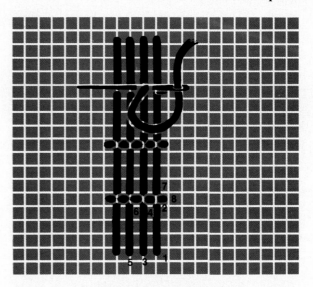

**Laid Stitch with Backstitch**

**Gobelin Stitch:** Consists of straight rows of the same length but may cover any number of canvas threads. Needle comes up through canvas at (1) then down through the canvas at (2). Follow the same sequence until all stitches are completed.

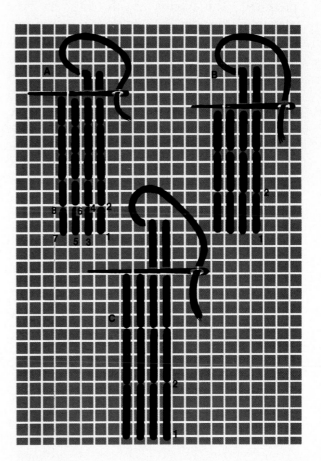

**Gobelin Stitch: Over 2 meshes (A); over 3 meshes (B); over 4 meshes (C).**

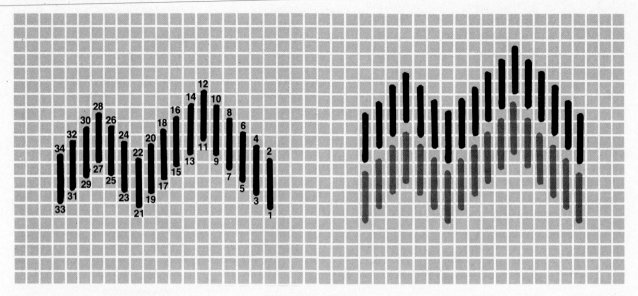

**Flame Stitch**

**Flame Stitch:** Similar to Gobelin except stitches are not worked side by side but form peaks and valleys. When worked in a gradation of shades and colors, the classic flame pattern is produced. The stitches usually cover an even number of threads. The stitches are worked in a progression, either up or down, each stitch advancing by half the number of that stitch. That is, if the stitch covers four threads of canvas the next stitch would be either up or down two threads of canvas.

**Hungarian Stitch:** The pattern consists of one short stitch, followed by a longer stitch, followed by a final stitch of the same length as the first stitch. The sequence of stitches is repeated and continued across the canvas. The second row of stitches dovetails into the first row.

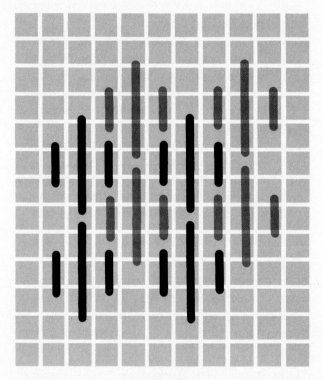

**Hungarian Stitch**

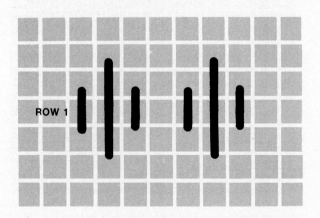

**Hungarian Stitch**

**Diamond Stitch:** Consists of a series of stitches beginning with a short stitch, followed with progressively larger stitches. When the longest stitch is determined, the length of the stitches is progressively shortened until the length of the first stitch is reached. Each progressively larger stitch will cover two more threads of canvas. An alternate type of diamond can be worked in a progression of shorter stitches as shown.

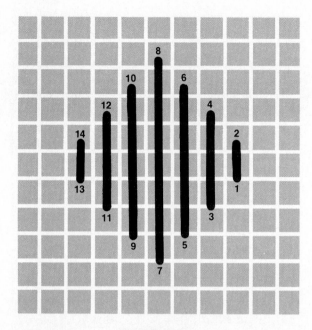

**Diamond Stitch**

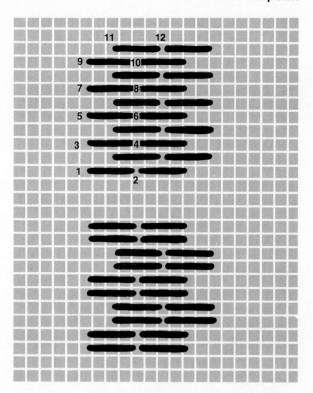

**Brick Stitch**

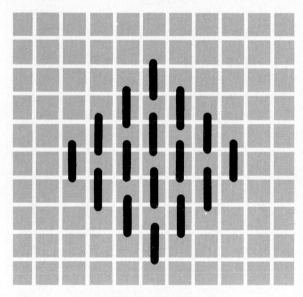

**Alternate Diamond Stitch**

**Brick Stitch:** Worked vertically, the Brick Stitch should be worked over an *even* number of horizontal meshes for length. The vertical height of the Brick Stitch can vary according to the desired effect. Skip the same number of vertical meshes each time to keep the symmetrical brick pattern. Bring needle up at (1); make first horizontal stitch over four meshes. Skip one vertical mesh. Bring needle up at (3) and make another horizontal stitch. Continue to end of row, skipping one vertical mesh between each stitch. The second row is worked just as the first so that the rows form interlocking brick patterns.

## BARGELLO TIPS

Since Bargello stitches are longer, it is a greater problem to fasten the first few loose stitches. Be sure to leave a longer end and fasten it by carefully stitching over it several times.

Yarn is used up quickly because Bargello stitches are much longer than basic needlepoint stitches. It is possible to use a slightly longer strand of yarn while stitching. However, a length of 15 to 16 inches is usually sufficient. Anything longer will be awkward to use and wear as the yarn is pulled through the canvas.

Long Bargello stitches should be flat on the front side of the canvas. If the yarn twists as it comes through the canvas, loosen the stitch with the tip of the needle and straighten the yarn as the stitch is tightened again. If the yarn twists as work progresses, hold the canvas up and let the needle swing free. It will unwind. Twisted yarn will not cover the canvas and the stitches will be uneven. A light even tension will work best.

Since it is often difficult to differentiate between delicate shadings of color it is wise to mark skeins in a way that will make identification easy.

Mistakes should be ripped out and corrected as soon as they are discovered. Carefully insert the tip of the embroidery scissors under the stitches and snip them. The loose stitches can then be easily picked out from the wrong side. If only a few stitches must be removed, they can be picked out one at a time with the tip of the needle. Yarn should not be reused. It is usually too worn and thin to cover the canvas completely.

## CENTERING BARGELLO ON CANVAS

Bargello designs must be centered on the canvas correctly for best results. Divide the canvas into quarters then use a waterproof pen or a strand of yarn to make two perpendicular lines through the center of the canvas. The first row is worked from the intersection of the two lines to the left edge. At the left edge, end the yarn and go back to the center of the piece. Finish the row by working out from the center to the right edge. This will complete the first row. Only the first row need be divided to center the design. Subsequent rows can be worked all the way across the canvas in a continuous row.

In many cases the first row of a Bargello pattern will establish the design. It is very important that this first row be counted carefully because a mistake here will carry through into the rows that follow. To help eliminate the chance of error, draw a line on the canvas following the thread that the top stitch touches. Continue to work the row counting the stitches and checking as you go to make sure that the top stitch of each peak touches the same thread as marked. If you make a counting error, it will be apparent that the mistake is in the last few stitches and it can be corrected easily.

## FINISHING

At the edges of a piece there will always be portions of motifs that will not be complete. Finish the edges into a straight line by working only the portion of the design that would lie within the line.

For complete detailed information on the proper techniques for washing, cleaning and blocking Bargello projects, see page 405.

## NEEDLEPOINT COLOR CHART

| | |
|---|---|
| 1. Pale Pink | 24. Chrome Yellow |
| 2. Medium Pink | 25. Bright Yellow |
| 3. Dark Pink | 26. Gold Yellow |
| 4. Light Red | 27. Medium Yellow |
| 5. True Red | 28. Pale Yellow |
| 6. Dark Red | 29. Light Orange |
| 7. Maroon | 30. Medium Orange |
| 8. Red-Violet | 31. Red-Orange |
| 9. Purple | 32. Beige |
| 10. Lavender | 33. Sand |
| 11. Blue-Violet | 34. Light Brown |
| 12. Dark Blue | 35. Medium Brown |
| 13. Medium Blue | 36. Dark Brown |
| 14. Light Blue | 37. Black |
| 15. Turquoise | 38. Dark Gray |
| 16. Light Aqua | 39. Medium Gray |
| 17. Dark Green | 40. Pearl Gray |
| 18. Medium Green | 41. White |
| 19. Bright Green | 42. Ivory |
| 20. Leaf Green | 43. Coral |
| 21. Pale Green | 44. Gold |
| 22. Chartreuse | 45. Brown-Gold |
| 23. Olive Green | 46. Burnt Orange |

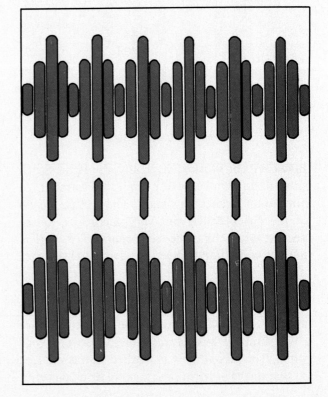

# NEEDLEPOINT PROJECTS

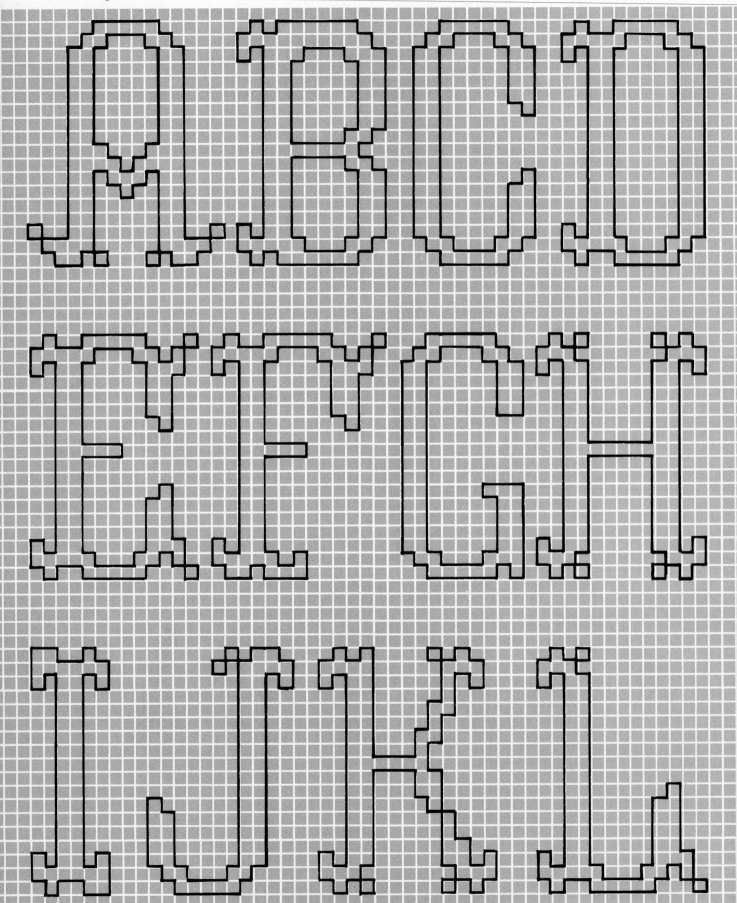

**NEEDLEPOINT ALPHABET AND BORDERS**

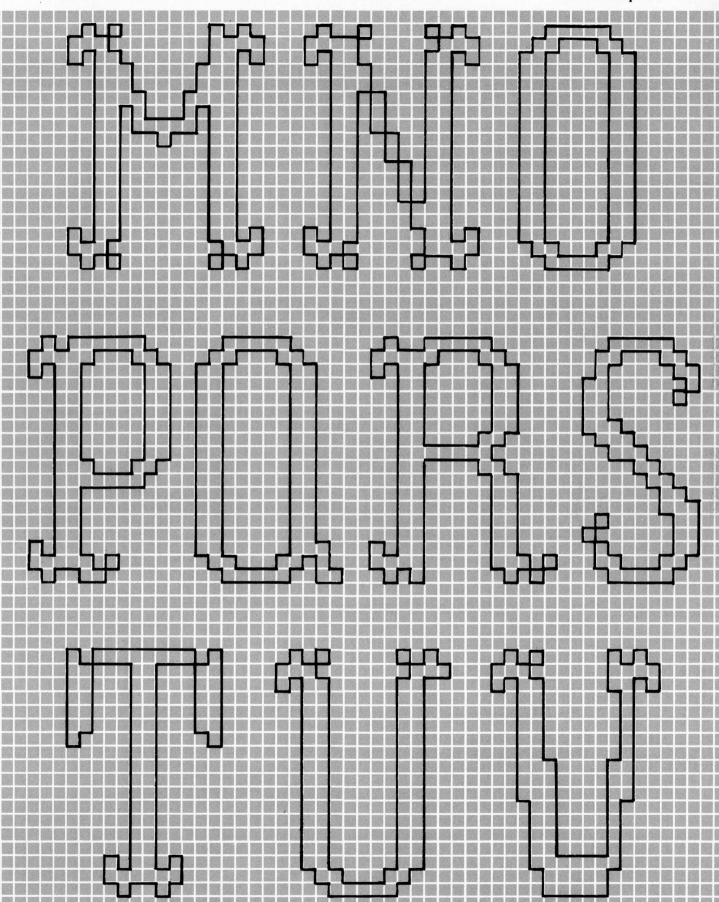

**NEEDLEPOINT ALPHABET AND BORDERS**

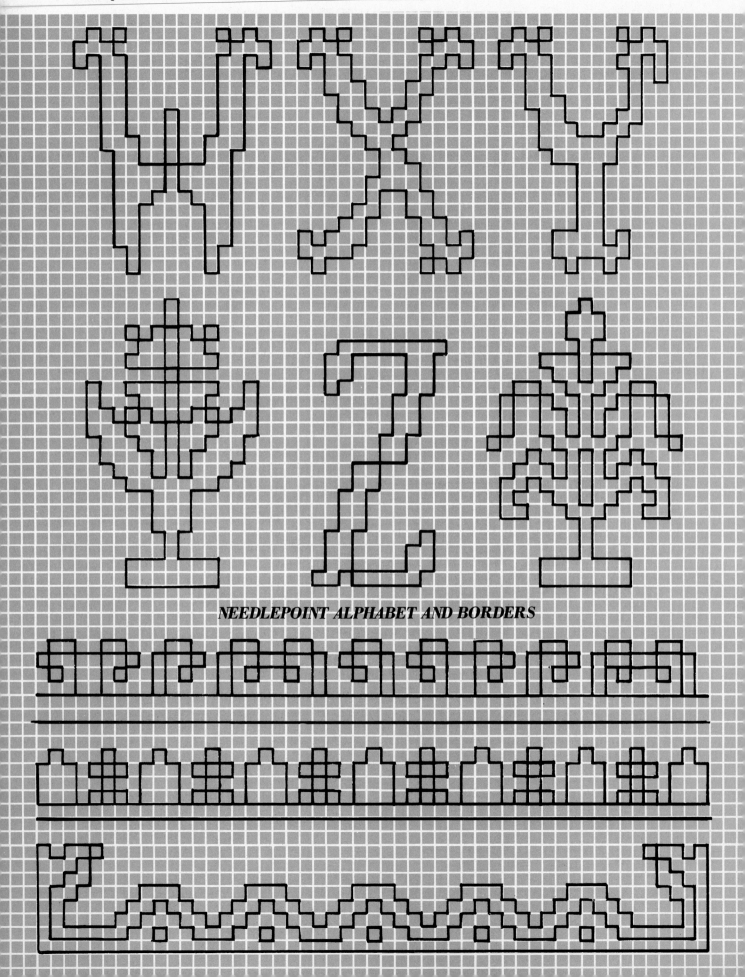

NEEDLEPOINT ALPHABET AND BORDERS

## NEEDLEPOINT ALPHABET AND BORDERS

A needlepoint nameplate or monogram on canvas with a handsome border around the edge is a unique idea. It can be sewn onto a straw bag or used as a nameplate on a door. There are upper and lower case letters from which to choose, as well as three different borders and two flower motifs. These can be used on samplers, linens and in Cross Stitch designs.

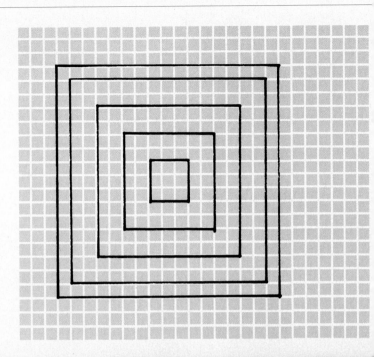

## SHADOW BOX PILLOW

### Designed and worked by Courtney Bede

The interesting shaded needlepoint design can be worked in any colors and combined in numerous ways for a variety of sizes and effects. The squares worked in rug canvas and joined together will make a fascinating rug for a modern room. Use five shades of each color with the lightest in the center and the darkest in the single row on the edge.

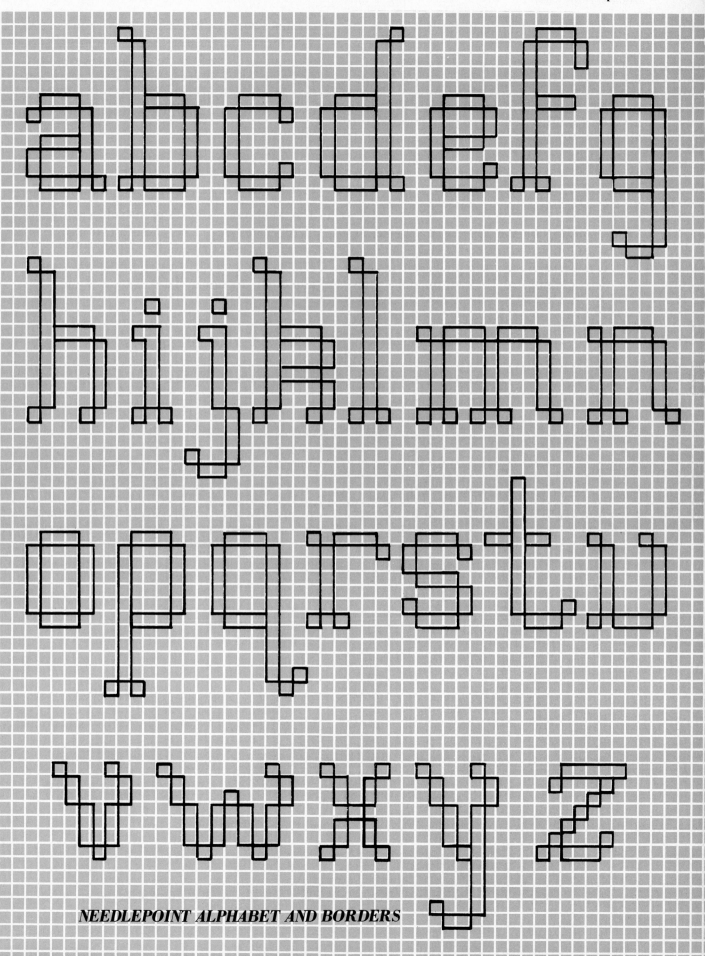

**NEEDLEPOINT ALPHABET AND BORDERS**

## PETIT POINT ACCESSORIES

### Designed and created by Joe Ann Helms

These delicate evening accessories are worked in shades of green, ivory and dark red on 16-to-the-inch canvas. The clasp on the bag is worked in metallics. We have given a little more than half the flap design of the bag on the pattern, just enough to include the clasp. Repeat across to the other corner and work the entire length of 17 inches in one piece.

Before making up the articles, finish the flat pieces by turning under the canvas edges about 1/2 inch and steam. Baste a very thin interfacing to the back of each piece, before turning the edges,

for more body if needed. Cut a lining the size of the canvas with the same seam allowances. Turn the lining under a little more than the canvas and slip stitch or blind stitch in place. Fold the bottom edge up 5 1/2 inches and join the sides. Fold the top edge of the flap over and sew a large snap underneath.

Work the glasses case continuously, repeating at the opposite end. The total length is 7 inches. Finish each piece separately and join the sides.

The comb case is made of stripes in ivory and three shades of green. There are five rows of stitching in each stripe and the whole piece is 3 by 5 1/2 inches. Line the case. Fold lengthwise and join along the side and across the bottom.

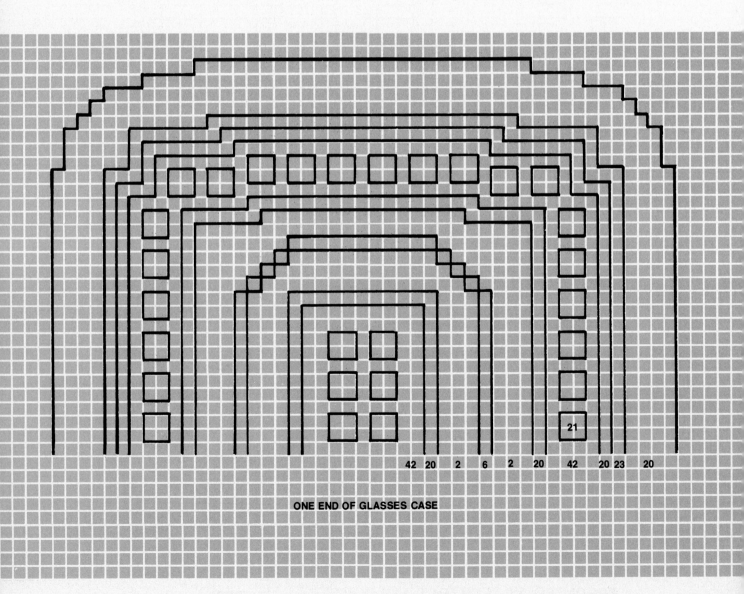

21

42  20    2    6    2    20    42    20 23    20

**ONE END OF GLASSES CASE**

**PETIT POINT ACCESSORIES**

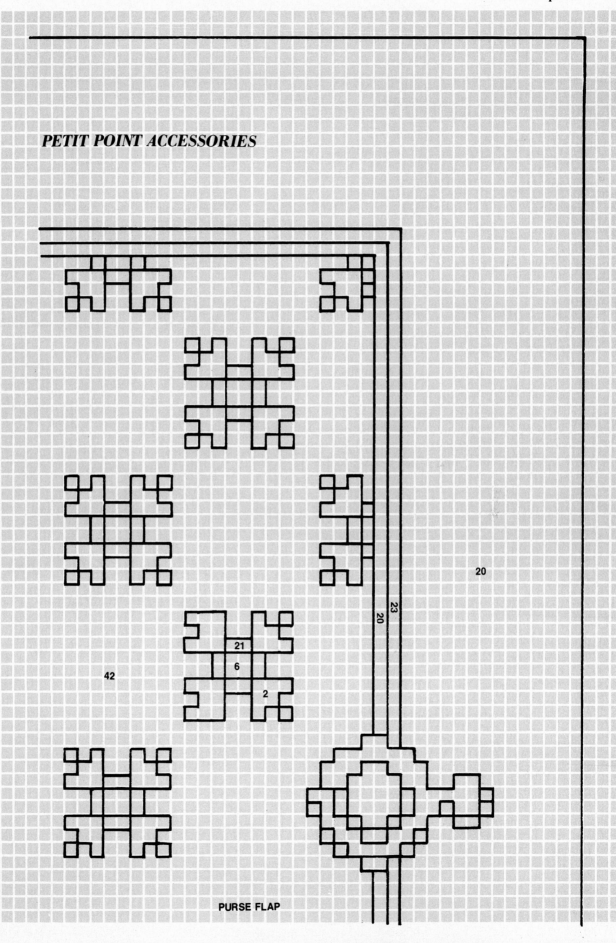

**PURSE FLAP**

**TOP**

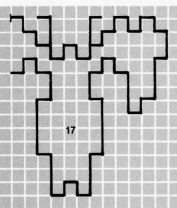

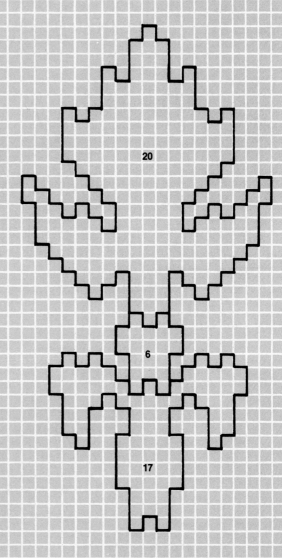

## FLEUR-DE-LYS BARGELLO TAPESTRY

### Designed by Carter Houck, worked by Kathy Crowe

The three-color designs are worked in over-two Brick Stitch, and the background in over-two and over-four Hungarian. Work the designs first, then fill in the background stitches. Do not worry if some of the over-four stitches have to be cut back to over-two in order to fit around the design.

26

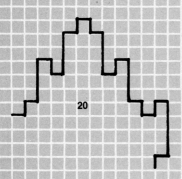

**BOTTOM**

## TWO DOOR STOPS AND A PILLOW IN BASIC STITCHES

*Door stops worked by Grace Harding*

*Pillow worked by Claire Harris*

These interesting and varied designs can be created by using three basic stitches and three colors. These can be used for chair seats, bags and, on a finer canvas, belts, glasses cases, etc. The gauge used here is 12-to-the-inch.

The pillow is worked in the Hungarian Stitch in dark, medium and light colors. The medium and the light colors are alternated to form the inside of the diamonds, outlined in the dark color. The corded piping is made of wool knit fabric.

The door stops are covers made over real bricks. Fold brown paper around a brick to make a pattern. Mark on a canvas so that the corners miter nicely; turn under the bottom on each edge about 1 inch. Blind stitch a piece of vinyl leather to the bottom as a finishing.

One brick is worked in a Florentine Stitch of the traditional Flame treatment, over four canvas threads per stitch, up three stitches, down three stitches, etc. We used three shades of red. The second brick is worked in Scotch Stitch, using five threads of canvas for each square, and two shades of red.

## CHAIR SEATS SUGGESTED BY A NAVAJO RUG

### Designed and Created by Marion Moffat

The repeating squares of double over-four Brick Stitch are worked in a pattern reminiscent of the log cabin quilt pattern. Four shades of blue and four shades of brown and tan are used in the squares and the outline is worked in white. The design can be worked continuously for as large or small piece as you wish.

Mitered pomegranate designs, with color reverses, seem almost to move around the center of the chair seat. They are also worked in over-four Brick Stitch; single, double, triple and four times. The center pomegranates are worked in five shades of brown and tan and five shades of blue, outlined in a paler blue. Beyond these are the same designs worked in cream. The cream is used for four paths in needlepoint in the miter lines.

Twelve-to-the-inch canvas is used for both designs. The repeating squares would also make a very nice petit bargello design on fine canvas.

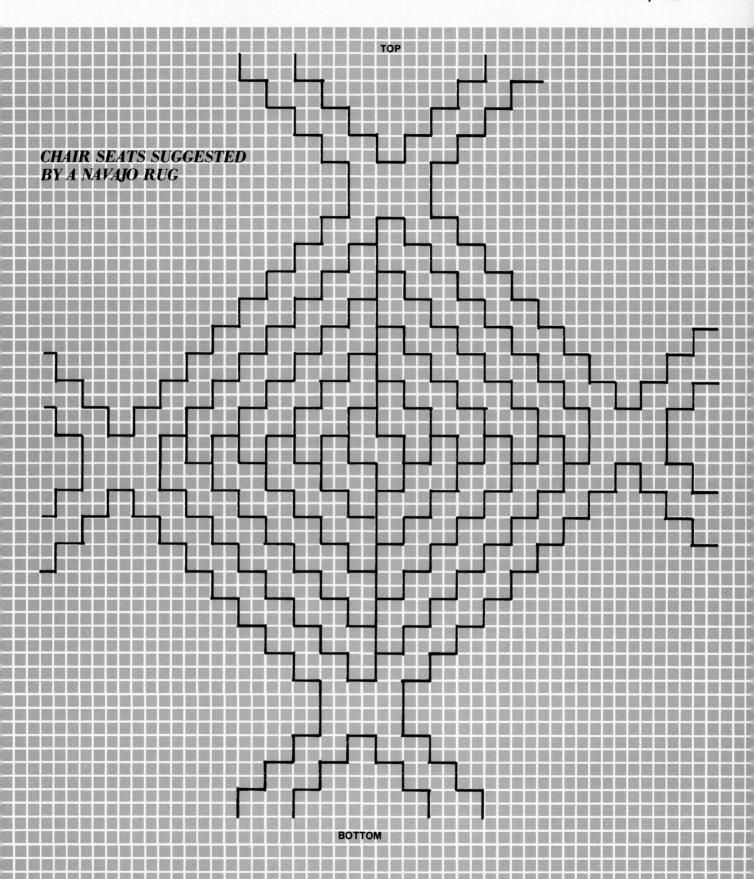

**TOP**

CHAIR SEATS SUGGESTED
BY A NAVAJO RUG

**BOTTOM**

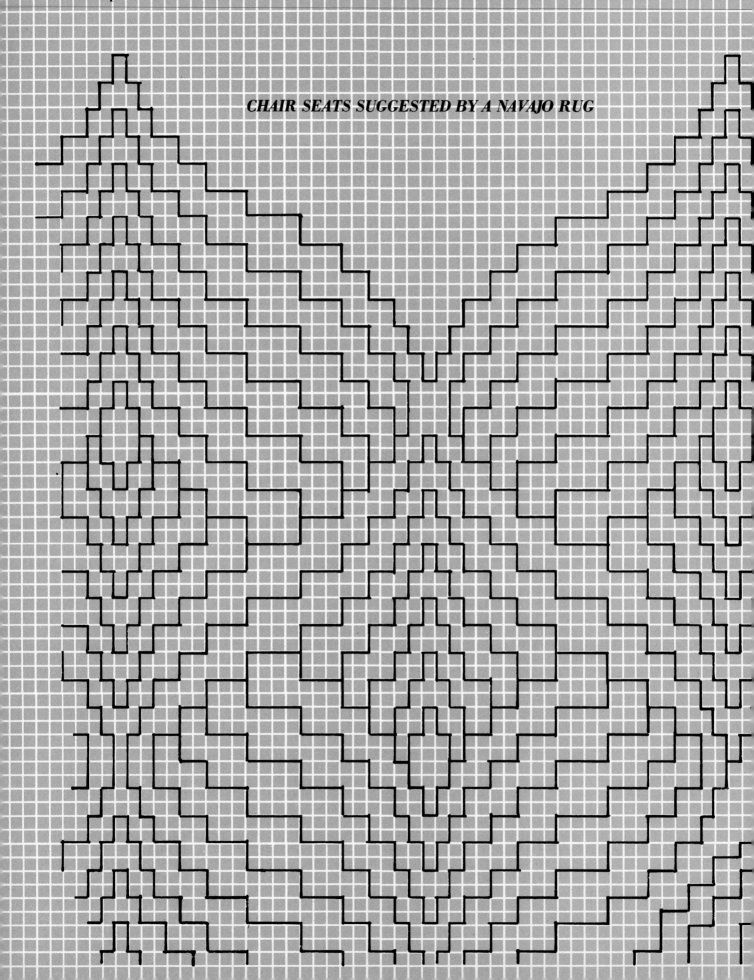

CHAIR SEATS SUGGESTED BY A NAVAJO RUG

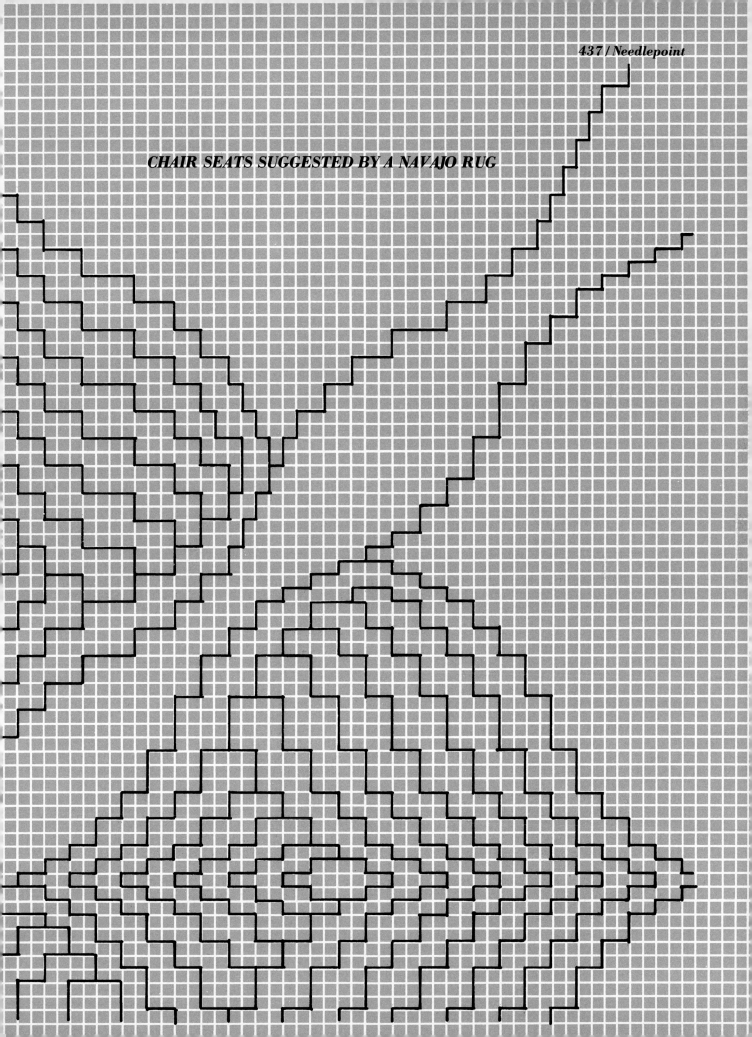

CHAIR SEATS SUGGESTED BY A NAVAJO RUG

## BARGELLO SCREEN OR BLINDS

The wave design, worked over four threads, can be expanded in length to fit any size blind panel. Keep the crest of the wave at the center and repeat the design at each end as far as necessary. Ours is worked in eight colors on 10-to-the-inch canvas. The colors, from the top down are: lime green, olive green, dark olive green, bright pink, dark red, light blue, medium blue and dark blue.

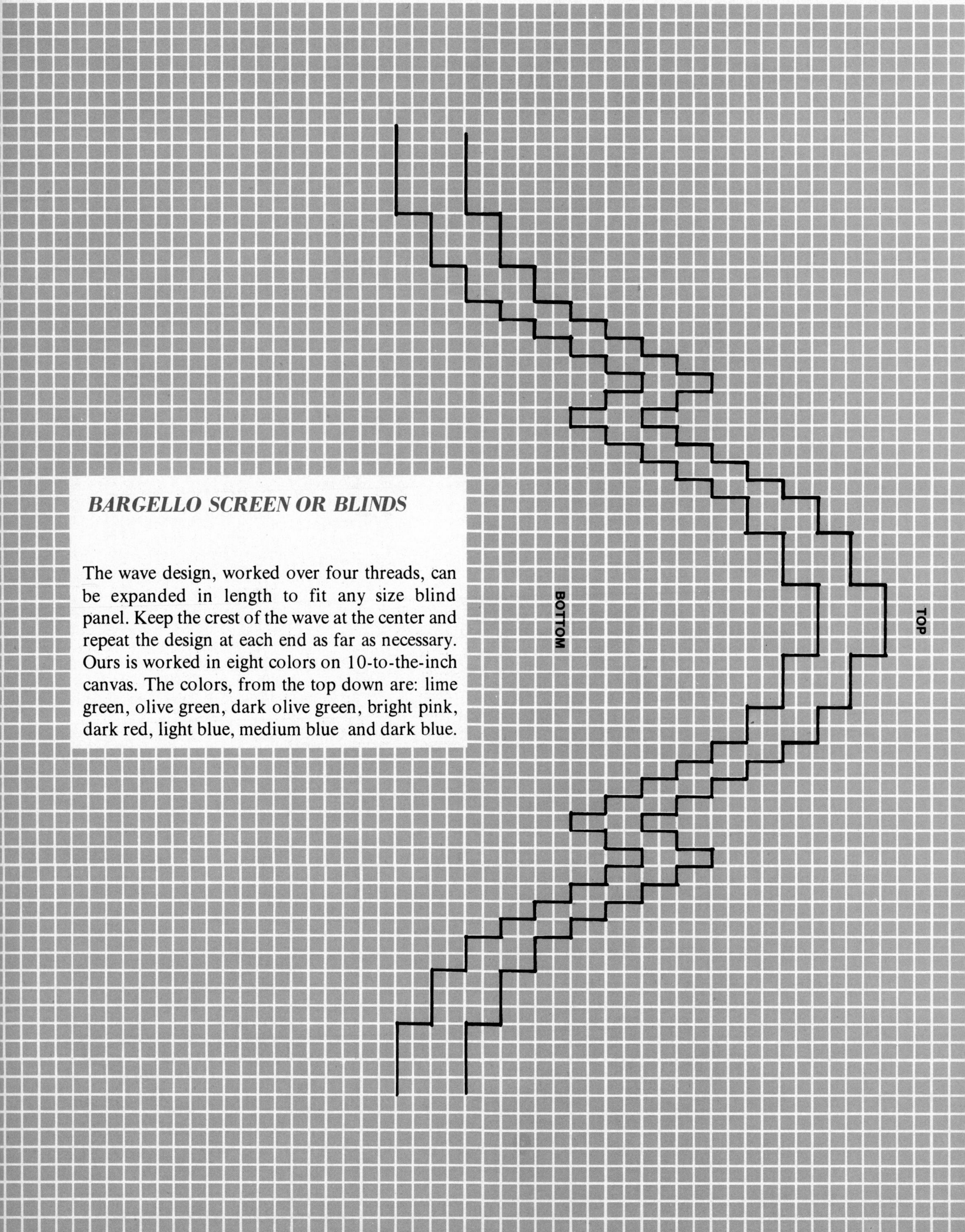

BOTTOM

TOP

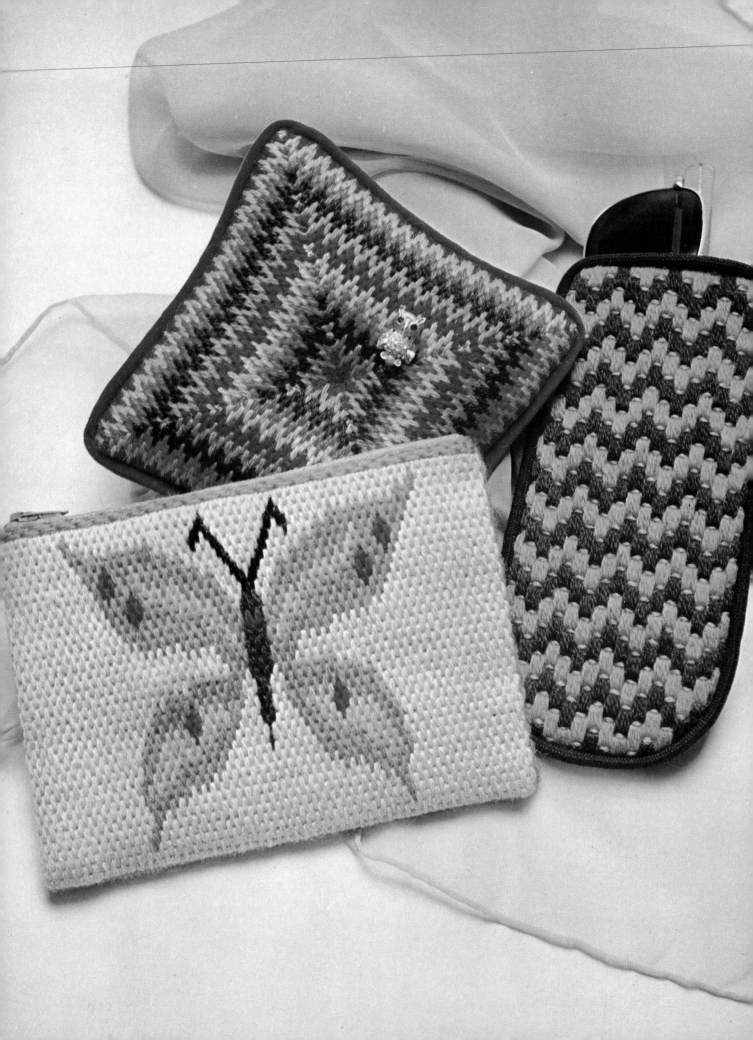

## A SAMPLING OF BARGELLO

### Designed and created by Carter Houck

Each of these small gift pieces is in a different type of Bargello, all on 16-to-the-inch canvas. The purse is a pictorial piece, worked in over-four Brick Stitch. The back of the purse is over-four Hungarian in two shades. It has a zipper set in the top by hand and a silk lining cut and seamed to size, blind stitched in against the zipper. The purse itself is whipped together with yarn.

The glasses case is an over-six Florentine varia-tion with bars worked across the top and bottom of each wave. The case is not lined but is finished with a corded piping of wool knit. The back is made of wool knit. The piping edge and the back are hand-finished at the top. The pincushion is mitered in over-four Flame, using five shades. It is finished with a corded piping and the back is of velveteen. After it is stuffed, tack through the center.

Any of these designs will increase $1\frac{1}{2}$ times if worked on 10-to-the-inch canvas. The pin-cushion and the butterfly in a larger canvas will make attractive pillows.

## CANVAS-WORK PILLOW WITH DIAGONAL DESIGN

Quickpoint canvas and a simple Cross Stitch is used to make this effective patchwork design. We have charted only the frame so that odds and ends of yarn can be used to make the inside patterns in any way desired. The lines defined with Xs are the large ones in the picture with the extra cross worked double and upright over four stitches.

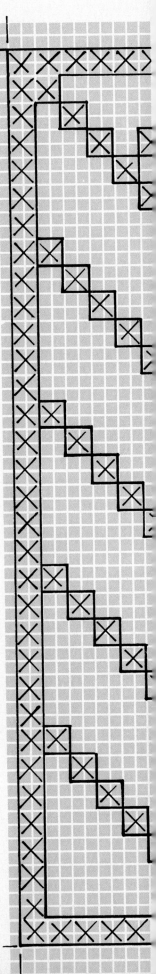

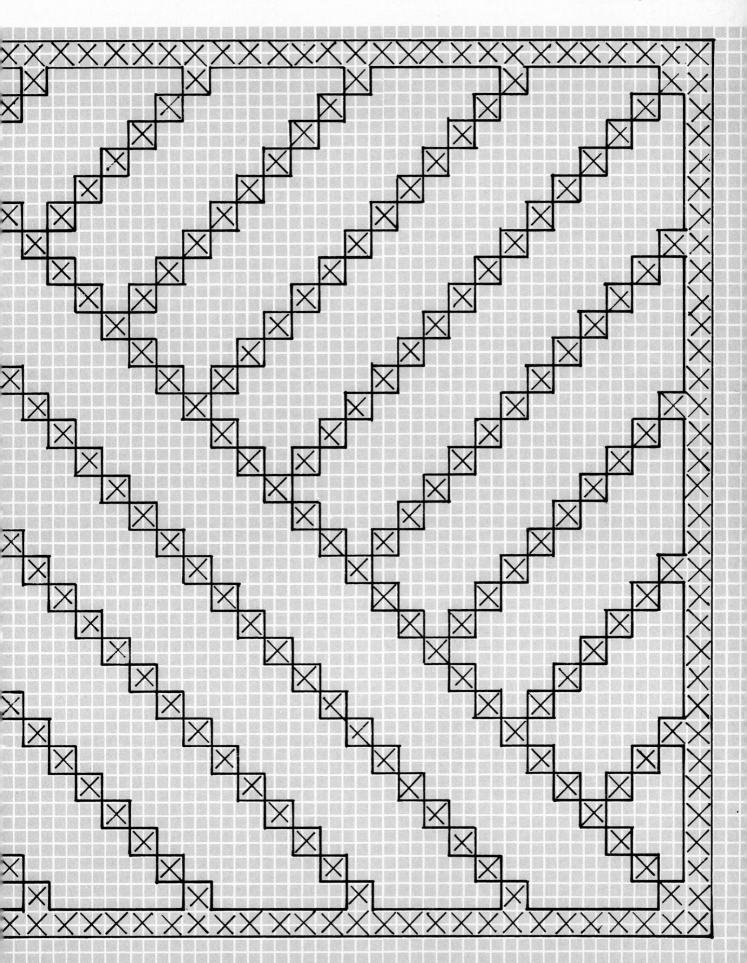

BUTTERFLY

TOP

*A SAMPLING OF BARGELLO*

BUTTERFLY

BOTTOM

A SAMPLING OF BARGELLO

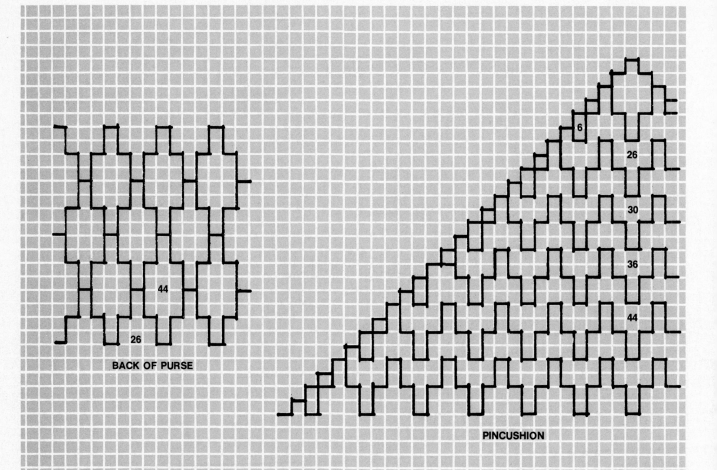

BACK OF PURSE

PINCUSHION

*A SAMPLING OF BARGELLO*

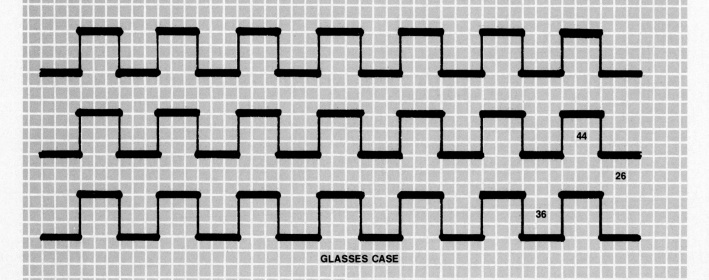

GLASSES CASE

## AMERICAN INDIAN DESIGN

### Designed and Created by Marion Moffat

The designs on baskets, pottery and rugs of the American Indians translate perfectly into needlepoint. This repeating one can be used for a pillow, bag, wall panel or vest. It is worked here on 14-to-the-inch canvas but can be done even in rug size.

## LEOPARD NEEDLEPOINT BELT
### (for man or woman)

### Designed and Created by Joe Ann Helms

Once this design is started, you can take off on your own in the arrangement of the spots or you can make a repeat of this first section. It is worked here on 16-to-the-inch canvas which makes it 1¾ inches wide. When sufficient length has been worked, use an iron-on stiffening and then back it by hand with grosgrain ribbon. The link-type buckle shown is most practical for tapestry belts because it is less bulky than a pull-through type.

# BIRDS IN FLIGHT

**Adapted and created by Joe Ann Helms**

**Courtesy of United States Postal Service**

Everywhere there are designs that are beautiful and simple enough to translate into needlepoint.

The indicia from a U.S. aerogramme makes a wonderful three-shade piece, worked here on 12-to-the-inch canvas. The back of the bag is made in matching velveteen, a zipper is hand applied to the top and a silk lining, cut to size, is blind stitched in around the edge of the zipper. A shoulder chain makes a nice finishing touch.

## AS-YOU-LIKE-IT TAPESTRY SAMPLER

### Designed and worked by Grace Harding

Anyone who has been doing needlepoint and bargello for a while is apt to have a fine collection of leftover yarn. Samplers can be worked in many styles and put to many uses and will accommodate a surprising number of colors. The little medallion and stripe design worked in needlepoint is a good divider for the chair seat and back. The canvas is 10-to-the-inch but 12-to-the-inch will also work nicely. The panels between the stripes are roughly 3½ inches in any bargello or needlepoint stitch desired.

Use the seat and back of a director's chair as a pattern, working the seat only wide enough to go to the edge of the seat clamp. When the canvas is worked, back it with any strong woven interfacing, basted lightly to the canvas. Line the pieces to the edge with a strong sailcloth or canvas in a matching color. This can be machine stitched to the edges and then turned right side out. On the seat piece, leave the fabric long enough at the ends to create the casing for the rods to slip in. Fold the lined ends of the back piece around to form a casing at each end and secure with hand stitches that do not show through on the right side.

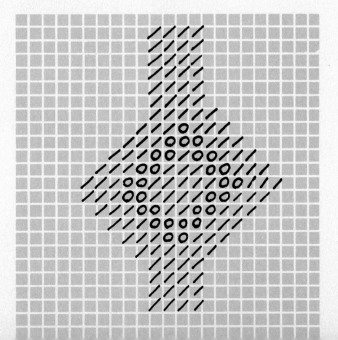

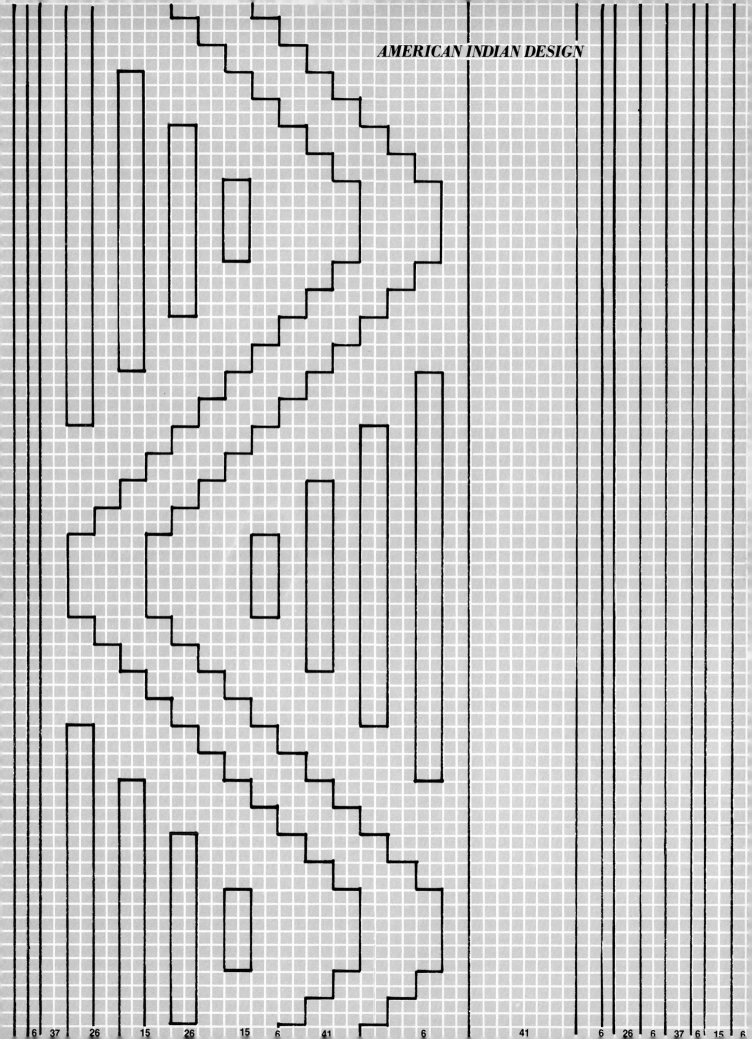

AMERICAN INDIAN DESIGN

**BIRDS IN FLIGHT**

BIRDS IN FLIGHT

## LEOPARD NEEDLEPOINT BELT

Background = Cream
- = Light Gold
/ = Dark Gold
O = Dark Brown
X = Black

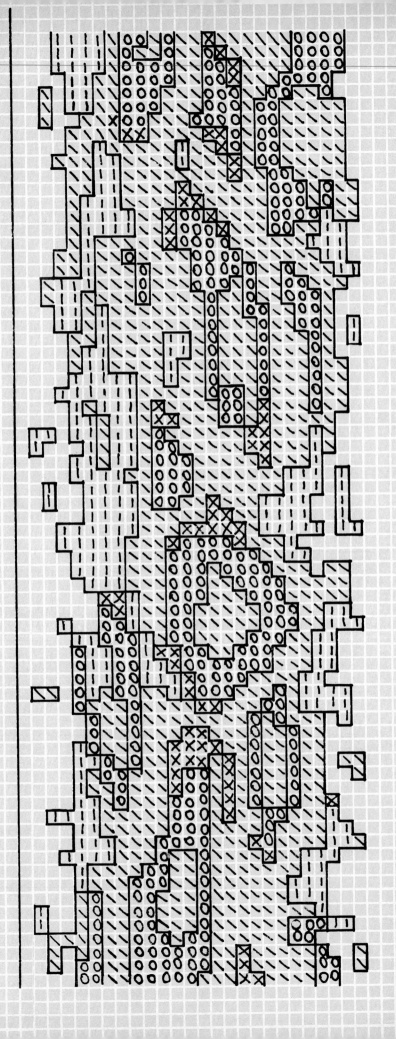

## NEEDLEPOINT PILLOWS IN EARTH TONES

### Designed and Created by Joe Ann Helms

An Oriental abstract design of trees and a repeating motif borrowed from wallpaper are both worked in an economy of colors. The trees are in tan, brown and black on cream and the repeating design uses only brown and black on cream. Both are shown here on 14-to-the-inch canvas making tiny pillows of about 9 x 12 inches. By increasing to 10 or 12-to-the-canvas, the pillows can be considerably enlarged. The trees would also be effective in two strong shades of green and black on blue and the repeating motif could be worked in any color combination that fits the decorating scheme.

NEEDLEPOINT PILLOWS IN EARTH TONES

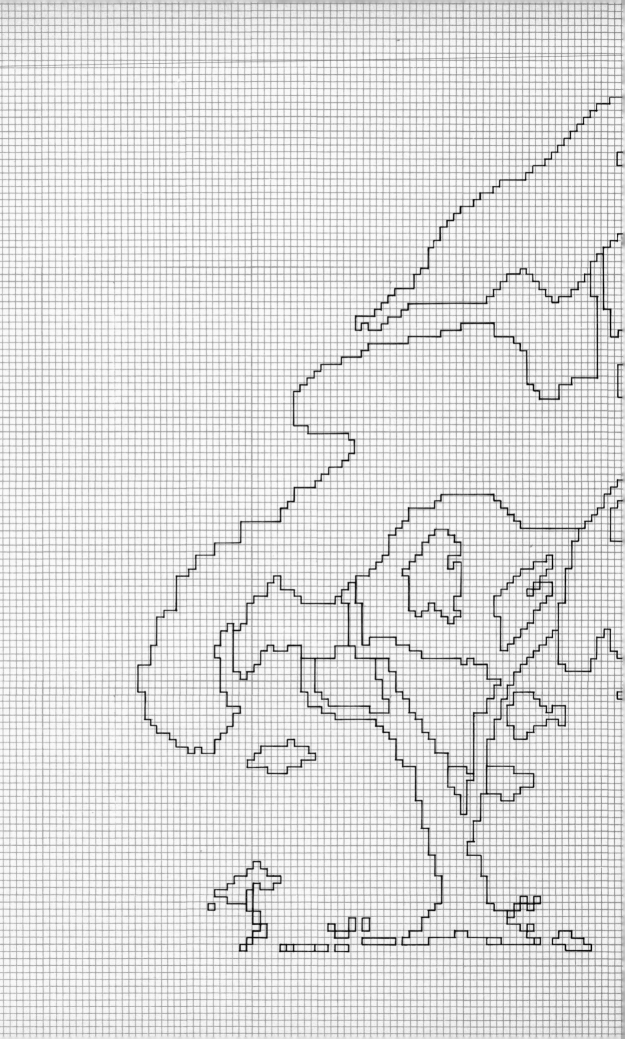

## CHAIR SEAT IN TRADITIONAL NEEDLEPOINT

Floral designs are the most traditional of all needlepoint motifs and are especially suitable to Victorian chairs and furniture. The only modern touch to this one is that it is worked on quick-point canvas. The size of the area covered can be controlled by changing canvas size or by enlarging the amount of background.

**Chair Seat**

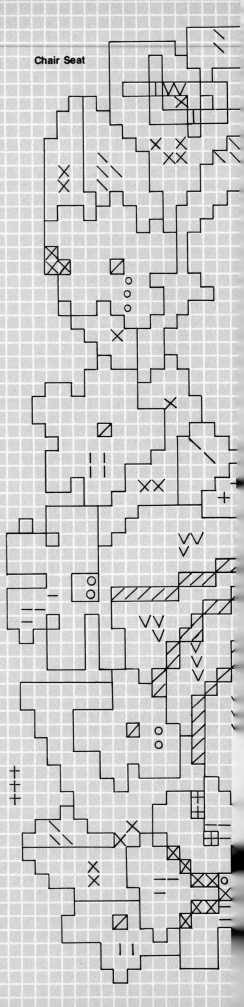

**FRONT**

## CHAIR SEAT IN TRADITIONAL NEEDLEPOINT

| | |
|---|---|
| + | DARK GREEN |
| × | MEDIUM GREEN |
| \ | LIGHT GREEN |
| — | BLUE |
| | | ORANGE |
| / | RED |
| = | ROSE |
| O | YELLOW |
| V | WHITE |

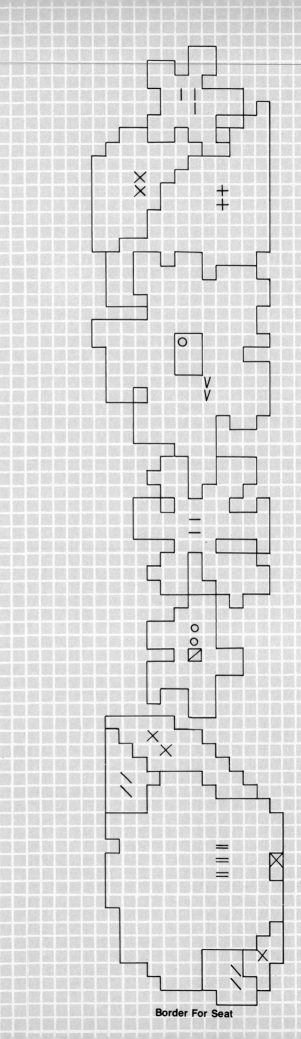

**Border For Seat**

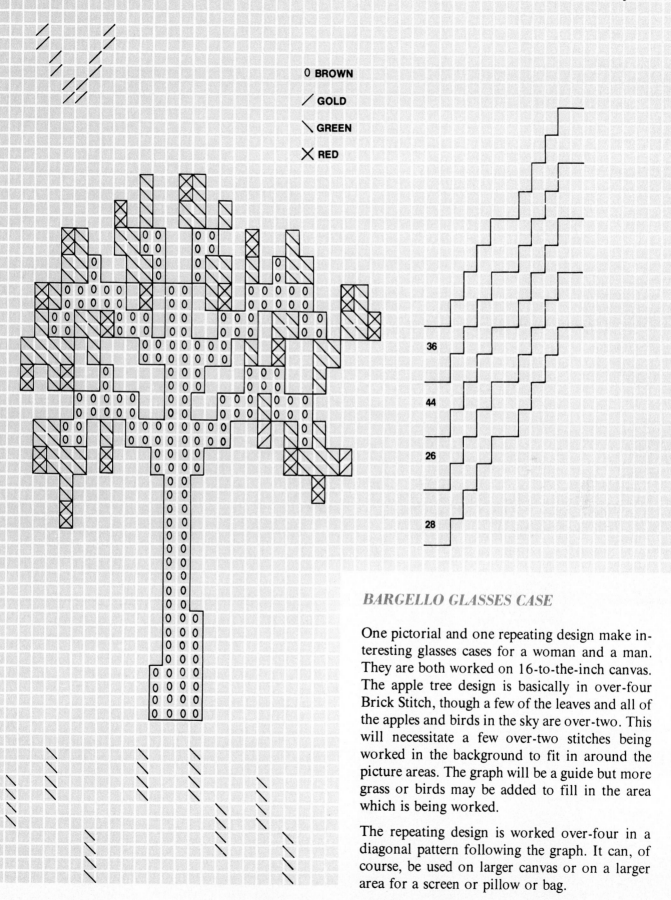

0 BROWN

/ GOLD

\ GREEN

X RED

36

44

26

28

## BARGELLO GLASSES CASE

One pictorial and one repeating design make interesting glasses cases for a woman and a man. They are both worked on 16-to-the-inch canvas. The apple tree design is basically in over-four Brick Stitch, though a few of the leaves and all of the apples and birds in the sky are over-two. This will necessitate a few over-two stitches being worked in the background to fit in around the picture areas. The graph will be a guide but more grass or birds may be added to fill in the area which is being worked.

The repeating design is worked over-four in a diagonal pattern following the graph. It can, of course, be used on larger canvas or on a larger area for a screen or pillow or bag.

## BARGELLO PINCUSHION

For a quick first project in bargello, try this dainty pincushion on 16-to-the-inch canvas. Three shades each of any two contrasting colors will work equally well. Use an over-four Brick Stitch and follow the graph. A repeating design of this kind can be applied to any larger area or to any larger canvas mesh.

The back and corded piping are made of wool knit fabric in a suitable color. The finished cushion can be filled with polyester or cotton batting or with cedar sawdust. If the latter is used, it is wise to treat the cushion like a pillow and make an inside form of tightly woven cotton fabric.

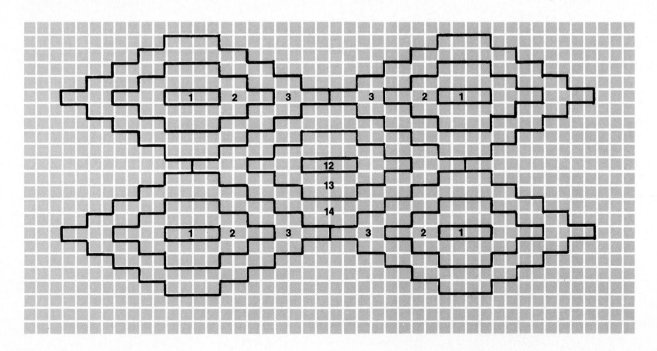

# Rug Making

Rug making existed in Egypt 2000 years before Christ. The palaces of the Egyptian Pharoahs contained an array of hand-loomed rugs. Many of the concepts used in making these rugs still are used today. Egyptian rug making was very highly developed, but other cultures in different parts of the world were also experimenting with similar ideas.

Persian rug making was adapted from the Babylonians who had highly developed rug making techniques centuries before Christ was born. There is also evidence that in China and India as early as 1300 B.C., carpet weaving was an established craft.

In early centuries when many poor homes had hard, bare floors, rugs were used to provide warmth and a soft surface on which to walk. Rugs were also used in piles for sleeping; worn to provide warmth and protection from cold winds and

**FINE ART IN WOOL: "Sandringham" was designed and is in the process of being worked by Joan Moshimer who also dyes her own wools.**

dampness; and hung over windows and door openings in wealthy homes for decoration and protection. In churches and temples, whose walls were often adorned with rugs in which religious motifs had been woven, rugs were placed on altars and hard floors to protect the knees of worshipers.

By the sixteenth century, possibly the most magnificent rugs ever known were made in Persia and Turkey. They are still famous for their elaborate designs and unique colors, which were made from vegetable dyes. Since these dyes were rare and expensive, late in the eighteenth century aniline or synthetic dyes were introduced. Synthetic dyes were cheaper, easier to obtain and required much less work to produce color consistency. However, synthetic dyes do not mellow or age so the subtlety of ancient rug colors is lost.

When the colonists came to America, they were unable to bring many furnishings. Every scrap of material, especially wool or silk, was used to create floor coverings. Although some early rugs were woven, most were the braided or needle (knitted and crocheted) rugs, because these could be easily made with scraps of fabric, yarn or other materials salvaged from worn clothing.

There are two main classifications of handmade rugs; flat-woven and pile. Early rugs were made of coarse fabrics woven like ordinary cloth. Flat weaves are still used on braided or crocheted rugs. Pile rugs consist of a surface material attached by knots to a backing. The pile is inserted into the backing in such a way as to form raised loops which can be cut and shaped.

The famous Persian rugs, many of which had several hundred knots to the square inch, are examples of the pile technique. Other examples of the pile technique were found in the Scandinavian countries, dating back to the Vikings. The Scandinavians called the knotting technique *rya* and used it to make a thickly knotted material for lining in garments and as covering for beds, sleighs or doorways for protection against the cold. Early ryas were plain and practical, unlike the patterned, multicolored rya rugs made today. A rya pile, in comparison with the Persian or Oriental, is quite sparse, having about thirty knots per square inch.

Articles made by hooking loops of yarn into a woven fabric (called punchwork) were produced by various nationalities early in the Christian era. This method was used mainly for clothing, but hooked rugs were later made in the Scandinavian countries, England, Europe and the United States. Colonial housewives often dyed strips of old cloth to create decorative and durable hooked rugs.

The basic rug making techniques spread throughout the world, absorbing the character of many countries. This is the rich heritage upon which today's rug making is based.

## PLANNING A RUG

Beautiful floor coverings can be the focal point of decoration in a room. Aside from the obvious practical aspects of warmth, the use of bright, decorative rugs are an asset to the bare floors of any cottage or castle.

There are numerous techniques employed in making a decorative or protective rug. The fac-

tors that affect the selection of technique and design when planning a rug are the same as in buying a rug — the room in which it will be used, a style which will blend with the other furnishings, the size of the space to be covered, and the necessary durability of fabric or yarn and backing.

## SELECTING RUG COLORS

By working with fabrics and yarns, increased perceptivity to color and design will develop. Rug making provides unlimited opportunities for creative ideas. Colors can be brilliant and lavish or subtle and soft hued.

No matter which technique is selected for a rug, it is important to consider the arrangement of color within the design. There are several terms that will help in making color selections.

**Hue:** Refers to the name of a color such as red, blue and yellow. A hue can be changed by mixing with another hue. Red mixed with blue produces purple; blue and yellow produce green.

**Value:** Refers to the degree of lightness or darkness of the hue. Dark values are called shades; light values are called tints. The value of a hue can be changed without altering the basic color by using less color to get a lighter value and more for a darker value.

**Intensity:** Refers to the brilliance of a hue; its brightness or dullness. Intensity can be decreased by adding black or another dark color.

**Color Schemes:** It is possible to select either warm or cool colors to dominate the overall color scheme of the rug. Warm colors are those which are generally associated with heat — reds, oranges and yellows. Cool colors are those identified with cold — blues and greens.

Familiarity with recognized types of color schemes makes selecting colors less difficult. Many times a monochromatic color plan can be effective. With this scheme only one color is used in different values when color is to be subordinate to design. Pink and red or black and gray are effective in monochromatic color schemes. However, it is important to have sufficient contrast between the shades.

Analogous color schemes use several colors that have a common element, such as a combination of orange, green and yellow. A complementary color scheme can also be used with interesting results. Complementary colors accent each other, for example, green and red or blue and yellow. However, quantities of each color and their relationship to each other must be carefully worked out to avoid unattractive clashes.

**Shading:** The same basic principles that apply in drawing or painting apply to working with colors in a rug. To achieve depth, the dark areas of color seem more distant, lighter colors appear closer.

## DESIGN SELECTION

Ideas for designs come from many sources. When planning a rug design, keep in mind the decor of the room in which it will be placed. Inspiration for a design can come from any source — china patterns, drawings, paintings, geometric designs, motifs on drapery fabric or upholstery, and wallpaper patterns.

Portions of a design can be rearranged to suit the size of the rug. Cut apart the design elements and rearrange them to fit the square, oval or rectangular shape of the planned rug. One motif can be repeated in several areas — placed in the center, used as a border along the outside edges, or arranged at random.

**Enlarging and Reducing Designs:** Two simple methods are frequently used to make designs larger or to reduce them to proportions that will fit the required area. They are the photostat method and the square method.

The photostat method is the easiest method to use when changing the dimensions of a design. Take the design to a photocopy shop to be photostatically enlarged or reduced to the proper dimensions. Ask for a positive image; a negative is difficult to see. Several photostats can be pieced together for a large design. Photostating costs very little and is the most efficient, accurate way of changing design dimensions. (See Needlepoint, pg. 407.)

With the square method, the design is divided into one-inch squares. Outline the size of the project on a piece of paper and divide the outline into exactly the same number of squares. When this is done, although the number of squares is the same, their comparative size will be different. Working square by square, make a freehand copy in the matching squares of the original design. To enlarge the design, the portion of the design drawn in each square will be enlarged; to reduce the design, the part of the design drawn in each square will be smaller. A reasonably accurate reproduction of the original design is possible with this method. (See Needlepoint, pg. 407.)

**Transferring Designs to Backing:** There are two basic ways to transfer a rug design. Each can be used successfully on all rug projects, although transferring from a graph is more accurate.

With the first method, trace the design onto canvas, using a waterproof or indelible marker. A gray or neutral color is best because a darker marker will show through light-colored fabric or yarn. Areas of color can be indicated by coloring the entire section with the marker, such as on a needlepoint rug canvas. Burlap or monk's cloth backings usually require only an outline to indicate the design.

The second method involves working from a graph. It is a slower process, but more accurate since each stitch is placed in a designated position. No outlines are drawn on the backing. Close reference lines can be provided by marking both the graph and the backing in equivalent sections. Stitch positions are counted and located from these smaller areas.

First, draw vertical and horizontal center lines across the graphed design. Then draw heavy lines at one-inch intervals. Mark the center of the backing by folding it in quarters. Using an indelible marker or straight pins, duplicate the one-inch squares of the graph on the backing by marking at one-inch intervals.

## DYEING FABRICS

Commercial dyes are available in most of the colors required by the beginning rug maker. Light-colored fabrics are best for dyeing light shades, since the light covering color will not be affected by the color already in the material. Tints dyed over white or cream-colored fabrics are clear and brilliant; tints dyed over pastels of a different color may be slightly altered. Dark shades are usually not affected by the color previously in the material because the covering dye is so intense. A beige wool fabric, besides being comparatively plentiful, takes most commercial colors without altering them.

There are almost as many methods of dyeing as there are rug makers. No matter what method is used, it is important to dye only a small amount of material at a time. It is easier to handle small amounts because no bulky equipment is required. Also, by limiting the amount being dyed, if a mistake is made, only a small quantity of material will be affected.

There are several helpful hints that will make dyeing more successful. First, assemble all the equipment needed for one dyeing session; once dyeing is under way it is difficult to look for additional equipment. Read the complete instructions to determine the various stages of dyeing and the equipment needed for each step. White enamel pans in the proper size to accommodate the material should be used. These pans make it easier to see how much dye has been absorbed by the fabric. The pots and pans assembled for dyeing should be kept thereafter for that purpose only. Measuring spoons and cups, tongs, vinegar and detergent, rubber gloves and a full-length plastic or rubberized apron should be assembled before dyeing begins. Be sure to wear old clothes.

When dyeing shades of one color, do the lightest shade first, then the next darker and finally the darkest coloring. This method eliminates making up a number of dye solutions. It is possible to mix several colors when dyeing. However, this takes a professional eye and some knowledge of how colors react to each other.

Test the color mixture on a small piece of the selected fabric before adding the rest of the material. Costly mistakes are minimized by being cautious. If more chemical must be added to the dye solution, remove the material, add the dye and then replace the fabric.

Experimentation can lead to interesting results and creates familiarity with dye combinations and how dyes react to various hues in the fabric. Keep records of what each batch of dye contains. It is frustrating to obtain a lovely color and have no way of duplicating it because various ingredients were added haphazardly.

Entire books have been written on the procedures used for obtaining various colors, the types of commercial dyes available and the use of natural vegetable materials to obtain beautiful colorations. If this aspect of rug making is of great personal interest, consult the local library or bookstore for additional references.

## HOOKED RUGS

The hooking technique produces handsome, useful articles for the home, the most favored of which are hooked rugs. These durable rugs, created from little more than fabric or yarn scraps, are a pleasure to work and become more attractive with use and time. Rug hooking is an ideal project that can fill small segments of time, does not require much space and need not cost a great deal.

Basically, rug hooking consists of pushing yarn or fabric strips through a backing, leaving a surface loop that serves as the rug pile. The selection of yarns or fabrics, their placement and the resulting textural effects make rug hooking a favorite activity.

### SUITABLE MATERIALS

**Fabric:** Fabrics used for hooking should be considered in relationship to the effect one wishes to create and the suitability of the fabric to the design. Fabric for a rug should be readily available, durable, relatively inexpensive and easy to hook. The wearing quality of a well-made rug depends in large measure on the strength of the original fabric. If the rug will eventually reside in a heavily trafficked area, the fabric selected should be exceedingly durable and soil resistant.

Cost per square foot for a hooked rug varies according to the choice of fabric. Whether the fabric is old or new, an expensive wool or a relatively inexpensive blend determines the amount spent on the rug project. One of the advantages of rug hooking, however, is that it is possible to make just as attractive a rug from inexpensive or old materials as from costly new fabrics if care is taken during hooking.

**Burlap and Monk's Cloth**

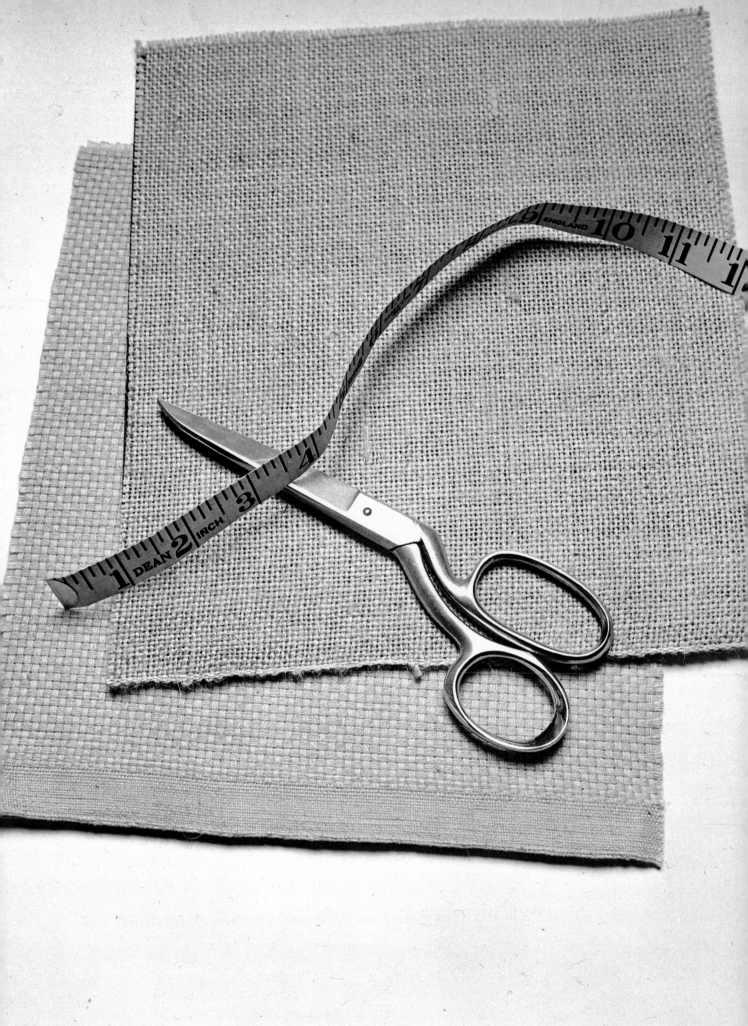

Some materials are easy to obtain in a variety of weights, textures and colors and are quickly prepared for hooking. Certain other fabrics are particularly easy to pull through the backing.

Different fabrics produce different effects in a hooked rug. Lightweight flannel, for example, produces a flat, even surface when hooked and works well when a subtle texture is required. Coarser weaves and tweedy fabrics produce a nubby surface which creates a textured effect. Either light and delicate or heavy, rough effects can be created by the choice of fabrics.

Fabric from old clothing and bedding makes excellent rug hooking material after it has been correctly prepared. Fabric should be inspected thoroughly and all worn or permanently soiled pieces cut away and discarded. If the material appears durable but of uncertain strength, cut a strip in the width required and then pull from both ends. The material should not stretch or break under the strain since it would also stretch or break during hooking. All material should be washed before being cut into strips to insure that it is shrinkproof, clean and colorfast. Machine washing in hot water will often tighten the fabric weave so that it can better stand the strain of hooking.

One of the disadvantages of using old materials, aside from the time spent in preparing the cloth, is the difficulty in obtaining enough of the same weight. To make a rug of even texture, different weights must be combined. To do this, cut heavy, closely woven material into narrow strips and lightweight material into wider strips. Since it is difficult to obtain enough old fabric in the same color or to match a color, be sure to have enough of one color to complete a particular area.

Problems arise when trying to obtain enough of one weight or color for the background since it is usually a large area. When it is not possible to get all the necessary material in the same color for a large area, slight differences can be concealed by dyeing all the material for the background. Even a slight tint of dye will help blend the minor differences, and unmatched materials will have enough similarity to be used together successfully.

Another way to combine fabrics for the background is to divide the background area into four parts. One quarter of the material should be used for each quarter of the background, working it in from the outside edge toward the center. Be careful not to end each line of hooking at the same place. If additional material is required to complete the four sections, purchase as close a match as possible. Divide and hook the additional material in the same way as before, working from the uneven edge of the previous hooking toward the center of the rug. In this way, the different materials are spread evenly over the rug with no sharp line of demarcation. Variegated effects are often used in backgrounds and these marbleized or swirled patterns conceal the difficulties in matching colors or materials.

Wool or cotton rug yarn is sometimes used in hooking, however, it is more expensive than fabric scraps. Either a smooth or textured surface can be obtained with rug yarn. Wool yarn is available in many colors; it is easy to dye, durable and soil resistant. Cotton rug yarn is less expensive than wool, available in many colors, easy to dye and washable. Cotton yarn, however, lacks the resilience of wool so it does not cover the surface as fully. Cotton yarn is also less durable than wool and has a tendency to absorb dirt.

Yarn is worked most successfully with a speed hook. Speed hooks require a continuous flow of material so rug yarn is available in skeins or in balls.

## EQUIPMENT

Hooking a rug does not require elaborate tools. There is one essential tool and several others that are optional but helpful. Other items are incidental but may make work more pleasurable.

**Rug Hook:** This is the essential tool needed for rug hooking. There are several types of hooks on the market with different size tips, short or long shanks and straight, bent or grooved handles. The handle of a hook should fit the hand comfortably. If the hook handle is too large or small, the

**RUG HOOKS: From top left, clockwise, punch hook or needle, speed hook, latch hooks (bent and straight), Moshimer's rug hooks, Rya needle.**

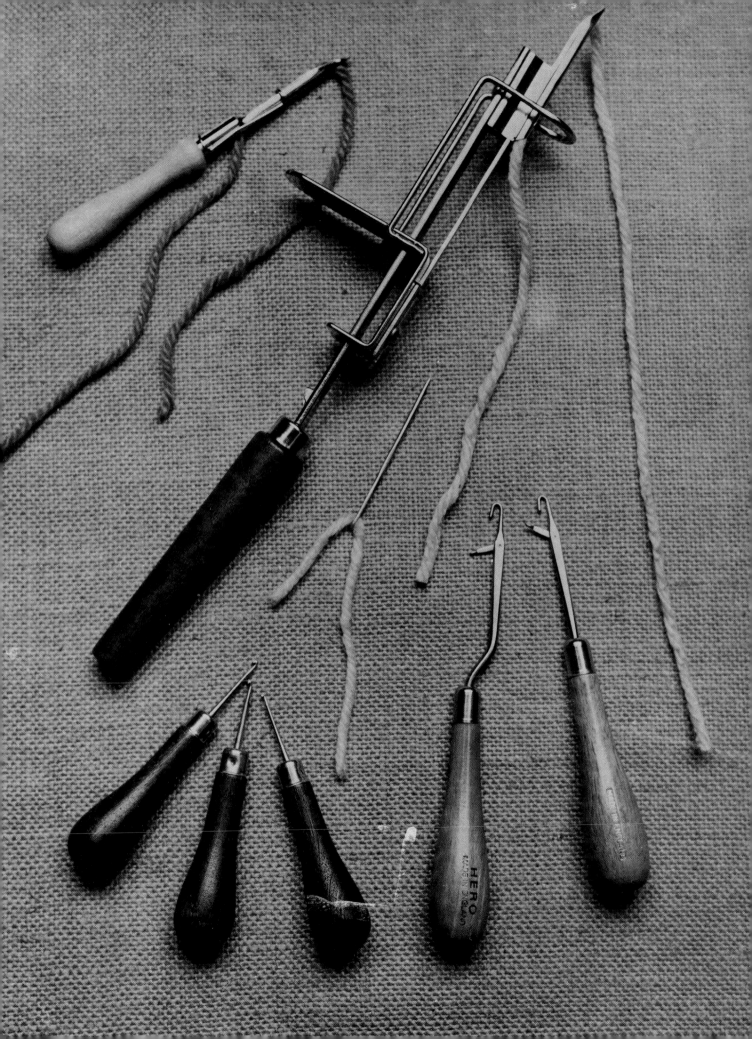

hand muscles strain while trying to hold it. To work well with different weights and thicknesses of material, the tip should be large enough to grasp a variety of fabrics but of a size that will fit through the mesh of the burlap backing without stretching it. A conventional or standard rug hook has a handle of medium length and a tip suited to strips of various widths; it is readily available in most needlework and craft shops.

**Speed Hooks:** These hooks are designed for fast work for those who want to make rugs quickly. One kind of speed hook has two points for use with strips of different widths. The metal end of the handle of this speed hook is grooved for adjusting to make loops of different heights.

**Backing:** In addition to the proper hook, it is important to have suitable material upon which to work. The two standard types of backing are burlap, which is made of jute, and monk's cloth, which is made of cotton.

Burlap is the most commonly used backing. Readily available, most commercial patterns are printed on burlap. When selecting burlap, buy a good grade of closely woven material. Burlap is available in either a double or single weave. Double-weave burlap is fine for narrow strips; the single weave is best with wide strips that require a more open mesh if they are to be drawn through easily.

Monk's cloth for rug hooking is rather soft and can be used with either wide or narrow strips. The weave is uniform and the material can be stretched tightly on a frame without breaking threads. Cotton fabric does not crack or dry out so the edges of a finished rug can be hemmed instead of bound. Monk's cloth is available in widths up to fifteen feet. Therefore, it is ideal for ambitious projects since separate pieces of a rug do not have to be joined by sewing or hooking through double thicknesses of backing. Monk's cloth is sold under a variety of trade names by rug and craft suppliers.

**Frames:** A frame is a great aid in rug making because it stretches the backing tight and allows freedom for both hands. There are two kinds of frames — standing frames and lap frames.

A standing frame can be folded and the top section lowered without disturbing the project under way. Standing frames are also relatively easy to carry or to store. The top of most standing frames can be lowered to a comfortable height and tilted to any desired angle for hooking. On the better models, the top section also revolves so that the underside of the work can be inspected; the top section is also removable. Hardware on a frame should be sturdy enough to hold even a room-sized rug firmly. Although a number of sizes are available, a forty-inch frame will accommodate most projects easily. **Fig. 1.**

Fig. 1

**Standing Frame**

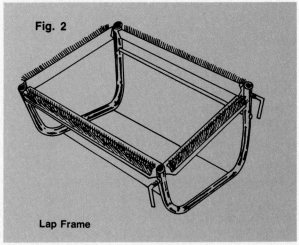

Fig. 2

**Lap Frame**

Lap frames are small enough to be set on a table, held in the lap or used by those confined to bed. Made of rounded metal bars, lap frames are open squares set on round metal legs. Equipped with many close-set teeth, the bars have handles on the back and side. A rug piece is placed over these teeth and tightened evenly by turning the handles. It is possible to make sizable rugs on this frame by lifting off one section and replacing with a different section of the same rug. **Fig. 2.**

The lap hoop is an inexpensive circular frame. Usually these frames are about fourteen inches in

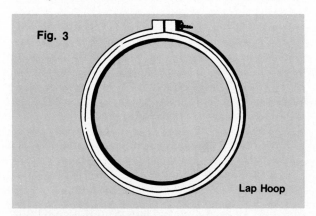

Fig. 3

Lap Hoop

circumference and equipped with a screw in the top of the hoop for tightening the outer band around the inner one. A lap hoop is somewhat awkward to work with since one hand must hold the hoop steady. Hooking, particularly by beginners, needs the use of both hands. **Fig. 3.** A picture frame or canvas stretcher can also be used for hooking. It is also inexpensive but, like the lap hoop, is hard to hold steady while working.

**Fabric Cutters and Scissors:** While many rug makers cut materials by hand, mechanical cutters produce strips easily and quickly. There are several varieties of cutters, and while all are relatively expensive, they should last forever. Some models can be set on a flat surface, others clamped to a table top. Most models are fitted with various blade sizes that cut either narrow or wide strips.

Scissors with bent handles are made especially for cutting rug-hooking yarn. The bent handles make it easier to cut drawn up ends on the surface of the rug. A small groove in the tip of these scissors makes possible the insertion of the blade into a loop to cut through it.

## TECHNIQUE

**Preparing the Backing:** Before putting the backing on the frame, make a one-half-inch fold along the raw edges of the material. Either hand or machine stitch this hem to keep the edges from raveling. This type of edge will suffice on any frame except the hoops, on which there is not enough material extending beyond the edge of the design to fasten between the hoops. To solve this problem, stitch the one-half-inch fold on all edges as previously explained; then sew a six to eight-inch strip of material onto each side of the piece. Use cotton muslin or scrap fabrics. This extra "border" increases the size of the piece when working near the edge so that it can be fastened between hoop sections. After the piece is finished the additional outside fabrics are removed and the rug is hemmed or bound.

**Placing Backing on the Frame:** For best results, the backing should be stretched tightly on the frame. Center the area of the design that will be worked first and stretch as evenly and tightly as possible. Then tack the backing onto the frame. Instructions accompanying individual frames will tell specifically how to pull the backing taut prior to starting work. Hooking will be more even and work will go faster if the backing is properly placed on the frame.

**How to Cut Strips:** Begin by cutting three-inch wide strips about twelve inches long. The material should never be torn because this leaves threads which make the rug look fuzzy when completed. Each strip can then be cut into very narrow strips, using scissors or a mechanical cutter. The average width of a strip is one-eighth inch, but strips as narrow as five-thirtyseconds of an inch can be cut with a mechanical cutter.

**Estimating the Amount of Material:** The amount of material needed for a rug can be estimated by weight or by measurement. It generally takes about one-half pound of fabric or yarn to fill one square foot of backing. However, it is best to allow a bit more than this standard amount to compensate for individual techniques. The tightness of the loops determines the exact amount of material needed.

To estimate by measurement, lay four thicknesses of fabric over the portion of the pattern to be hooked. This is the amount of fabric needed to fill the area. Again, a little extra material should be included to allow for individual technique.

**Holding the Hook:** The hook is held in the same manner as a pencil or else in a grip called the whole-hand grip. Either method is correct so the choice of a grip depends solely on personal preference. **Fig. 4.** The whole-hand grip consists of grasping the wooden handle of the hook firmly in the palm of the right hand. Place the index finger on the steel shank about halfway between the curved tip of the hook and where the shank is set into the handle. With the left hand,

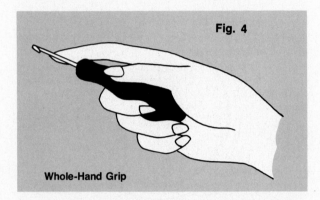

Fig. 4

Whole-Hand Grip

pick up a strip of material and hold it between the thumb and index finger. **Fig. 5.** Put the left hand under the backing against the spot where hooking is to start. Place the right hand on top of the backing with the tip of the hook just slightly to the right of the left hand.

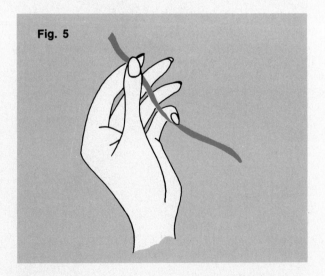

Fig. 5

## HOOKING

**Inserting the First Strip:** Insert the curved tip of the hook into the mesh facing in the direction

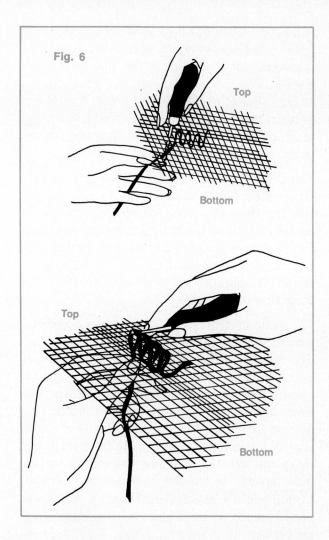

Fig. 6

Top

Bottom

Top

Bottom

being worked. With the left hand, lay the end of the strip across the tip of the hook and draw this end up through the backing. Continue to hold onto the strip with the left hand and let the part that is being pulled through glide between thumb and index finger. Hook in a straight line, working from right to left. Make a row of loops that follow a horizontal thread in the backing.**Fig. 6.**

A short length of the strip is now standing up in the backing of the rug, ready to make the first loop. Using the horizontal thread of the backing as a guide for a straight row, skip one hole in the mesh and insert the hook in the next opening. Lay the strip across the tip of the hook and gently ease a section of it up into a loop on the surface of the backing. Continue in this manner and make a row of closely placed loops. At the end of the strip, draw the end through the front of the backing. After a small area is filled, the ends can be clipped to the same height as the loops.

To hook the second strip, bring the end up in the same opening that the first strip stopped in. Continue hooking another line of loops. Make a second row just above the first by starting two backing threads above the lower row.

**Filling and Packing:** Hooking is the process of pulling fabric strips or yarn through openings in a foundation fabric or backing. Strips are pulled from the back of the fabric to the front, resulting in a series of loops. Putting a number of loops into a backing is called "filling."

Close filling of the backing with loops of another fabric is called "packing." Packing begins when two rows of loops are completed close together. By placing many loops in the backing, the mesh of the backing will tighten and hold the loops so snugly that they cannot slip out. Single rows of loops pull out quite easily by pulling one end of a strip; it is rather difficult to remove a strip from a packed area.

**Loop Placement and Height:** The most common loop height is $\frac{1}{4}$ inch. Fine-textured rugs look best with a shorter ($\frac{1}{8}$-inch) pile while heavier textures should be $\frac{1}{2}$ inch. All loops should be the same height unless the sculptured technique is being used.

Keep loops close together but do not try to count the threads of the backing. Instead, attempt to judge how close to set the loops to make a firm rug and cover the backing. Loops are left uncut when fabric strips are used.

Even loops are desirable, but since rugs are generally seen from a distance, a slightly uneven pile will not be noticed. Slight inconsistencies in pile length can be pressed out with a steam iron when the rug is finished. Once the rug is in use, many of the slightly uneven loops disappear.

**Developing a Rhythm:** Attempt to develop a synchronized set of movements when hooking. Steady motions will help to prevent loops of different heights, and previous loops will not be pulled out while attempting to place the next loop. Speed will develop as familiarity with the technique increases and awkwardness disappears.

**Directional Hooking:** Hooking becomes more difficult when attempts are made to reverse direction. Usually hooking moves from right to left; it

**FINGERING, shown in the leaf, is used to mingle colors or shades. DIRECTIONAL patterns, moving with the basic outline of the pattern, (as in the cherry), give texture and light changes in a straight row background. SAWTOOTHING, making an occasional stitch to one side of a line, (as on the yellow line), blends two neighboring colors subtly.**

is difficult to reverse that direction. Do not attempt to change direction, but instead cut off the strip, draw the end to the top of the backing and start again in the same direction even if just a few loops are needed.

Place each loop close to the preceding loop. Do not draw a strip along under the backing, pulling up a few loops a short distance from the previous work. These short lengths drawn across the backing are called "crossovers." Because they lie slightly above the rest of the hooked area on the back of the rug, they should be avoided.

A special effect can be created by hooking continuously in one direction. This type of "directional hooking" accents curves and other parts of designs. For example, a portion of the rug is hooked in the direction of the design; the remainder of the rug or the background is done in straight rows using standard filling techniques. Areas of straight lines contrast with areas of curved lines. To make the background of a rug unobtrusive, do not hook continuously in one direction. Work the entire area in short curved lines called "rivers." Then join these areas with rows of hooking that go in a different direction. Fill in the remaining spaces called "lakes."

A hooking technique used to blend different colors is called saw-toothing. A row of single loops is hooked just to one side of the row that is being worked with space in between. A zigzag effect is created similar to the teeth of a saw. The spaces between the "sawteeth" are filled with the color in the adjoining section thereby blending the adjacent colors.

The density of the packing will determine to a large extent how attractive and durable the rug will be. However, overpacking will result in a lumpy rug that will not lie flat on the floor and backing that will stretch and weaken. Underpacking, on the other hand, allows the backing to show through the surface and decreases the durability of the rug.

The width of strips and the weight of the material determines the number of holes in the backing that must be filled for proper packing. Wider strips result in fewer loops and heavy materials require fewer loops than lightweight fabrics. The fiber content of the fabric also influences the number of holes to be filled. Materials with elasticity, such as wool, are fluffier and cover more surface area than just the space over the hole through which the loop has been drawn. Cotton, linen and other tight weaves do not expand as much, so more loops are needed to cover the surface.

Fingering is another special hooking method in which single flat rows are hooked into an area that is to be filled. These single rows give the appearance of narrow lines or veins. Sometimes these rows can be clipped across the top to appear even finer.

## FINISHING

The finished rug should be bound around the edges with cotton rug tape. The sew-on rather than the iron-on type is best. Since rug tape comes in different colors, get a color that matches the background or the predominant color of the rug.

**Binding:** To bind the rug, trim the backing about 3/4 inch from the hooked edge. Lay the cotton tape on the right side of the rug with the outer edge of tape even with the outside row of loops. Use heavy cotton thread and a close overcast stitch to sew through the outside row of loops about ⅛ inch from the edge of the tape. Turn the binding to the back of the rug and sew down with widely spaced overcasting stitches. To bind a round or oval rug use bias cotton tape. If rug binding or wide bias tape is not available, it is permissible to use cotton strips cut on the bias. **Fig. 7.**

**Hemming:** One of the easiest methods for hemming a rug, particularly when monk's cloth has been used for the backing, is to first cut away excess backing material leaving an even margin of approximately 2 inches from the hooked area. Using the zigzag stitch on the sewing machine, stitch around the edges of the material. Fold under carefully so that no backing fabric will show and hem in place using wide overcasting stitches. If a sewing machine is not available, overcast the raw edges of the backing by hand. **Fig. 8.**

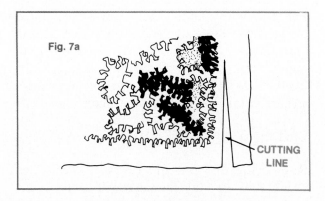

Trim edges of rug, leaving ¾ inch.

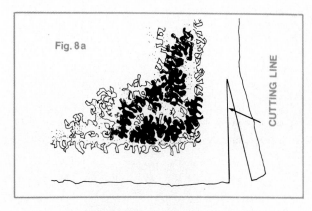

Trim edges of rug, leaving 1½ to 2 inches.

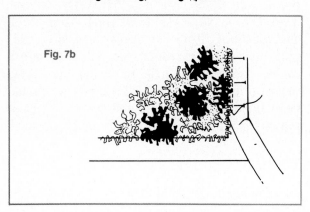

Pin tape in place on right side of rug very close to hooked loops and stitch.

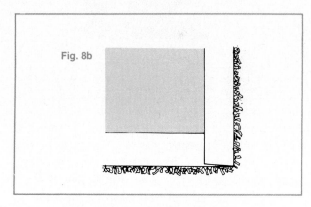

Fold against outside edge of hooking.

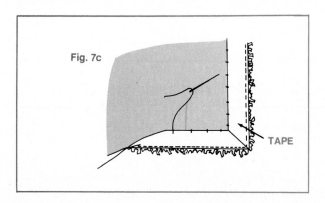

Turn tape to back, miter corners and overcast or Blind Stitch in place.

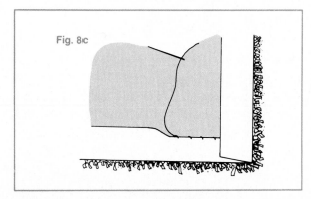

Fold under ½ inch along raw edge and overcast or Blind Stitch in place with strong thread (carpet warp).

**Binding Before Hooking:** To bind a rug before hooking it, machine stitch rug tape on all edges. The outside row of loops is then hooked close to the tape. When the hooking is completed, the tape is turned back and stitched against the underside with widely spaced overcasting. This method insures that no binding shows on the surface of the rug and provides a very secure edge that takes a lot of wear. **Fig. 9.**

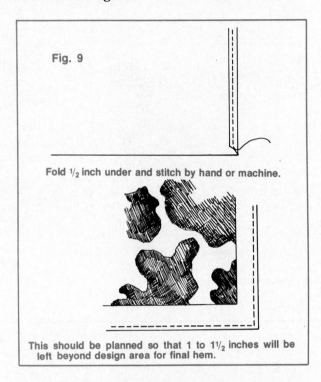

Fig. 9

Fold ½ inch under and stitch by hand or machine.

This should be planned so that 1 to 1½ inches will be left beyond design area for final hem.

**Padding:** A pad can be placed under a hooked rug for added resiliency and to protect the rug from excessive wear. To keep rugs from slipping, particularly scatter rugs, use thin sheets of foam rubber for padding or sew canning jar rings to the corners of the rug.

## PUNCH NEEDLE RUGS

This method differs from hooking in two ways though the final result is much the same. Yarn is usually used for the "punch" technique rather than fabrics and the work is done from the back of the rug rather than from the top as in hooking.

### EQUIPMENT

A punch or shuttle-type needle is used. The punch needle is a tube-like affair through which the yarn runs. It is made in different sizes for different weights of yarn. There is always some sort of adjustable guard on the shank to prevent the needle from being pushed too far and to regulate the length of the loop. In addition to the standard punch hook, there are also several speed hooks that hasten the work. The rug yarns used for hooking and punch needlework are the same.

### TECHNIQUE

Punch hooking requires that the design be placed on the wrong side of the backing. The backing must be placed on a frame because punching requires a firm surface. The needle should not be lifted above the surface before pushing it in again a short distance away to make another loop.

### CLIPPING & SCULPTURING

Rugs made of yarns are often clipped. This should be done while the rug is still on the frame. Using long narrow scissors made for this purpose, slide the points into the loops. Several loops can be cut at one time using this method. The cut loops or pile can also be shaped by clipping into a sculptured surface. The same effect can be created while making the rug by varying the loop length. Exaggerated sculpturing should be avoided; however, a limited amount of shaping can produce attractive and interesting results.

## BRAIDED RUGS

Braided rugs, like old quilts, have a subtle charm and warmth which makes them an integral part of the craft heritage. In addition, braided rugs, particularly those of the small-sized "scatter rug" variety, are ideal users of scraps and old clothing.

### COLOR SCHEMES

Braided rugs are worked in bands or stripes of graduated or shaded colors. Therefore, it is necessary to decide generally how a series of colors will be arranged prior to starting a rug. The necessary colors may be dyed or collected from wool scraps — old blankets, suits, etc. The colors within the individual braid, as well as those within a band, should be repeated for a coordinated effect. If a rug is worked which incorporates

**SCULPTURING gives a high-low effect that adds dimension to many types of rugs. This one is done with the two settings on a punch needle.**

many colors in a scattered manner, even this pattern should be continued evenly throughout the rug.

## CHOOSING MATERIALS

Wool fabrics are the most suitable for braiding. Cotton and silk can also be used, but cotton soils easily and silk wears quickly. A medium-weight flannel-like fabric in a soft but tight weave is best. The best weight is that found in old coats, suits or skirts. This type fabric is often found at remnant stores or mill outlets sold by the pound.

Do not use knits or jersey-like fabrics, except for small washable rugs, because they stretch too much and do not wear well. Nylon panty hose can be used for small washable scatter rugs.

## EQUIPMENT

Heavy multi-stranded carpet thread and a blunt needle are used to lace the braids together. A special clamp for holding braid ends and cones or braid-aids for folding the braiding materials are also useful.

## ESTIMATING FABRIC REQUIREMENTS

Each square foot of rug requires about $3/4$ pound of wool. Very heavy braids require about 1 pound of wool per square foot. To estimate the length of strands needed for each braid, remember that $1/3$ to $1/2$ the length of a strip will be taken up in braiding. Using the spiral method, each braid in an oval or round rug is 7 to 8 inches longer than the one in the preceding row. If complete rows or closed braids are being made, allow approximately 7 inches for interweaving ends of braid.

## PREPARATION OF STRIPS

The size of the rug should determine the size of the braid. Narrow braids are used for small rugs and large, wider braids for large rugs. The thickness of the fabric determines the size of the braid.

Strips are usually from 1 to $1^1/2$ inches wide. Strips should be cut or torn crosswise (selvage to selvage) because crosswise fabric has more give. Strips cut lengthwise tend to wrinkle more.

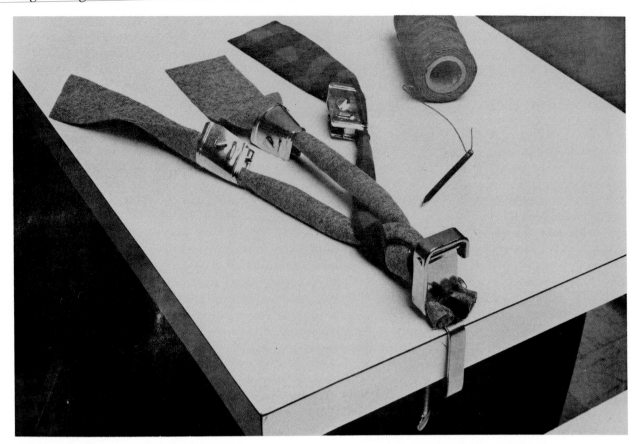

**BRAIDING EQUIPMENT: Clamp, braid-aids, lacing needle and thread are the simple tools needed for rug braiding.**

Separate colors and roll the strips into balls to keep them neat.

To piece strips, cut the ends on the diagonal and seam them together with small running stitches.

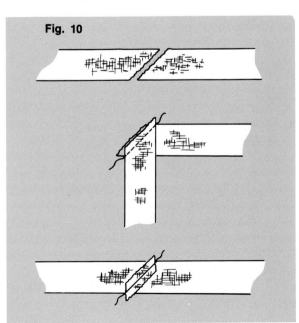

Fig. 10

To avoid tangling while braiding, the pieced strips should be no more than 2 yards long. When braiding, to keep bulges from forming, be sure that piecing seams on the three strips fall in different places. It may be necessary to cut and repiece at least one strip. **Fig. 10.**

## BRAIDING

The simplest braiding uses three strips of fabric. Four or more strips can also be used in what is called multiple braiding. Before starting a rug, practice to achieve a tight, uniform braid. Prior to braiding slip on cones or braid-aids before enclosing the braid ends in a clamp. If braid-aids are not used, there are two easy techniques that will keep raw edges from appearing while working a braid. The first technique involves a method of joining the strips in a "T" prior to placing them in a clamp.

Piece the ends of two strips together diagonally, fold the strip in half and place on a flat surface with the open edges down. Slip the end of the

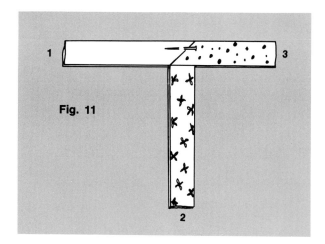

**Fig. 11**

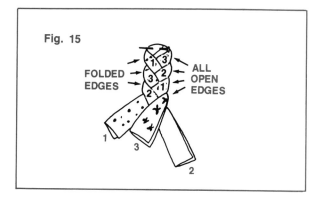

Fig. 15

FOLDED EDGES → | ALL OPEN EDGES ←

third strip into the fold. Pin or sew in place. **Fig. 11.** The top of the braid can consist of one or two colors; the third strip can be in another color or one of the previous two.

Start braiding with strip number 3. **Fig. 12.** Pick up number 1 and twist it once before crossing over and placing it between numbers 3 and 2. **Fig. 13.** This keeps open edges on all strips to the right. Continue to braid alternating left and right. **Figs. 14 and 15.**

Another technique frequently used requires that the raw edges of each strip be turned in and Slip Stitched. Fold each strip inward, then slip all three ends, with open edges to the right, onto a safety pin or into a clamp and start braiding. **Fig. 16.**

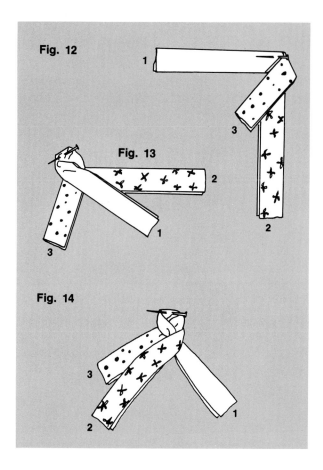

**Fig. 12**

**Fig. 13**

**Fig. 14**

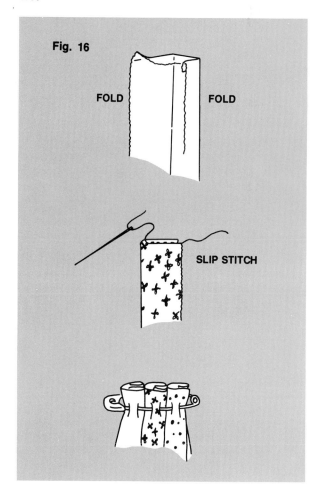

**Fig. 16**

FOLD     FOLD

SLIP STITCH

**Plaiting:** While braiding, keep the strip flat and always have the same side of the strip up. Do not twist the strip over each time; keep the open edges of strips to the right. **Fig. 17.**

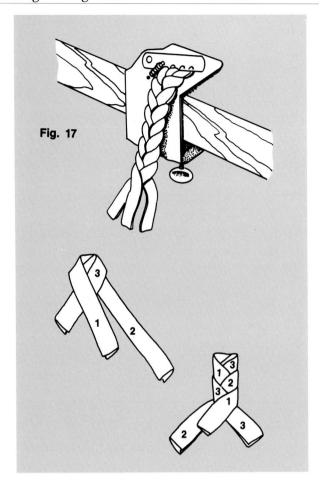

Fig. 17

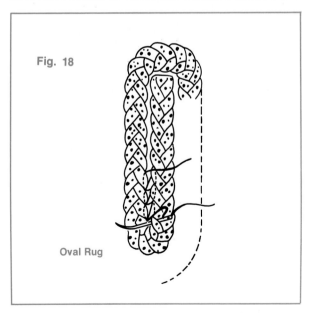

Oval Rug

**How to Start an Oval Rug:** Subtract the width from the length of the rug to get the length of the center starting braid. Then braid the few yards needed for the center color. The first braid must be twice the length of the center since it has to be doubled around to form the center. Measure the length of the center braid and then turn it back on itself with the open-edged sides of the braid together. **Fig. 18.**

**How to Start a Round Rug:** Start with the end of the braid and turn and twist it in spiral fashion to form a circle. Hold it in place with pins and then begin to lace from the center. **Fig. 19.**

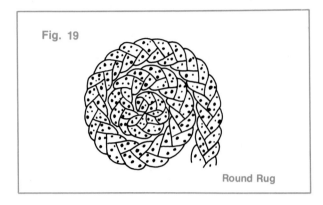

Fig. 19

Round Rug

## LACING

This method of attaching braids produces a strong, attractive rug that looks interwoven because the braids are wrapped around each other.

Tie a knot in the end of the lacing thread. Using a heavy darning needle, bring the knot through the braid where it will be hidden. Rethread with the lacing needle. Slip the needle through one loop of the first braid, then through a loop of the adjoining braid. **Fig. 20.** Work back and forth,

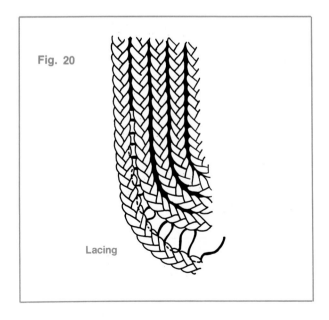

Fig. 20

Lacing

pulling the thread tight so that the joining can barely be seen. Proper lacing completely hides the thread.

To lace round or oval rugs, the curves must be increased so that the rug will lie flat. The outside braid must be longer than the previous one. The curve is made by skipping loops while lacing. Do not skip loops on the straight sides of an oval; on the curves skip only one loop on the braid being added to produce the correct curvature. Usually three increases on the shoulder of a curve is sufficient. If a rug gets too full, add a row or two with no increases. Do not skip loops except on curves.

## FINISHING

Remove braid-aids or cones after last row of the rug is completed. With scissors, taper off each strip to a long point. **Fig. 21.** Continue to braid to the end and finish facing, working the end slightly under the previous braid or into the ends of the adjacent braid for an invisible finish. **Fig. 22.**

## BUTTING

This is the process of joining each round of braid so that it forms a complete circle around the rug, whereas the spiral rug is a continuous braid from beginning to end.

The oldest method of butting is to sew the ends of each round together. The rug will not be reversible because the ends of the braid are brought together at the back, sewn together by hand, turned back and pressed. **Fig. 23.** A second method brings the ends together in a perfect braid, keeping each strand flat. The ends are sewn together by hand in diagonal seams. **Fig. 24.**

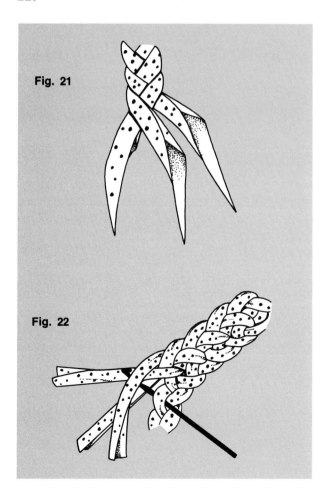

Fig. 21

Fig. 22

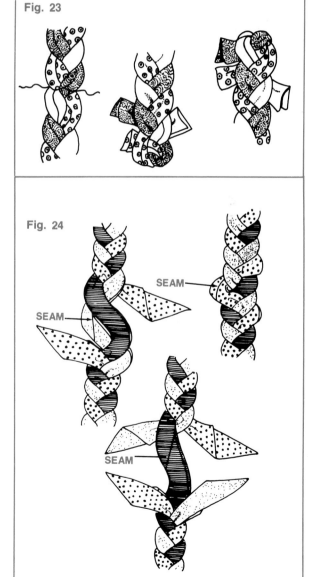

Fig. 23

Fig. 24

SEAM

SEAM

SEAM

## LATCH HOOK RUGS

This technique employs a hook to pull short strands of yarn through a canvas backing and gives a deep pile surface to a rug. The hook is used to make a special type of knot that secures the yarn to the backing.

### EQUIPMENT

**Yarn:** Rug yarn for latch hooking is available in acrylic or wool. Wool yarn is usually more expensive but it has greater durability and resilience. Rug yarn for latching is packaged according to color in precut 2¹/₂-inch lengths. If convenience is not important, rug yarn can be cut to the correct length from a skein or cone. A yarn thinner than rug yarn has less bulk when latched; therefore, the rug surface is less dense and luxurious.

To make correct yarn lengths, wind yarn around a strip of cardboard that is about 1¹/₄ inches wide and approximately 10 inches long. Cut along one edge of the cardboard strip and 2¹/₂-inch lengths of yarn will result. Keep colors separated for convenience.

**Canvas:** Large mesh canvas of the type used for needlepoint (quickpoint) is necessary. Double mesh canvas with 3 to 5 holes per inch works well with most rug yarns available for latch hooking. The yarn is knotted on the weft threads which are those running across the canvas from selvage to selvage. Patterns for latch hooking are available already printed on canvas or a design can be drawn on the canvas with felt markers.

**Latch Hooks:** The latch hook is a wooden or plastic-handled tool with a movable prong (latch) near the stationary hook. These hooks are available with two types of shanks — a shorter straight shank and a bent shank. Each hook works the same way and the choice of shank is one of personal preference.

### TECHNIQUE

To make knots on canvas with a latch hook, first fold the yarn over the shank of the hook holding the ends of the yarn with the left hand. **Fig. 25a.** With the hook grasped in the right hand holding the latch down with the index finger, push the hook down through the canvas from the top under the double horizontal threads and up again through the mesh. **Fig. 25b.** Place yarn ends inside the hook and close the latch. **Fig. 25c.** Draw the hook back through the canvas pulling the ends of the yarn through the loop; tighten the knot by pulling the yarn ends with the fingers. **Fig. 25d.**

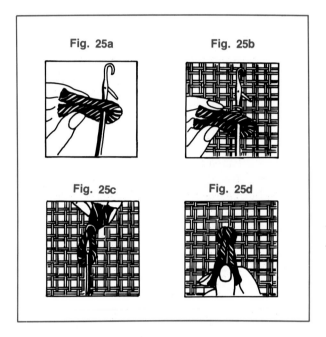

Fig. 25a      Fig. 25b

Fig. 25c      Fig. 25d

### FINISHING EDGES

Prior to latching, fold five rows of canvas on the lengthwise edges over to the front. Work through the doubled canvas for the first 5 rows of knotting — this will form a finished edge. Work the width of the canvas if this is the desired size of the rug, leaving 2 inches on each side for selvage hems.

For selvage hems, turn under the side edges 2 inches and Slip Stitch to the back of the rug with heavy-duty or carpet thread. If there are more than 2 inches of hem, cut away the excess. Place rug binding over the edge of canvas and Slip Stitch along both sides of binding to give a neat finish.

### JOINING RUG SECTIONS

It is possible to join squares or strips for larger projects. Latch hook each square or strip, leaving 2 inches on the edge of each piece. Join two sections in the same manner as for needlepoint (pg. 400) and work the latching over the lapped portion of the canvas. When planning various portions of a rug, be sure to allow the correct number of inches on each section to permit joining them.

## CROCHET & KNIT RUGS

Anyone who has mastered the most basic skills in crocheting or knitting can apply them to making area rugs with leftover yarns from other projects. To make it even easier, crochet or knit rugs are often done in segments which are sewn, knitted or crocheted together. Sometimes one pattern is used and repeated in various color combinations, such as the "granny square" used in crocheting. At other times more than one pattern is used in combination or a chart is followed to make a particular design.

Because of its thickness, rug yarn is best for making knitted or crocheted rugs. However, knitting worsted can be doubled or tripled or combinations of other yarns can be used to create the desired effect. To sew together sections of knitted or crocheted rugs, use braided rug lacing techniques but with yarn instead of carpet thread.

## RYA RUGS

The luxurious pile created by the rya method makes this rug a welcome and attractive addition to any home. However, a rya's long pile uses more yarn than most other methods so a large rya rug may be expensive to make. Leftover skeins of yarn from knitting and weaving can be incorporated into any rya rug and textured yarns produce especially interesting results. The backing is a large weave material like burlap or homespun. There are special backings available for rya that have a strip of close weave alternating with strips of open weave.

### TECHNIQUE

To work rya, thread a large-eyed rug needle with a length of yarn, 16 to 18 inches long. Work on the facing side (front) of the rug backing. Starting at the bottom of the rug backing and working up, work each row across from left selvage to right selvage.

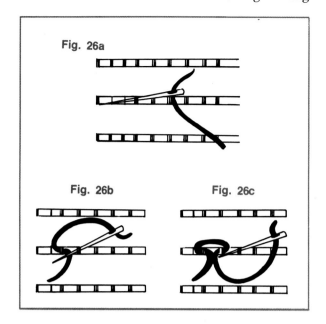

Fig. 26a

Fig. 26b          Fig. 26c

Starting at left edge, skip the first two spaces in selvage and insert needle right to left under the next group of warp threads. **Fig. 26a.** Pull yarn through until the end is the required pile length, about 1 3/4 inches. Holding the end below this row with the left thumb, insert needle under next group of threads from right to left and pull tight to make first knot (stitch). **Fig. 26b.**

Holding yarn below this row with left thumb, insert needle under the next group of warp threads, right to left. **Fig. 26c.** Pull yarn up, leaving 1 3/4-inch loop below this row. Continue across row to right selvage, working as in Fig. 26b and c making each loop the same length. At right selvage, stop two warp threads from edge.

Cut each row of loops with scissors as it is completed to be sure that all loops are cut. The loops can be cut evenly, but for the real rya effect loops are cut in different lengths or some remain uncut. When colors are to be changed, work across the row to the color change and cut yarn to length of loop after completing the knot of the first color. Start new color as in Fig. 26a under next group of threads. Work across the entire row in the pattern before starting on the next row up.

When using Swedish backing, the edge is finished when the last knot is made. If edges at top and bottom are rough, fold under and hem. To finish rug edges when the backing is burlap or monk's cloth, use instructions given for finishing selvages of latch hook rugs.

## NEEDLEPOINT RUGS

This type of rug is a favorite of needleworkers because of its flexibility of design. Any subject can be depicted in needlepoint and design arrangements are as numerous as the individuals that work them.

### EQUIPMENT

**Canvas:** When selecting needlework canvas for rugs be sure the mesh is even and has no weak threads or knots. Canvas comes in widths from 36 to 54 inches; the larger sizes are usually more appropriate for rugs of sizable dimensions. Piecing canvas should be avoided if possible because it is time consuming and exacting work. Therefore, many needleworkers prefer to work on smaller rug squares because of the ease of handling.

**Rug Yarns:** Needlepoint yarn contains long staple fibers that resist wear. Rug yarns, now often called quickpoint yarn, are more rough and wiry in texture. They are available in cotton, synthetics and wool sold by the pound or in skeins. Pure wool is the finest and most durable of the rug yarns with high resilience and soil resistance. Needlepoint rugs are usually worked in gros point on ten-mesh-to-the-inch canvas or in quickpoint on three- to seven-mesh-to-the-inch canvas.

**Needles:** Use a rug needle with a blunt point and an elongated eye to accommodate the larger yarns.

### ESTIMATING AMOUNT OF YARN

Work a 1-inch square using the selected yarn and canvas. Multiply the amount used to work the 1-inch square by the number of square inches to be covered. Do this with each color to get the approximate yardage needed for that color. Then divide the yardage by the number of yards in a skein to get the number of skeins needed.

### BASIC STITCHES

**Half Cross Stitch:** This stitch can be worked only on double mesh canvas; it will slide unless it has the double threads of the mesh to hold it in place. The Half Cross Stitch does not provide a

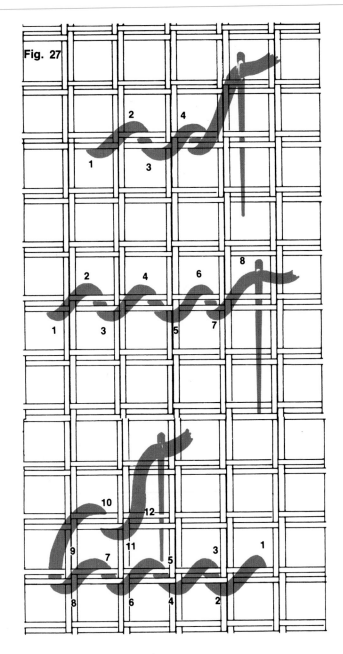

**Half Cross Stitch**

thick backing on the reverse side so it has a tendency to wear more quickly. This stitch also pulls the canvas out of shape and therefore requires more blocking. On the favorable side, it does take less yarn to work and is easy to do.

Always work from left to right. Start at the bottom of a stitch. Cross over one mesh of the canvas (diagonally from 1 to 2) and insert needle for next stitch (bring needle up at 3 and then diagonally to 4). **Fig. 27.** The needle is always inserted in the vertical position. When the row of

**Continental Stitch**

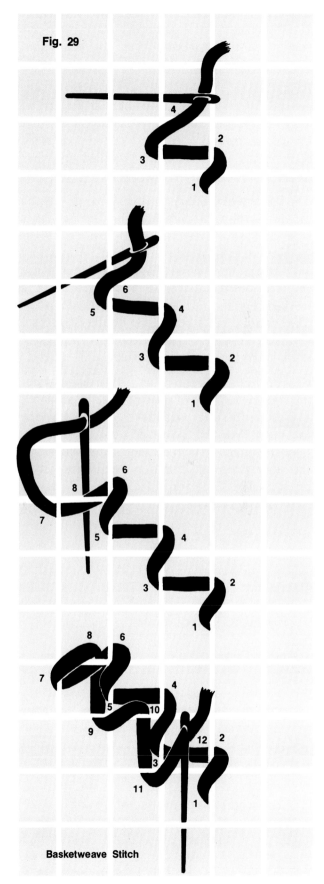

**Basketweave Stitch**

stitches is completed, turn work upside down so that the next row can be worked from left to right (9 to 10).

**Continental Stitch:** This stitch works well on either single or double mesh and provides sufficient backing on the reverse side of the canvas to insure durability. When worked over a large area, this stitch has a tendency to pull the canvas out of shape and blocking is needed.

The Continental Stitch requires more yarn than the Half Cross Stitch. It looks like the Half Cross Stitch but it is always worked from right to left. Bring needle out at bottom left corner of a stitch, (up at 1) and then diagonally to upper right corner. Insert needle (down at 2) and cross behind stitch just completed to new stitch (3) on left. **Fig. 28.** When one row is completed, turn work upside down so that next row can also be worked from right to left (9 to 10).

**Basketweave Stitch:** This is a favorite background filler stitch. It does not pull the canvas out of shape and can be worked without turning the canvas around. The firm backing takes a lot of wear and the stitch can be worked on either mono mesh or double mesh canvas.

The Basketweave Stitch is actually woven into the canvas, forming a durable web. The needle is brought up and over one mesh to the right (1 to 2). Note that the needle is inserted horizontally and brought up again (3). **Fig. 29.** These steps are repeated on the diagonal, across space being worked. On the next row, also worked on the diagonal one mesh below, the needle is inserted vertically (8 to 9). Each succeeding row has one more stitch than the row before.

**Cross Stitch:** This stitch can be started at either the right or left side of the work. Make a slanted row of evenly spaced stitches of equal length, one to a mesh. Work back over these stitches from the opposite direction with the same stitch, slanted in the other direction. Both steps result in a row of cross stitches. The back of the canvas will show a row of upright stitches.

## STARTING A RUG

Allow 2-inch margins on all sides of the design. Before starting to stitch, bind all raw edges of the canvas with masking or hemming tape or use overcasting to prevent raveling.

## JOINING RUG SECTIONS

Unfortunately large rug sections are almost impossible to carry about and smaller segments necessitate many joinings. While the initial planning of the design and layout of a rug is being done, it is wise to consider where the joining of segments of canvas will take place.

The least complicated method of joining is to sew the two pieces together like a seam, matching mesh for mesh using a Backstitch. Sew through the last row of worked stitches. Then trim the excess canvas away and Blind Stitch the edges to

keep them flat. Another method of joining is to leave three mesh rows unworked on either side of the piece. Lay one mesh over the other and baste together with carpet thread to hold it in place. Work five rows of the design over this joint. **Fig. 30.** This method is used successfully when joining four pieces of canvas as in joining squares. First join two squares; treat them as one piece and join to another section. **Fig. 31.**

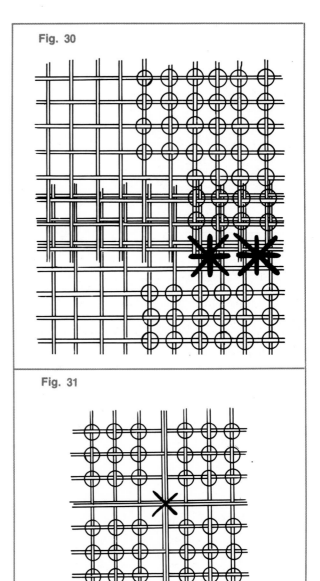

Fig. 30

Fig. 31

## JOINING BORDERS

A centerpiece of needlepoint may be attached to its border by laying it in place and stitching through two layers as when joining squares. Liquid latex can be used on the very outside meshes to hold them in place and prevent raveling.

## BLOCKING

Sections of a needlepoint rug should be blocked before being joined because some distortion occurs. Place each piece of the rug or the entire rug face down on a board marked horizontally and vertically with lines. Dampen the needlepoint on the wrong side using a sponge and cold water. Fasten it down on all sides with rustproof tacks about 1 inch apart, straightening and stretching at the same time. Tack the top, the other two sides and then the bottom. The needlepoint should remain on the board until thoroughly dry, even if it takes several days. If the piece is not perfectly straight, restretch, wet and dry again. When dry, remove from the board and steam lightly using a slightly damp cloth.

## FINISHING

To finish a canvas, fold the hem to the underside, trim down to 1 to 2 inches depending on the size of the rug and firmly Blind Stitch with

carpet thread to the backs of the nearby stitches. The corners should be mitered as you come to them. To miter a corner, fold the corner of the canvas back towards the center of the canvas. Cut the tip of the corner off to within ½ inch of the nearest Wool Stitch. Fold the sides down so that a short diagonal seam is formed and Whip Stitch with carpet thread. **Fig. 32.**

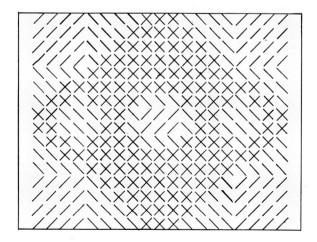

### RUG MAKING COLOR CHART

| | |
|---|---|
| 1. Pale Pink | 24. Chrome Yellow |
| 2. Medium Pink | 25. Bright Yellow |
| 3. Dark Pink | 26. Gold Yellow |
| 4. Light Red | 27. Medium Yellow |
| 5. True Red | 28. Pale Yellow |
| 6. Dark Red | 29. Light Orange |
| 7. Maroon | 30. Medium Orange |
| 8. Red-Violet | 31. Red-Orange |
| 9. Purple | 32. Beige |
| 10. Lavender | 33. Sand |
| 11. Blue-Violet | 34. Light Brown |
| 12. Dark Blue | 35. Medium Brown |
| 13. Medium Blue | 36. Dark Brown |
| 14. Light Blue | 37. Black |
| 15. Turquoise | 38. Dark Gray |
| 16. Light Aqua | 39. Medium Gray |
| 17. Dark Green | 40. Pearl Gray |
| 18. Medium Green | 41. White |
| 19. Bright Green | 42. Ivory |
| 20. Leaf Green | 43. Coral |
| 21. Pale Green | 44. Gold |
| 22. Chartreuse | 45. Brown-Gold |
| 23. Olive Green | 46. Burnt Orange |

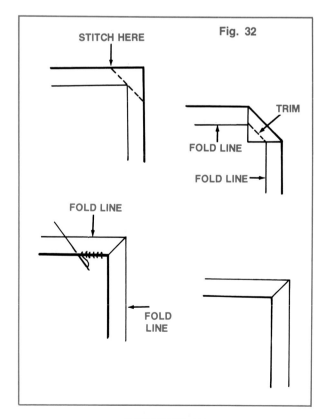

STITCH HERE  Fig. 32

TRIM

FOLD LINE

FOLD LINE

FOLD LINE

FOLD LINE

**A Mitered Corner**

# RUG MAKING PROJECTS

# KNITTED FRINGE RUG

### Designed by John Bade

**SIZE:** Approximate size 18 x 54 inches

**MATERIALS:** Rug Yarn — 100-yd skeins; 3 skeins Yale Blue for background, 1 skein White for fringe, 1 skein Olive for fringe, 1 skein Lt. Blue for fringe, 1 skein Yale Blue for fringe.

Size 15 Knitting Needles for background, Crochet Hook K for Fringe.

**GAUGE:** 2 sts = 1 inch

Work background in double yarn. With Yale Blue cast on 36 sts. Rows 1, 3, 5 and 6 are knitted. Purl rows 2 and 4.

Repeat these 6 rows for pattern and work even until there are 27 ridges including first and last row. Bind off.

*Fringe:* Wind yarn around an 8-inch piece of cardboard and cut at both ends. Take two 8-inch strands for each end; fold in half. Pull through first st of first row on left side with K crochet hook from front to back, about 1 inch. Pull cut ends through folded lp to form fringe. Fringe may be uneven but do not trim, uneven fringe is desirable.

Fringe is worked in every st in first and last row and every ridge row in between. Follow chart for color scheme for each ridge row to be fringed. Repeat chart twice for 3 large "V"s.

x = YALE BLUE

o = WHITE

/ = OLIVE

I = LT. BLUE

**Each line = a ridge row**
**Cross of Rug Complete**

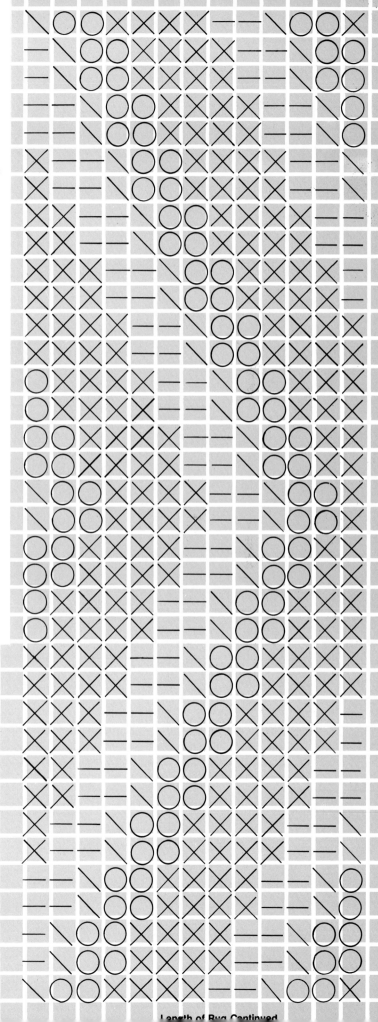

Length of Rug Continued

## LOOP CROCHET RUG

Fabric scraps or jute twine from the stationery store will make highly colorful or nicely neutral rugs of any size. Necessary equipment includes a size K crochet hook or any size hook which gives the correct gauge and a piece of firm cardboard or plastic, 1½ x 12 inches.

**GAUGE:** 2 sts = 1 inch, 1 row sc + 1 row loop = 1 inch

**Stitch Pattern:** Chain desired number of stitches for base (end) of rug.

*Row 1:* Sc in 2nd ch from hook, sc in each chain across row, ch 1 for turning, turn.

*Row 2:* Sc in first st, *hold cardboard in back of work, insert hook in next sc, bring yarn over from back to front of cardboard strip; yo and draw a loop through st, yo and draw through first loop, yo and draw through 2 loops on hook (loop st made). Repeat from * across to last st, sc in last st, ch 1, turn.

*Row 3:* Sc in each st across, ch 1, turn. Repeat rows 2 and 3 until desired length is reached. (Move the strip along as needed, pushing the finished loops off the end.)

A remnant rug is made of ½-inch pinked strips of lightweight plaid wool. Other light to medium-weight fabrics, remnants, old clothes in good condition, etc. can be used. Cut sample pieces and check gauge. Varying the fabric colors, join strips with machine stitching on flat overlap of ends. Roll in a ball like yarn. A rug 3 feet by 5 feet requires approximately 17 yards of 36-inch fabric, 14 yards of 45-inch fabric or 11 yards of 54-inch fabric, all cut crosswise.

The jute rug is made from 3-ply jute twine. A rug 4 feet by 6 feet requires approximately 20 pounds of twine. Try to find it in the more economical 10-pound tubes or balls.

Either rug can be blocked on a piece of plywood or other wallboard or very heavy corrugated cardboard. Tack in place and steam with a steam iron held lightly over the surface. Leave to dry in place.

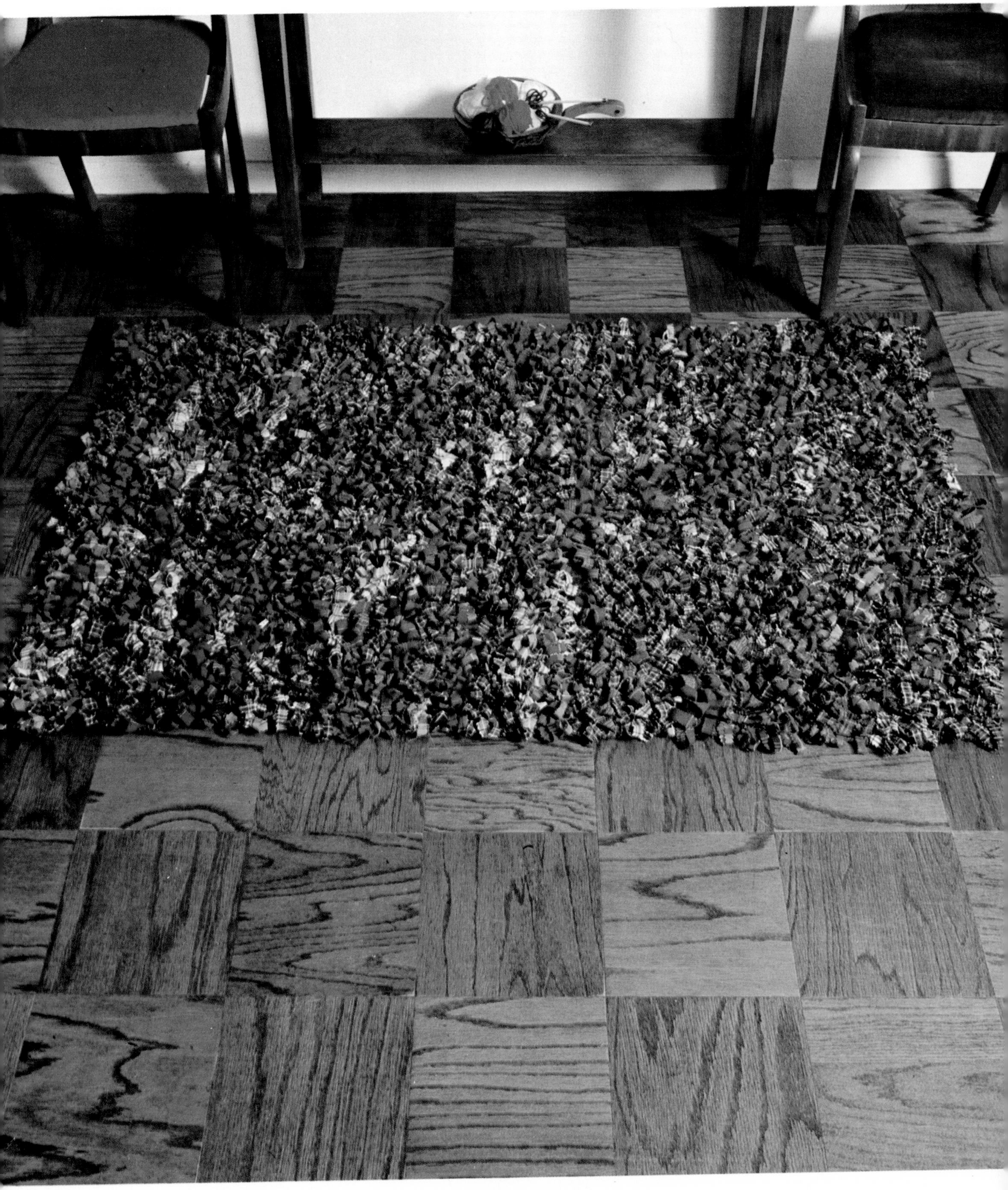

## HOOKED RUG OR RUNNER

### Worked by Martha Anne Crowe

Any color can be used and, depending upon which is predominant, the rug can be made to fit in the decor of any room. The squares are four inches each, outlined in black and alternating in direction, checkerboard style. The design can be used for a stair runner, small door mat or room-size rug.

## RUG CROCHETED IN STRIPS

**SIZE:** Approximately 58 x 36 inches

**MATERIALS:** Lily Soft Sheen (Art. 441) 4-ounce skeins, seven each of Cream (A), Avocado (B), Orange (C) and Rose (D). Crochet hook J, or any hook that gives the gauge below.

**GAUGE:** 12 sc = 4 inches, 14 rows = 4 inches

Crochet rug in three 12-inch wide strips.

### Strips 1 and 3

With Rose ch 37 sts loosely.

*1st Row:* Sc in 2nd ch and in each ch thereafter (36 sc).

*2nd Row:* Ch 1 for turning. Work 1 sc in each sc. Color striping pattern: *4 rows D, 4 rows A, repeat from * four times. Work 4 rows D, 13 rows B, 7 rows A, 13 rows B, 13 rows C, *7 rows D = center of strip,* then reverse order starting with 13 rows C and work all the way back.

### Strip 2

Working in same stitches as before, use color striping pattern as follows: 13 rows C, 7 rows D, 13 rows C, * 4 rows D, 4 rows A, repeat from * four times, 4 rows D, 13 rows B, *7 rows A = center of strip,* then reverse order starting with 13 rows B and work all the way back.

Sew strips together. Pillows may also be covered with any variation of the striping pattern.

## CROCHETED RUG WITH CLOTH STRIPS WOVEN IN

**SIZE:** 50 x 30 without fringe

**MATERIALS:** Lily Sugar 'n Spice, 2½-ounce balls, five balls pink and four balls eggshell. Each square also requires about 7 yards of medium-weight fabric strips in unbleached and shades of pink, 1½ inches wide (approximately 30 yards, cut crosswise, can be made from 1 yard of 45-inch fabric). Fabric should be washable and is easier to handle if it has been washed several times. Crochet hook H.

**GAUGE:** Each square = 10 inches

Make eight squares pink and six squares eggshell. Make fringe in pink.

**To crochet one square:** Ch 45 sts loosely.

*1st row:* Dc in 5th ch * ch 1, skip 1 ch and dc in next ch. Repeat from * (21 loops).

*2nd row:* Ch 3 for turning, dc in 1st loop, *ch 1, dc in loop. Repeat from * across. Repeat 2nd row until square is 10 inches deep.

Turn the two raw edges in toward the center of the fabric strips and then fold again along the center so all raw edges are hidden. Weave strips in and out, continuing to turn edges in as much as is possible all the way.

Sew the squares together in checkerboard pattern and make looped fringe on each end.

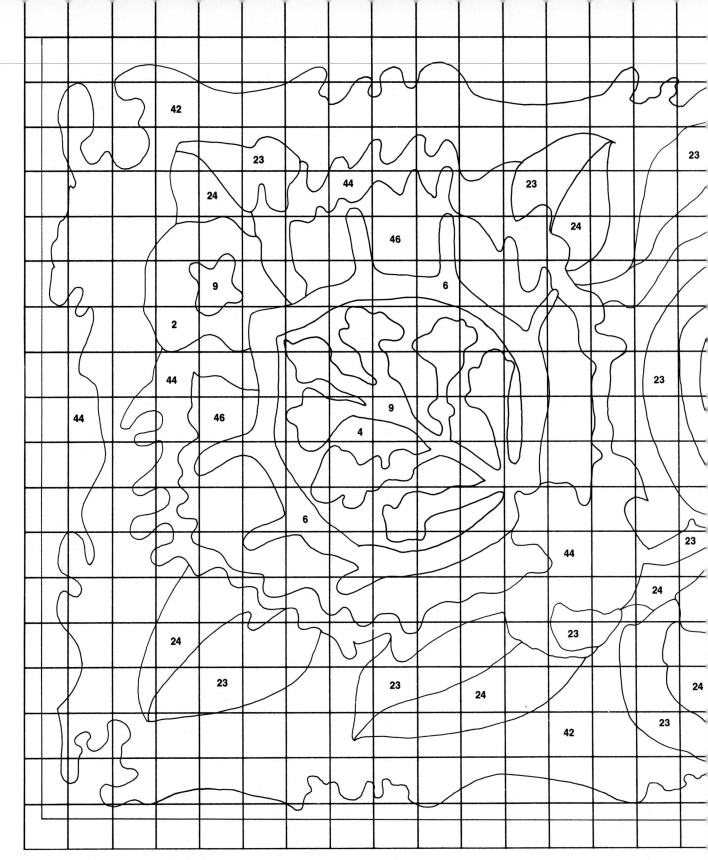

**Each ½-inch square = 2 inches**

## DESERT FLOWER LATCH HOOK RUG

Use precut latch hook rug yarn or cut your own
in 2¼-inch lengths. There are eight colors and
ivory for the background. Enlarged as suggested,

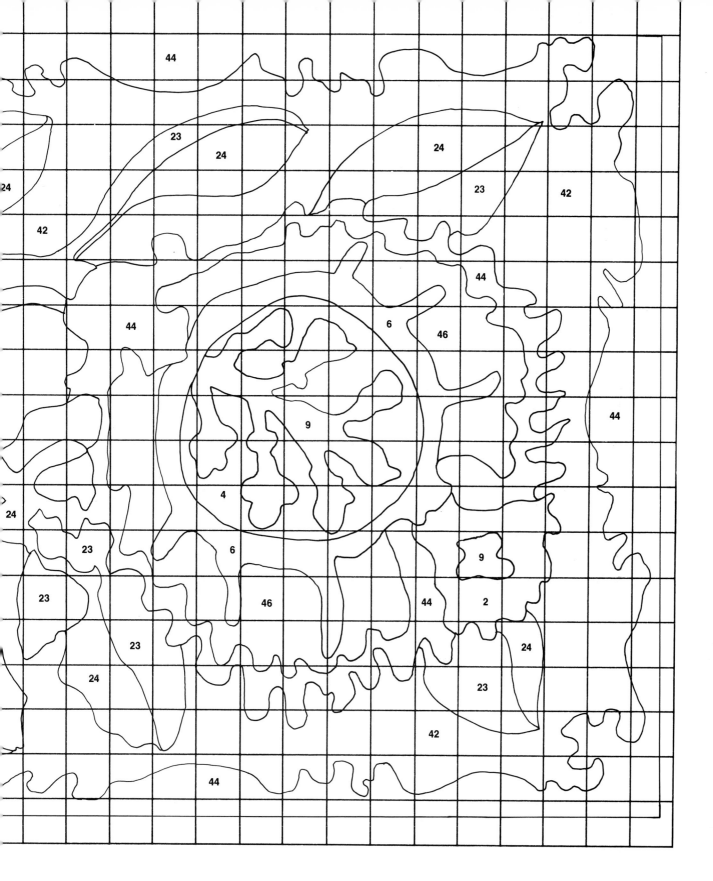

the size will be 58 inches by 33 inches. If each
square equals 3 inches, instead of 2 inches, the rug
will be 87 inches by 39¹/₂ inches. To enlarge the
rug slightly, work the gold border wider.

**BLUE IRIS PUNCH NEEDLE RUG**

Each ½-inch square = 1 inch

## BLUE IRIS PUNCH NEEDLE RUG

### Designed and created by *John Bade*

Only three colors are used on a white base for this 24-inch by 36-inch bedside rug. The graph is half size; the remainder of the measurements are worked in background white. If desired, the rug can be enlarged to 36 x 54 inches.

## LIONS AND TIGERS NEEDLEPOINT RUG

### Designed and created by Alice T. Bullard

What child wouldn't delight at waking every morning to his own private jungle! The room-size rug is worked in rug yarn on 5-to-the-inch canvas. Use the animals and leaves in this arrangement or in any other arrangement that fits the room size and mood.

## LIONS AND TIGERS NEEDLEPOINT RUG

**Work on 5-to-the-inch canvas.**

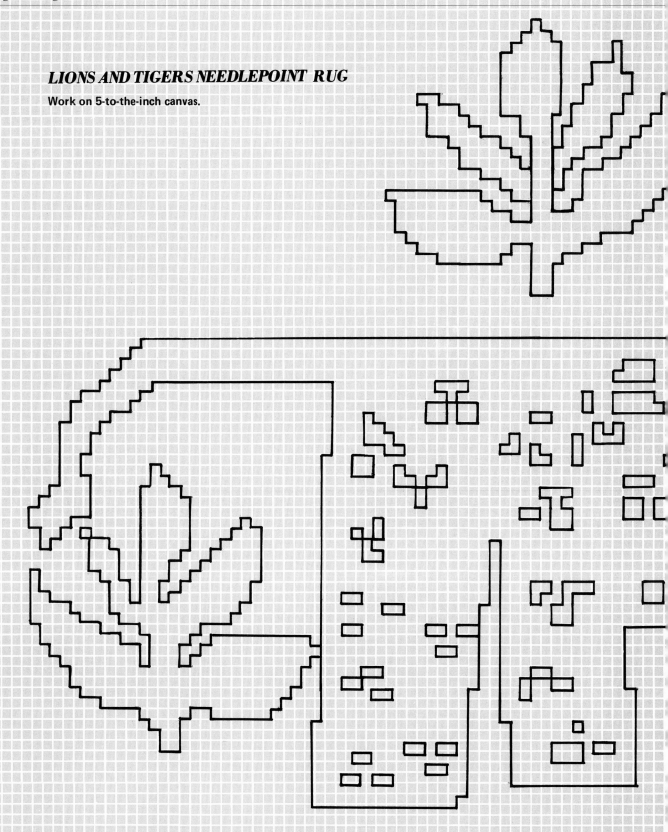

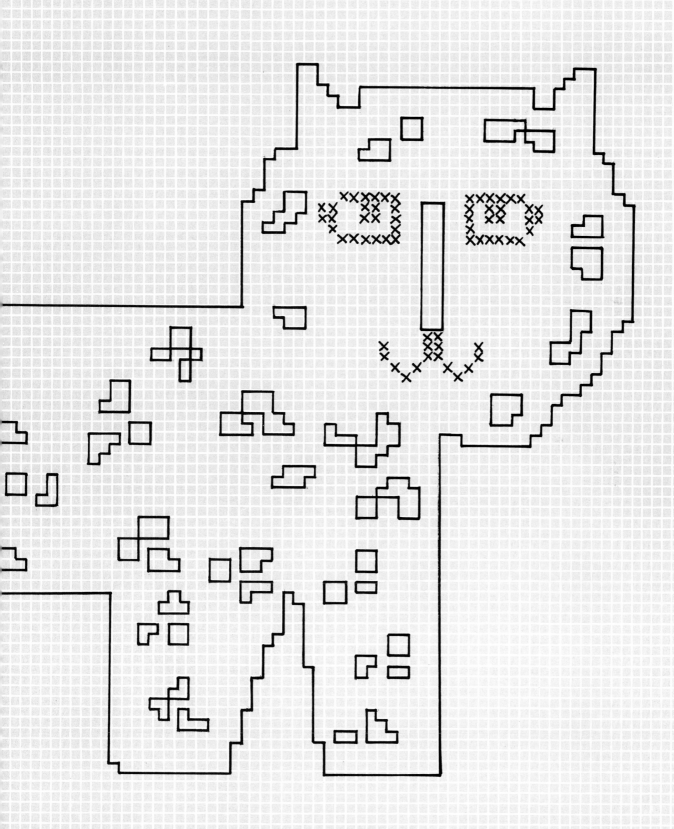

**LIONS AND TIGERS NEEDLEPOINT RUG**

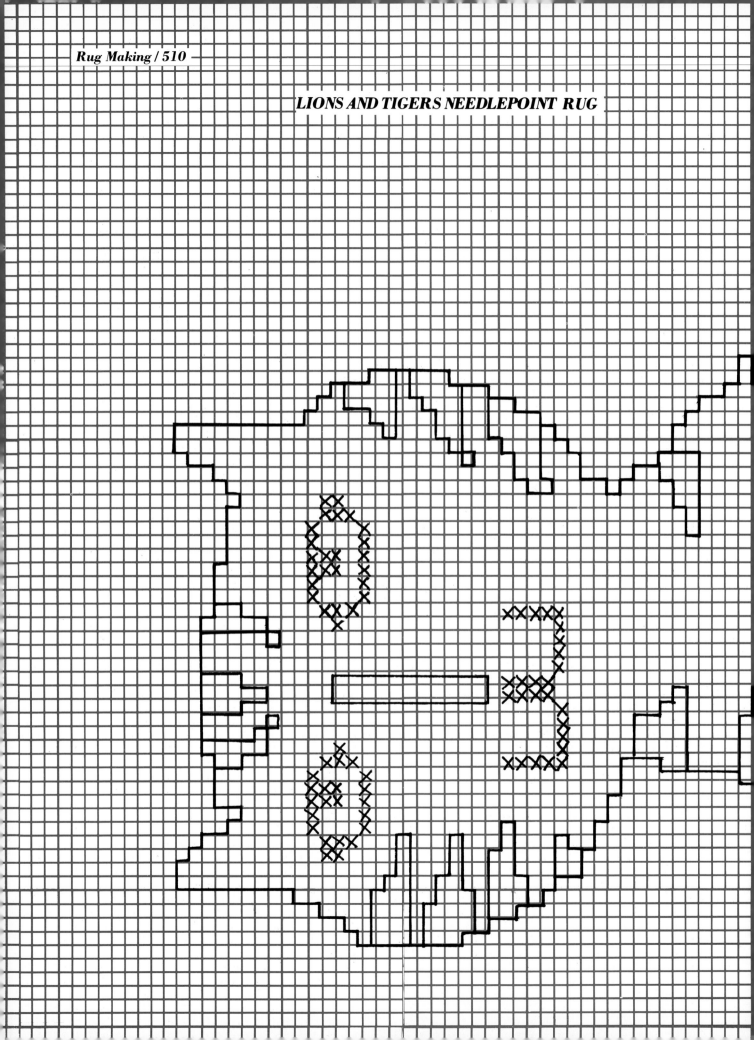

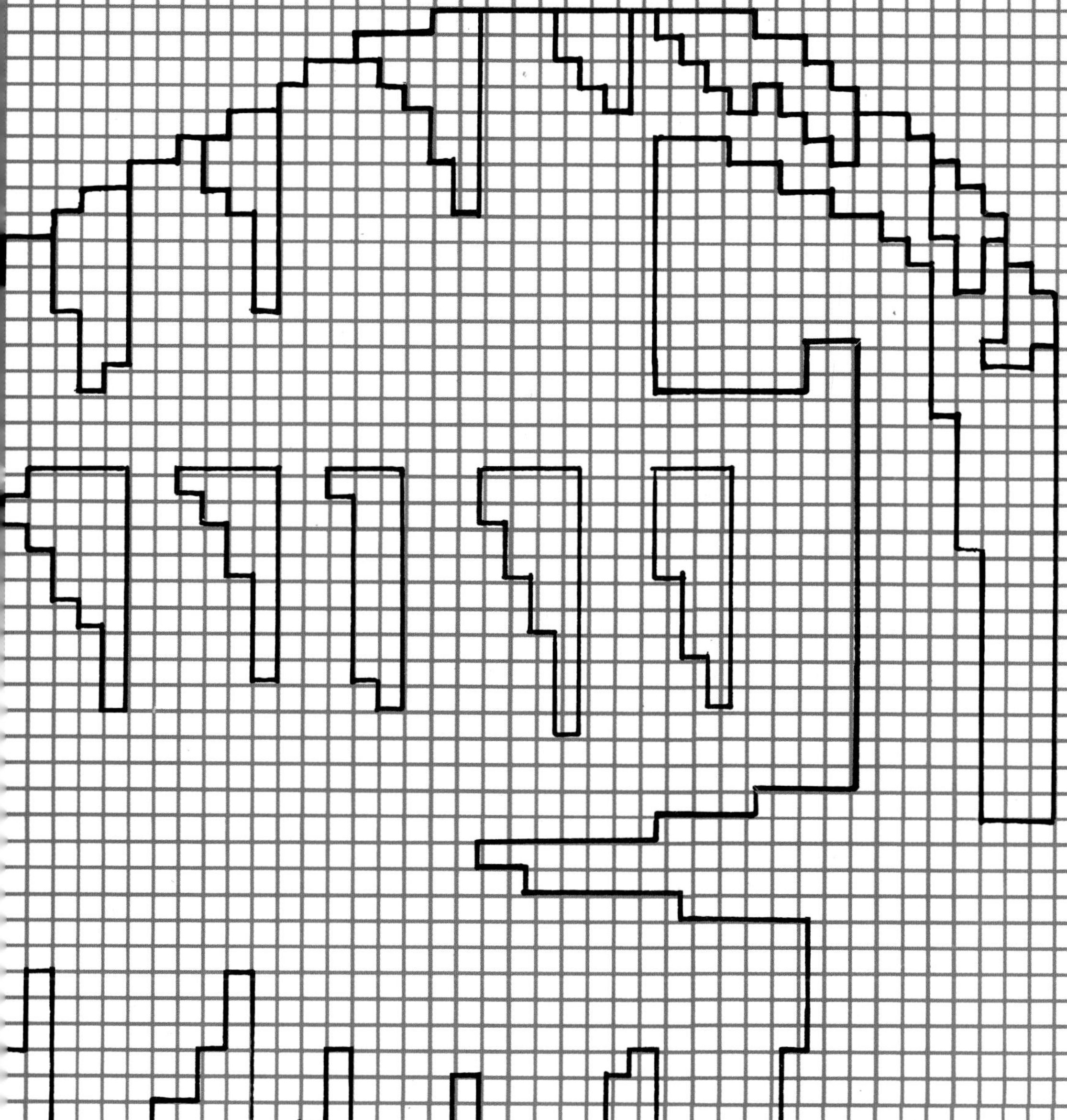

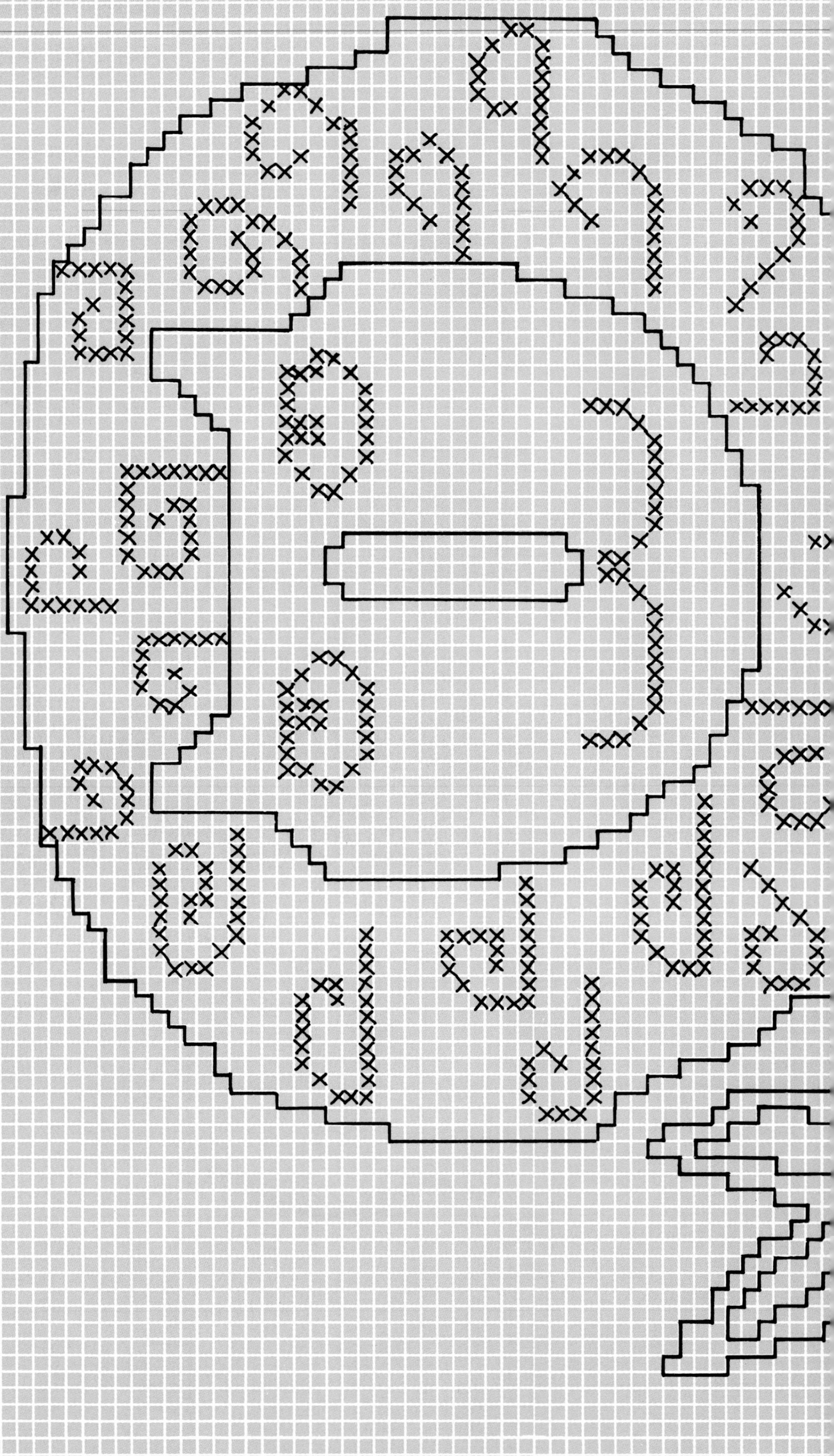

# LIONS AND TIGERS NEEDLEPOINT RUG

**Work on 5-to-the-inch canvas.**

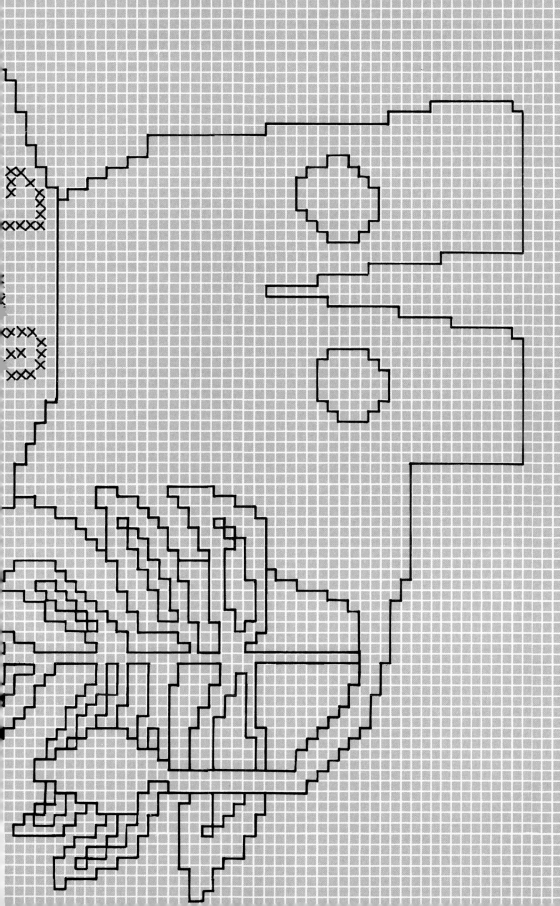

## STRAWBERRY RUG MADE IN SQUARES ON CANVAS

A 24 x 36-inch rug can be made in six squares of 5-to-the-inch canvas or it can be increased to any size desired by adding squares. With rug yarn, work in needlepoint — Basketweave Stitch or Cross Stitch. The same design can be worked in Cross Stitch on linen for other uses.

Background = Cream

X = Cream

O = Dark Olive in entire area

Berries, except X spots = Red

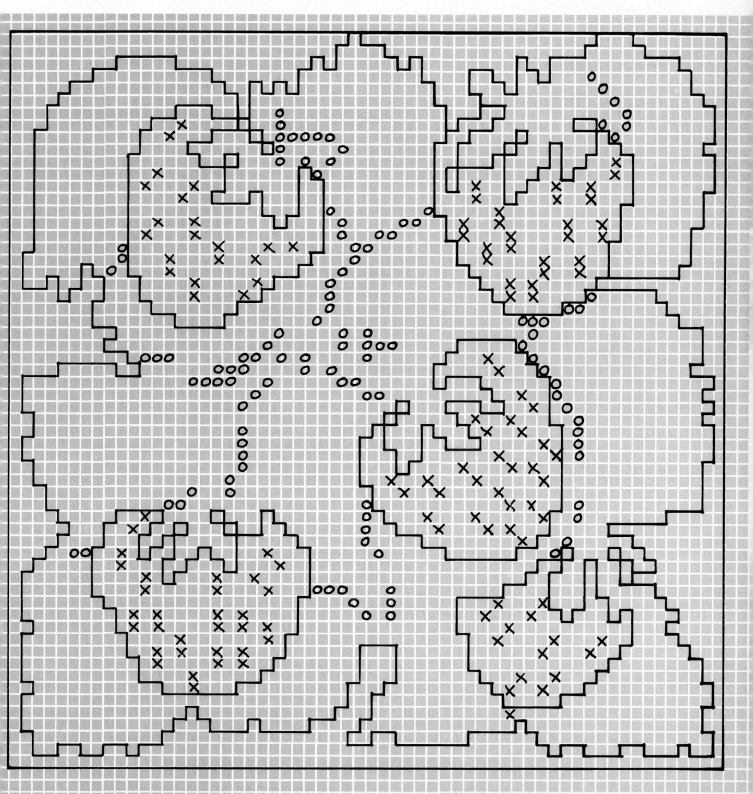

## GUARDSMEN THREE

### Designed by Joan Moshimer, worked by Jeanette Darisse

Even a beginner can work the simple lines and colors of this charming child's hooked rug. The diagram for the figures is given half size to be worked for a 24 x 36-inch rug with 1½-inch borders.

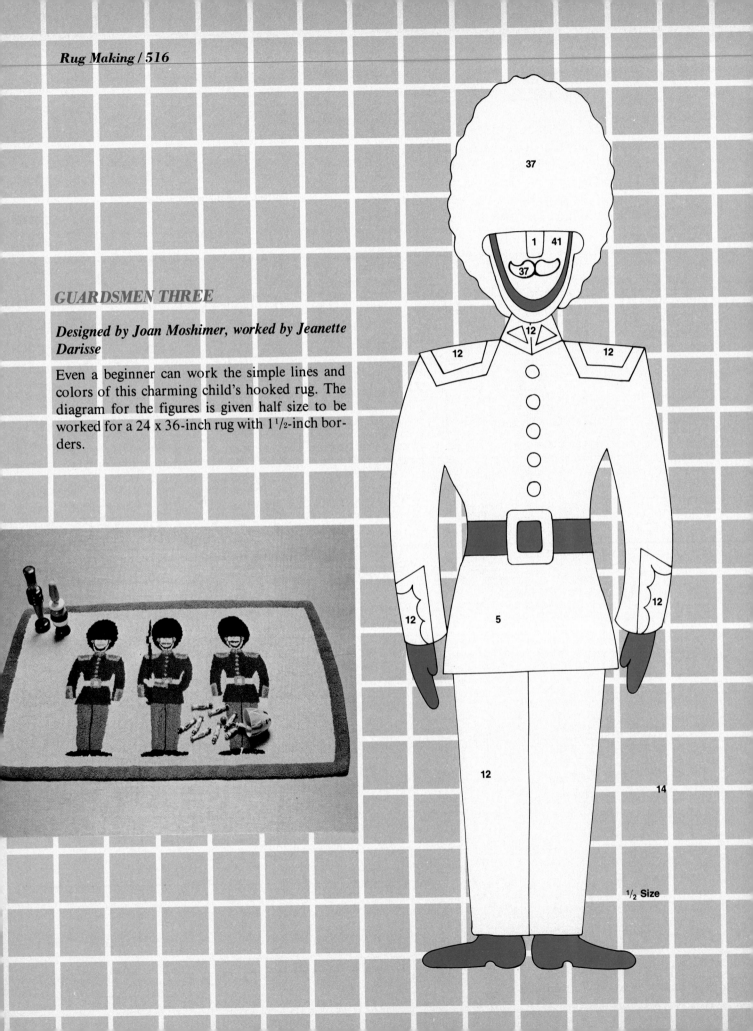

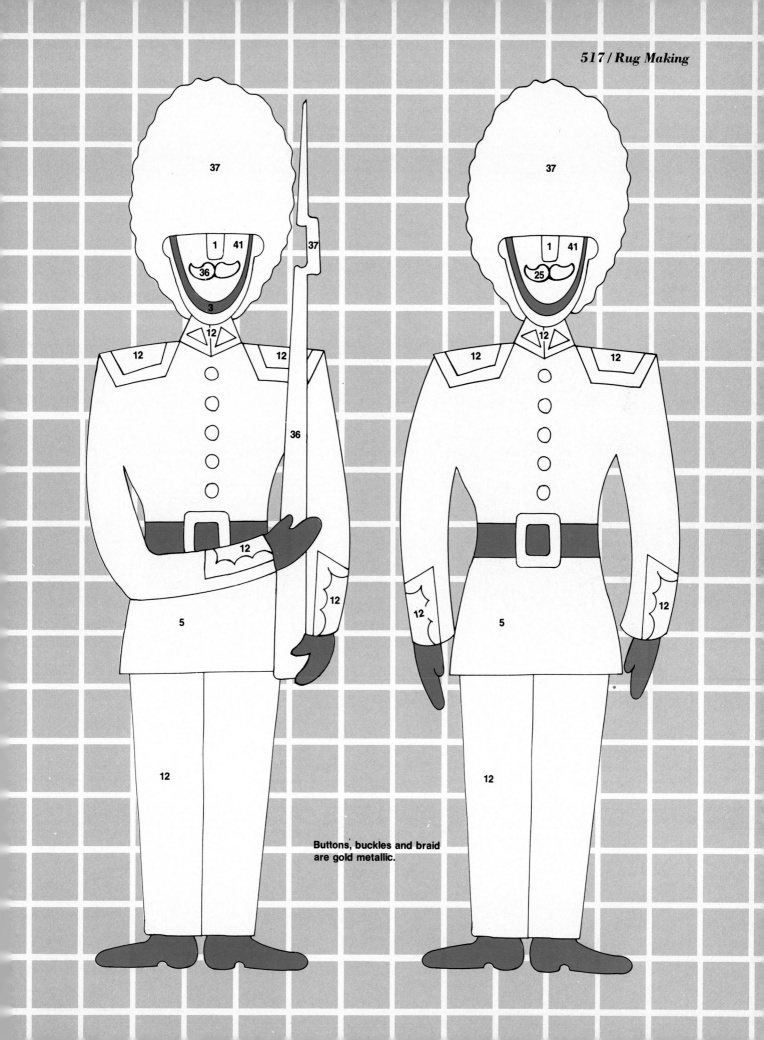

Buttons, buckles and braid
are gold metallic.

**TOP**

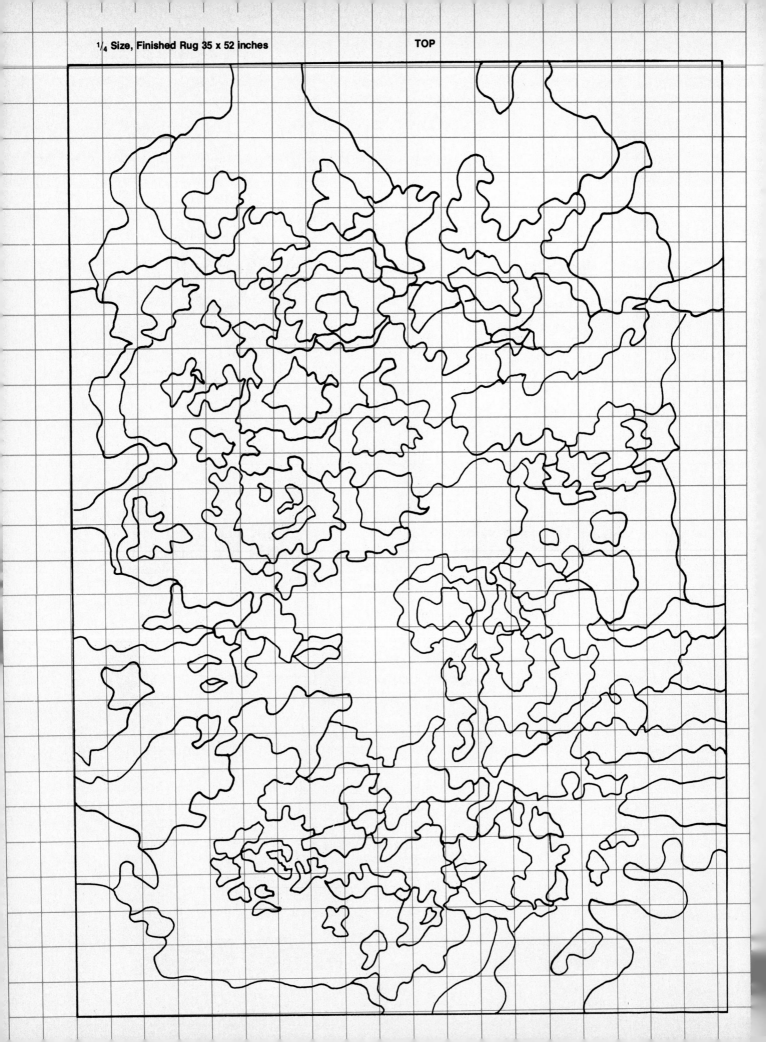

**TOP**

## *RYA RUGS*

The designs of rya rugs are free and imaginative, so we have given only rough sketches for reference. The effect will be very much like those pictured, though much of the final effect depends on the way colors are blended.

A.  Use two shades of gold, two shades of orange, three shades of red and three shades of brown. Use the colors as shown in the picture, blending for extra shades.

B.  Use four shades of green and five shades of blue. Blend the shades to make the extra shades shown.

## BRAIDED "RAG RUGS"

### Designed and Created by Susie Terry

The early American braided rug has really grown to be a decorator's dream when the colors are as controlled and the patterns as well-planned as in these examples. Planning from the center out on the round or oval ones can change shades and colors and achieve many interesting effects.

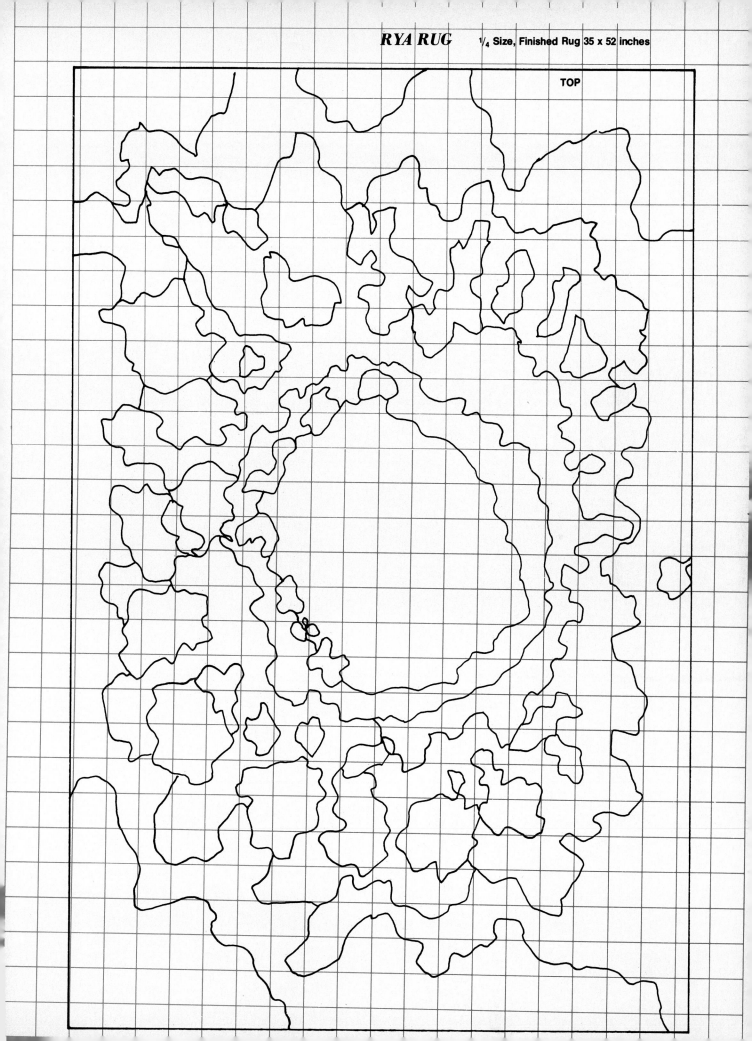

**RYA RUG**  ¹/₄ Size, Finished Rug 35 x 52 inches

TOP

# Macramé

Macramé, the art of knot tying, has been practiced since the time of prehistoric peoples. As people became more civilized, knotting became a decorative art. There is much evidence that artistic knotting existed as early as 3000 B. C. Ancient warriors went into battle with knotted trim on their uniforms. Ancient Egyptian tombs show figures wearing knotted trimmed robes. Assyrian sculptures show entire robes made of knots. The most common use of knotting in ancient times was to decorate the end cords of fabric instead of using a hem.

Although knotting began as a utilitarian function, it developed into one of the earliest forms of decorative art. From its rise in the Arab countries of the Middle East, macramé spread across northern Africa and eventually to Europe. The Moors introduced it to Spain; the returning Crusaders brought the craft to Italy and France. In Renaissance Italy, it came to be known as "punto a gropo" or knotted lace. Mary, wife of William of Orange, introduced knotting to England where it quickly became a favorite drawing room pastime.

**MACRAMÉ, THE SEAMAN'S ART: James Lorier shown in The Seaman's Church Institute of New York with part of a collection made by him and other seamen.**

The Spaniards introduced macramé to Mexico where it became known as "Mexican Lace." The Indians of eastern Canada were introduced to decorative knotting by French sailors and explorers. In the time of Queen Victoria, Macramé Lace was a necessary craft for all young ladies of high social standing. During this period, macramé was worked with very fine thread and was, in fact, a lace. Soon after the death of Queen Victoria, there was a revolt against the ornately decorative style of the period. Macramé was dismissed along with most other Victorian styles.

The word macramé came into use in the mid-nineteenth century — probably from the Turkish word "makrama," meaning fringed napkin, or from the Arabic word "migramah," meaning embroidered veil. Today the word macramé is applied to any form of decorative knitting.

Sailors and seamen, for several hundred years, have been working with "Sailor's Knotting," known also as "McNamara's Lace." While sailor's knotting is not exactly the same as macramé, they are very close cousins. The articles were made to either decorate the ship or to be sold in the next port of call. By the mid-1900's the best knotters in the world were the British

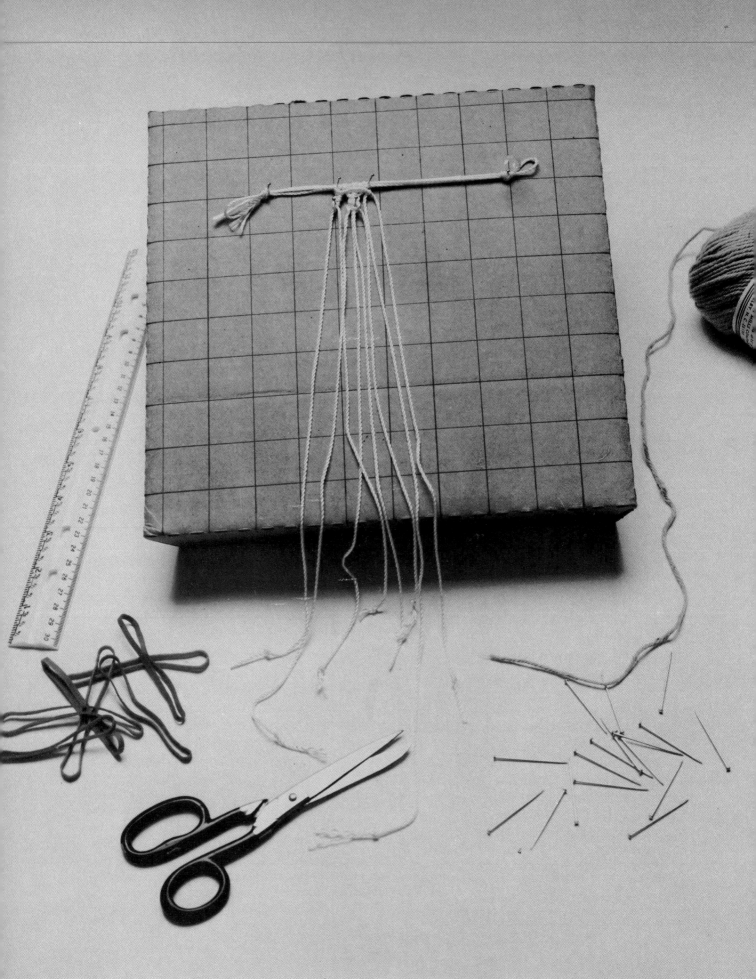

and American sailors. In this century the art of sailor's knotting has almost died out completely.

From the end of the 1800's until the mid-1960's, macramé was practiced by only a few nuns in eastern Europe and was, indeed, a nearly lost art form. Through the interest and work of Virginia Harvey, the craft was introduced again and has become more popular than ever. However, for current styles, macramé knots use larger cords, more color and more decorative items such as driftwood, feathers and beads. The development of synthetic fibers also introduced a wider variety of cords from which to select. Macramé looks complicated, but it is deceptively simple. After a short time of practice on two basic knots, it is possible to make the finest of laces or the boldest of wall hangings. Try it. The knots are genuinely easy, the materials inexpensive and the results truly spectacular.

The great charm of macramé lies in the ease with which the craft can be learned. The types of projects possible are limited only by the imagination. Make practical pieces such as clothing and household items, or enjoyable articles such as wall hangings and room dividers. The list of macramé possibilities is without limit — belts, tote bags, pocketbooks, lamp shades, window screens, pillows, rugs, hanging planters, hats, table runners, bell pulls, guitar straps, vests and covers for waste baskets, wine bottles and director's chairs.

Learn the Half Hitch Knot and the Square Knot first; these are the basic knots from which all projects are made. Practice with these knots and their variations and combinations on one-yard lengths of cord.

## BASIC MATERIALS

Macramé requires only a few materials, most of which can be found around the home. The necessary items are cord for knotting, a yardstick and scissors for measuring and cutting the cords, rubber bands for bundling the cords, gloves for working with very rough cords, straight pins and a knotting board. **Fig. 1.**

A macramé knotting board can be purchased at an arts and crafts supply store or made at home.

Anything into which pins can be easily pushed is suitable for a knotting board — a piece of cork or heavy cardboard, a padded clipboard, a ceiling tile or a tightly stuffed pillow. It is helpful to measure the board into one-inch squares to be used as guides while knotting.

### CORD

The variety of cords available for macramé is almost endless. There are natural cords such as manila, hemp, cotton and silk, and synthetic cords such as rayon, nylon, plastic, raffia and rattail. **Fig. 2.** Most of these cords are also available in a wide range of sizes.

Any cord is suitable that has a hard twist, is non-elastic and is strong enough to survive the tension necessary to pull the knots into place. Very thin cord such as buttonhole twist can be used for a lace effect. However, with cord this fine the knots will not show well. Leather strips can also be used, but it is very hard to find leather in long lengths. To use leather, it is usually necessary to buy a large piece from which strips can be cut. In cutting the leather, begin at the center and draw an exact spiral to the outer edges of the piece. Cut the spiral line with a small, very sharp blade.

When selecting cord be sure to choose a cord suitable for the finished macramé piece. A heavy, strong cord, such as sisal or jute, should be selected for hanging planter or tote bag. A soft, pliable cord, such as rattail or nylon, should be selected for a choker or a vest.

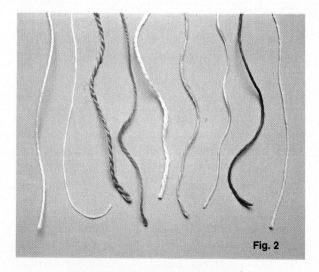

Fig. 2

Types of Cord Suitable for Macramé

Cord may be found in hardware stores, grocery stores, marine supply stores, sporting goods outlets, yarn and craft dealers — in short, anywhere cord, rope or yarn is sold. When working with very rough cord such as jute or sisal, be sure to wear gloves.

**Estimating Cord Length:** Determining cord length depends on the thickness of the cord, the individual style of knotting, and the macramé pattern to be used. A piece that is heavily knotted will require much more cord than an open pattern.

In macramé, the thicker the cord, the faster the yardage will be used up — the thinner the cord, the slower.

One method of estimating cord length is to work a test piece. Cut several lengths of cord about 2 yards long. Work these cords in the selected knotting pattern until all of the cord is used up. When completed the length of the test piece will help in estimating the amount of cord needed for the finished project. Example: A 2-yard piece of cord folded in half equals 1 yard per cord. If there are 12 inches of knotting when the cords are used up, figure each cord at three times the desired finished length. For a belt that is to be 25 inches long, figure 75 inches per cord for that style. Since each cord is usually folded in half, figure 150 inches per cut cord. If ties are to be used for the belt rather than a buckle, add the extra inches required for the ties to each cord before cutting.

Another method of estimating cord length is to figure four times per cord the length of the finished work. If each cord is to be folded in half, figure eight times the length of the finished work.

When measuring cord yardage always add an extra amount to be on the safe side. This will often be wasteful, but it is difficult to add new cord once the project has been started. After cord has been cut, tie the cord ends with an Overhand Knot to prevent fraying. If beads are to be used, dip the ends in clear nail polish so that they will slide on to the cord more easily.

**Bundling Cord:** Because of the long lengths of cord involved in macramé, it is necessary to bundle the excess cord. **Fig. 3.** Wrap each individual cord around the fingers in a figure eight, then

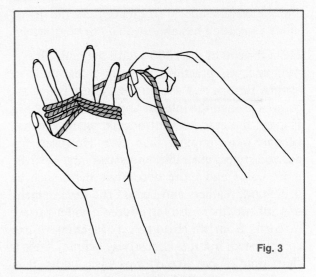

**Bundling Macramé Cord**

fasten the bundle at the center with a rubber band. As additional cord is needed while working, simply pull the bundle.

## TECHNIQUES OF WORKING

There are three methods of working macramé. The technique selected depends upon the item to be made. Use a knotting board, the "hanging free" technique or the "in the round" method.

**Method 1:** The knotting board is suitable when working with a small piece such as a belt, choker or small wall hanging. For the beginner, it offers the added advantage of pinning knots into place thus keeping the lines of knots straight while working. **Fig. 4.**

**Method 2:** For larger pieces such as a wall hanging or room divider, it is necessary to work with the "hanging free" method. Hang a dowel between two high back chairs, suspend it from two nails on the back of a door, or use a spring tension rod placed in a doorway. If a cord is used to hold the macramé piece rather than a dowel, tie each end of the cord to the back of a chair. **Fig. 5.** To keep the holding line taut while working, loop the holding line around your belt.

Smaller macramé pieces can also be tied using the hanging free method. The technique used is strictly a matter of personal choice. For a small piece, such as a belt, tie the buckle or the ties to a door knob for working. **Fig. 6.**

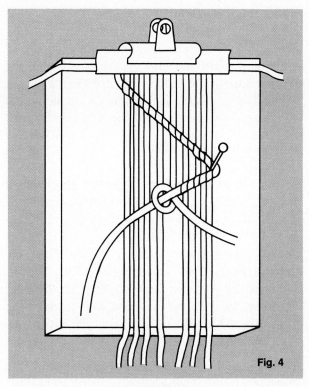

**A Knotting Board**

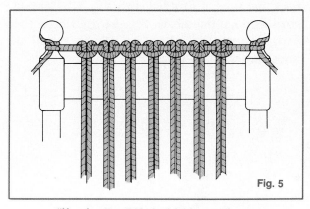

**"Hanging Free" Method for Large Pieces**

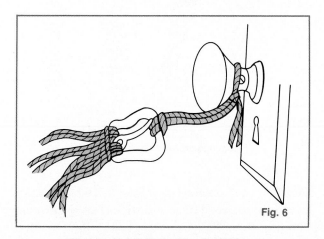

**"Hanging Free" Method for Small Pieces**

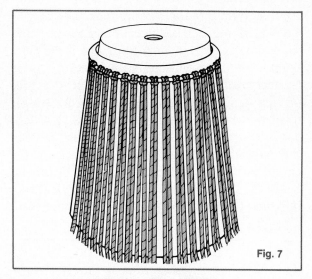

**Working "In the Round"**

**Method 3:** When working "in the round," it is easy to improvise with a padded block of wood, a flower pot or any article similar in size and shape to the planned design. **Fig. 7.** If the macramé is to be fitted around a specific object such as a wine bottle or a lamp shade, use the object itself.

## BEGINNING TO KNOT

As a beginner, practice the Half Hitch Knot and the Square Knot — the two basic knots — until working with them and handling the long lengths of cord is easy. If a mistake is made in knotting, simply untie the knot and try again. In macramé there is no correct or incorrect way to position the hands. Work in whatever fashion is the most comfortable.

Before beginning, know the meaning of the following terms: Holding Line and Tying Line. The holding line is the cord around which the knots are tied. The tying line is the cord with which the knots are tied. **Fig. 8.** These two lines may frequently exchange places during knotting.

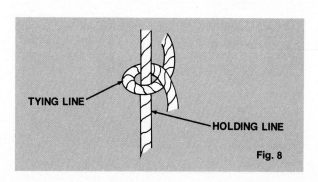

TYING LINE

HOLDING LINE

Fig. 8

Another term is Main Holding Line. This may be a dowel, a ring, belt buckle, another cord or anything suitable. The main holding line is the piece from which the work is suspended. If using another cord for the main holding line, cut three or four lengths of cord about 6 inches longer than the desired width of the work. Using several cords held together as one for the main holding line will add extra strength to the piece. At the end of each group of these cords tie an Overhand Knot. Pin the end knots to the top of the knotting board so that the main holding line is taut.

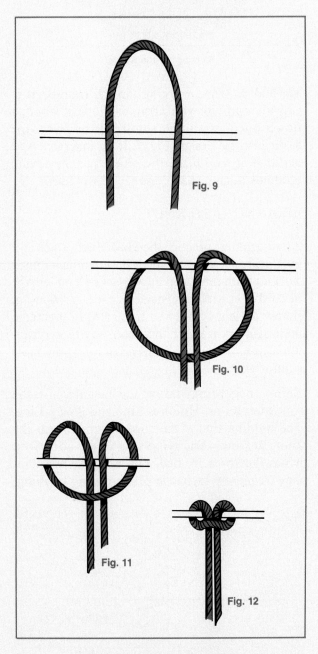

Steps in Tying the Lark's Head Knot

## THE BASIC KNOTS

Five knots are shown here as basic knots. The two main knots are the Half Hitch Knot and the Square Knot. The remaining three knots — the Clove Hitch, Lark's Head and Overhand knots — are actually variations of the Half Hitch Knot.

### LARK'S HEAD KNOT

(Known also as the Reversed Half Hitch Knot and the Mounting Knot.) The Lark's Head Knot is normally used to tie the cord to a main holding line. To tie the Lark's Head Knot, fold the cord in half forming a loop at the center. Place the loop in front of the main holding line. **Fig. 9.** Fold the loop to the back of the main holding line. **Fig. 10.** Pull the two cord ends through the loop. **Fig. 11.** Pull the knot securely into place. **Fig. 12.**

The Lark's Head Knot can also be set on fabric to work a fringe. Using a crochet hook to pull the cord through the fabric, insert the hook from the back and catch the folded cord. **Fig. 13.** Draw the cord through the fabric. **Fig. 14.** Pull both cord ends through the loop. **Fig. 15.** Now pull the knot securely into place. **Fig. 16.**

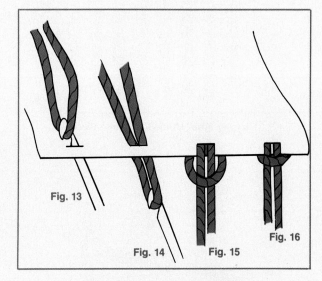

Lark's Head Knot Set into Fabric

Another method for tying the Lark's Head Knot is to fold the cord over and slide it onto the main holding line. To work the knot in this manner, use a main holding line that is straight. Fold the

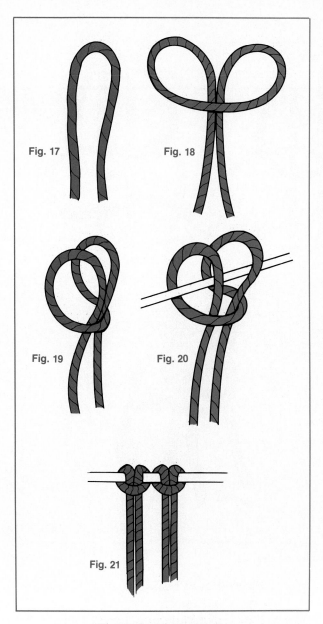

**Alternate Lark's Head Knot**

## HALF HITCH KNOT

(Known also as the Tatting Knot and the Simple Knot.) Usually used in chains and braids, the Half Hitch is simply the turn of one cord around another. **Fig. 22.** The Half Hitch Knot can be worked over as many holding cords as desired with as many tying cords as needed, and in either direction.

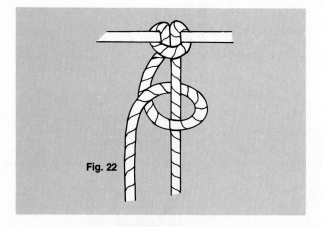

**Half Hitch Knot**

## CLOVE HITCH KNOT

(Known also as the Double Half Hitch.) The most versatile knot in macramé is the Clove Hitch — and mastering it is a necessity. It can be worked in any direction — vertically, horizontally or diagonally — and over as many or as few holding lines as desired. The Clove Hitch is actually made up of two Half Hitch knots. **Fig. 23.**

cord in half. **Fig. 17.** Turn the cord loop to the front to form two butterfly wings. **Fig. 18.** Fold the wings to the back (**Fig. 19**) and slide the main holding line through the two wings. **Fig. 20.** Pull the knot securely into place. **Fig. 21.**

**Reversed Lark's Head Knot:** the Lark's Head Knot with the loop tied at the back. It is tied the same way as the Lark's Head Knot with all the steps reversed.

The Lark's Head Knot and the Reversed Lark's Head Knot are usually used to tie cord onto the main holding line. They can, however, be used within the design of the macramé piece itself.

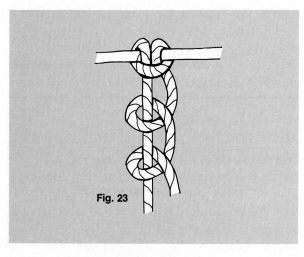

**Clove Hitch Knot**

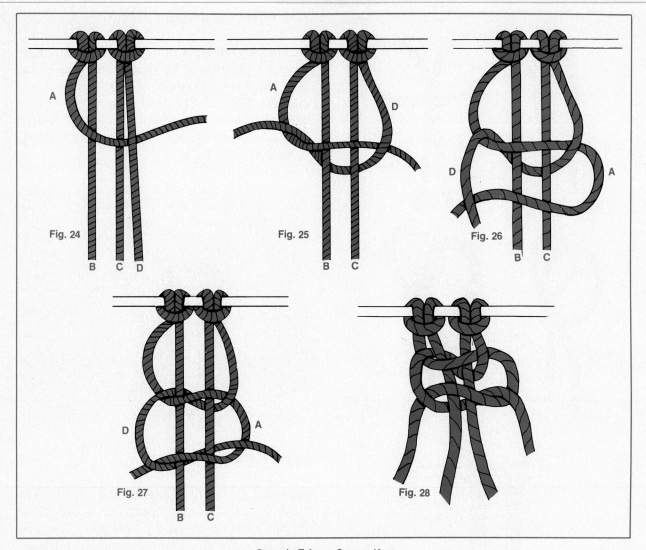

Fig. 24

Fig. 25

Fig. 26

Fig. 27

Fig. 28

**Steps in Tying a Square Knot**

## SQUARE KNOT

(Known also as the Flat Knot and the Reef Knot.) The Square Knot is another macramé knot often used. Learning it may go slowly at first, but once this knot is mastered, it can be worked with great speed. Work the Square Knot in either direction over one, two, three or as many holding lines as desired using any *even* number of tying lines.

The diagrams show the Square Knot made with four cords, the most common combination.
***Step 1:*** Following the diagram, place A cord over B and C cords and under D cord. **Fig. 24.**
***Step 2:*** Place D cord behind B and C cords and through A loop. **Fig. 25.**
***Step 3:*** Place A cord (now on opposite side) over B and C cords and under D cord. **Fig. 26.**

***Step 4:*** Place D cord behind B and C cords and through A loop. **Fig. 27.**
***Step 5:*** Pull knot tightly in place. **Fig. 28.**

## OVERHAND KNOT

(Known also as the Shell Knot.) The simplest knot in macramé, the Overhand Knot, can serve a variety of purposes. Tie it at the end of individual cords to prevent fraying or to prevent a bead from slipping out of place. Consider using it with a group of cords to form a tassel, or as a part of the design within the work. To tie the Overhand Knot, make a loop, then bring the cord end through the loop. **Fig. 29.** Pull the knot securely into place. **Fig. 30.** The Overhand Knot can be tied with one cord as already shown, with several cords (**Fig. 31**), or over another cord. **Fig. 32.**

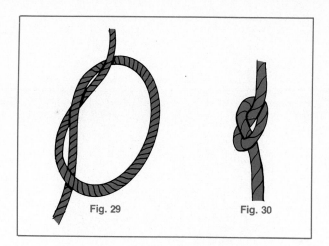

Fig. 29    Fig. 30

**Steps in Tying an Overhand Knot**

## LARK'S HEAD DESIGNS

While the Lark's Head Knot is usually used to tie cords to the main holding line, it can also be used within the macramé design.

**Lark's Head Braid:** Using one cord as the tying line, following the diagram, tie as many Lark's Head knots as desired around the holding line. **Fig. 33.** This variation may be tied using as many or as few cords as desired.

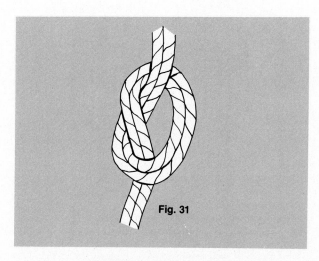

Fig. 31

**Overhand Knot with Two Cords**

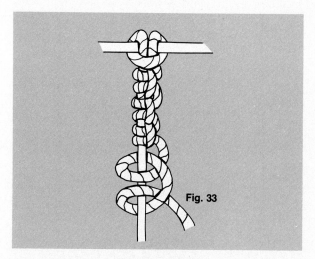

Fig. 33

**Lark's Head Braid**

Fig. 32

**Overhand Knot Tied around Another Cord**

## *VARIATIONS ON THE BASIC KNOTS*

With the few simple knots on the preceding pages, an endless variety of patterns can be formed. Here are a few — many, many more are possible.

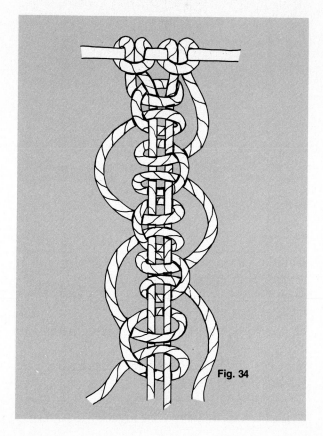

Fig. 34

**Alternating Lark's Head Braid:** Using four cords with cord at each outside edge, alternate Lark's Head knots over the two center cords. The knots may be alternated one at a time (**Fig. 34**), two at a time (**Fig. 35**) or in any combination that suits the design.

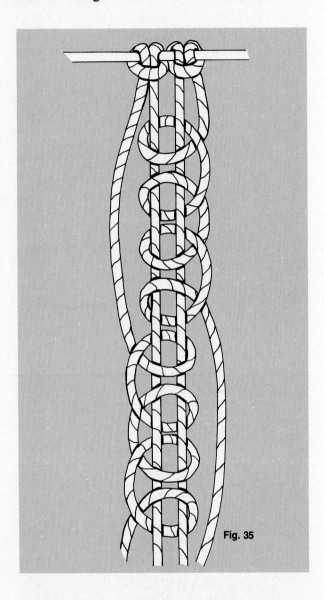

Fig. 35

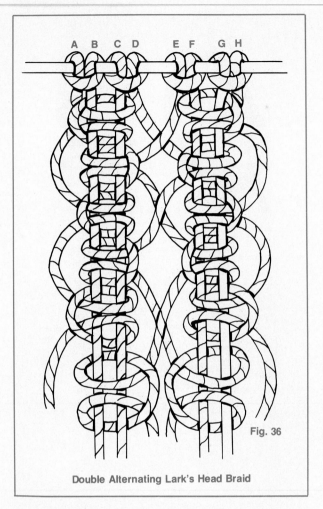

Fig. 36

Double Alternating Lark's Head Braid

**Double Alternating Lark's Head Braid:** This is worked with eight cords. **Fig. 36.**

*Step 1:* Using A as tying line, tie Lark's Head Knot over B and C cords.

*Step 2:* With H cord, tie a Lark's Head Knot over F and G cords.

*Step 3:* With D cord, tie a Lark's Head Knot over F and G cords.

*Step 4:* With E tie a Lark's Head Knot over B and C cords. Repeat Steps 1 through 4 for pattern.

## HALF HITCH DESIGNS

An incredible number of forms and shapes can be developed with this simple loop knot.

**Half Hitch Braid:** The Half Hitch Braid is made by tying several Half Hitch knots, one after the other. **Fig. 37.** When tied in this manner the Half Hitch knots form a braid that twists around the holding line. You may leave the braid twisted, or tie the knots a bit more loosely to straighten the braid.

**Half Hitch Chain:** Using two cords, work the half hitch chain by alternating tying and holding lines. **Fig. 38.**

**Alternating Half Hitch Braid:** Use four cords to make braid. **Fig. 39.**

*Step 1:* With right hand cord, tie a Half Hitch Knot over the two center cords.

*Step 2:* With left hand cord, tie a Half Hitch Knot over the two center cords. Repeat Steps 1 and 2 for pattern.

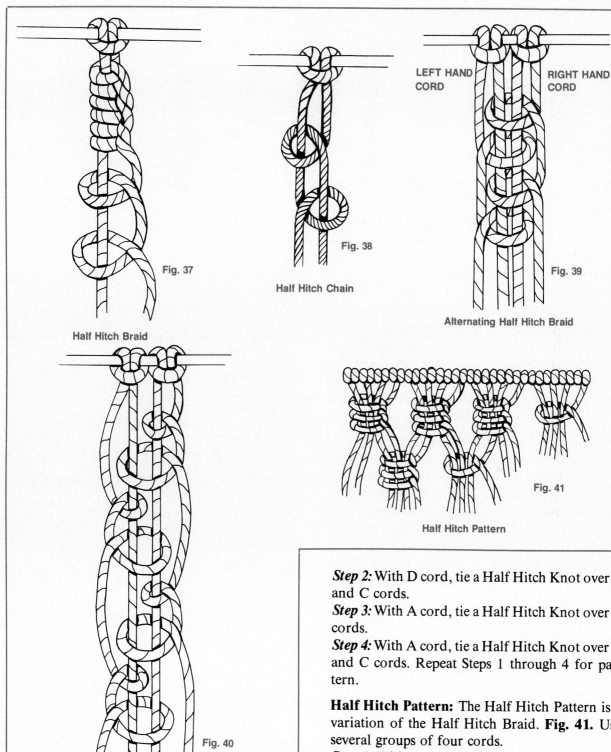

Fig. 37

Half Hitch Braid

Fig. 38

Half Hitch Chain

LEFT HAND CORD

RIGHT HAND CORD

Fig. 39

Alternating Half Hitch Braid

Fig. 40

A    B    C    D

Double Half Hitch Braid

Fig. 41

Half Hitch Pattern

**Step 2:** With D cord, tie a Half Hitch Knot over B and C cords.

**Step 3:** With A cord, tie a Half Hitch Knot over B cords.

**Step 4:** With A cord, tie a Half Hitch Knot over B and C cords. Repeat Steps 1 through 4 for pattern.

**Half Hitch Pattern:** The Half Hitch Pattern is a variation of the Half Hitch Braid. **Fig. 41.** Use several groups of four cords.

**Step 1:** With the right hand cord of each group, tie three Half Hitch knots over the remaining three cords of the group.

**Step 2:** Leaving two cords with each edge unworked, divide again into groups of four cords per group. With the right hand cord of each group, tie three Half Hitch knots. Repeat Steps 1 and 2 for pattern.

**Double Half Hitch Braid:** This is also worked with four cords. **Fig. 40.**

**Step 1:** With D cord, tie Half Hitch Knot over C cord.

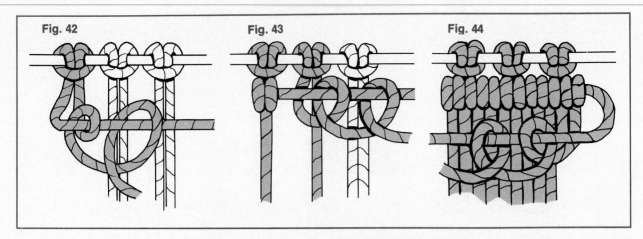

**Steps in Forming the Horizontal Clove Hitch Knot**

## CLOVE HITCH DESIGNS

The Clove Hitch Knot is the most versatile of all macramé knots. It can be worked diagonally, vertically or horizontally, and is the best knot to use for shaping and color movement. When working the Clove Hitch patterns, the holding line may be an entirely new cord added from the side or it may be a cord that is already a part of the work.

**Horizontal Clove Hitch Knot:** The Horizontal Clove Hitch Knot is very often the first row of knots tied after the cords have been mounted on the main holding line with Lark's Head knots. This additional row secures all Lark's Head knots and prevents the cords from slipping out of place. To make the Horizontal Clove Hitch Knot, place holding line across the top of the tying cords and tie a Clove Hitch Knot. **Fig. 42.** Repeat this step across. **Fig. 43.** When the end of the row is reached, place the same cord across the top of the tying cords again; and work back across in the opposite direction forming a second row of knots. **Fig. 44.**

**Vertical Clove Hitch Knot:** The Vertical Clove Hitch Knot is tied much like the Horizontal Clove Hitch Knot, except that the tying line is worked across from underneath the row of cords. Each cord in the row serves as a holding line, while the cord laid across serves as the tying line. **Fig. 45.** When the row is completed, work back across in the opposite direction with the same cord. **Fig. 46.** The Vertical Clove Hitch Knot takes a great deal of cord, so if the design contains a large number of these knots, extra cord yardage will be necessary.

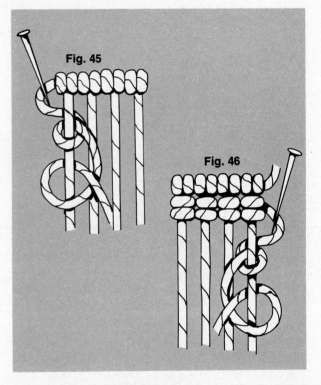

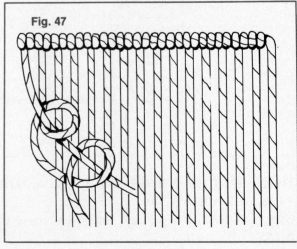

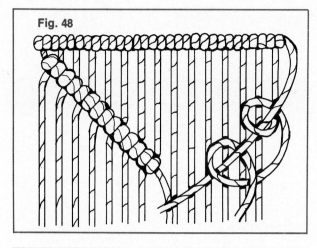

Fig. 48

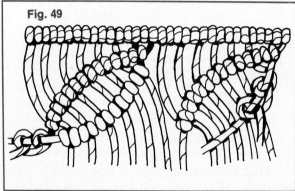

Fig. 49

**Chevron Clove Hitch Knot:** The Chevron Clove Hitch Knot is actually a method of tying two Diagonal Clove Hitch Knots as they intersect. **Fig. 50.** Once the knot has been tied, continue with the Diagonal Clove Hitch Knots. **Fig. 51.**

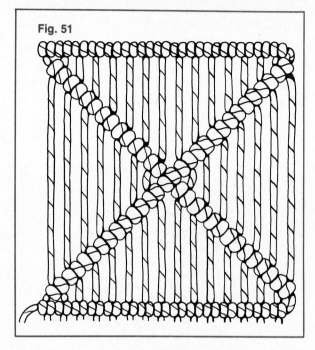

Fig. 51

Chevron Clove Hitch Knot

**Diagonal Clove Hitch Knot:** The Diagonal Clove Hitch Knot is similar to the Horizontal Clove Hitch Knot, except that the holding line is held in a diagonal position across the top of the cords. **Fig. 47.** The diagonal can be worked all the way across the piece, or just to the center. **Fig. 48.** The Diagonal Clove Hitch Knot may also be worked so as to curve (**Fig. 49**) by pulling up or down on the holding line in the center of the knotting.

*Shape and Color Movement with the Clove Hitch Knots:* In macramé work the easiest way to move color from one area to another is with any of the Clove Hitch Knot variations. The Horizontal Clove Hitch Knot is shown here. **Fig. 52.** However, the same results will take place using the Vertical or Diagonal Clove Hitch Knots. In addition to moving color, the Horizontal Clove Hitch Knot will also add shaping to the design.

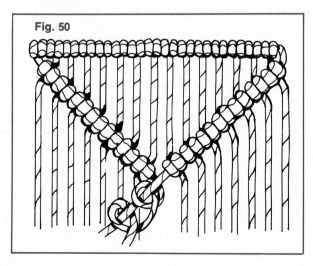

Fig. 50

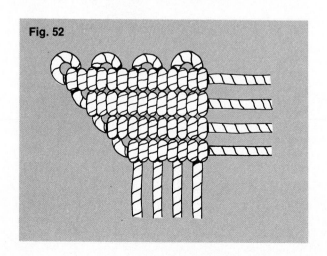

Fig. 52

## SQUARE KNOT DESIGNS

The Simple Square Knot offers an incredible number of beautiful and unique combinations.

**Simple Square Knot Braid:** The Simple Square Knot Braid is made by making vertical rows, called sennits, of Square Knots. **Fig. 53.**

**Alternating Square Knot Braid:** The Alternating Square Knot Braid is made by alternating the holding and tying lines. This braid looks best when two colors are used. **Fig. 54.**

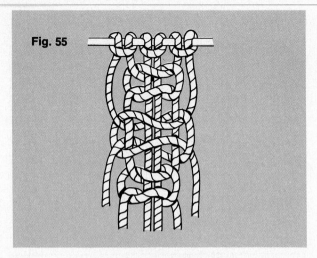

Triple Knot Square Knot Braid

**Step 2:** With cord at each outside edge, tie a Square Knot over the four center cords. Repeat Steps 1 and 2 for pattern.

**Looped Square Knot Braid:** The Looped Square Knot Braid is formed in the same way as the Simple Square Knot Braid — the knots, however, are separated on the holding line. **Fig. 56.** After working five or six Square Knots, each about one-inch apart, push the knots up the holding line so that the side loops form at the edges.

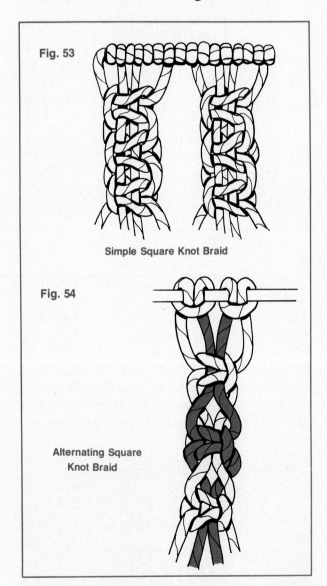

Simple Square Knot Braid

Fig. 54

Alternating Square Knot Braid

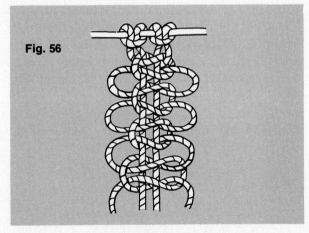

Looped Square Knot Braid

**Beaded Square Knot:** This is worked with four cords.
**Step 1:** Tie one Square Knot.
**Step 2:** Leaving a space about the size of one knot, tie three knots more. **Fig. 57.**
**Step 3:** Bring two center cords through the opening. **Fig. 58.**
**Step 4:** Pull cords tightly to form a button. **Fig. 59.**

**Triple Knot Square Knot Braid:** This is worked with six cords. **Fig. 55.**
**Step 1:** Leaving one cord with each edge unworked, tie a Square Knot over the two center cords.

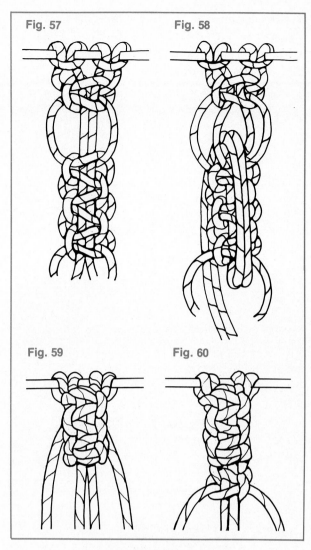

Fig. 57     Fig. 58

Fig. 59     Fig. 60

**Forming a Beaded Square Knot**

**Square Knot Pattern:** These steps make this pattern easy to work.

**Step 1:** Divide the cords into groups of four cords per group. **Fig. 62.** Tie one Square Knot on each group.

**Step 2:** Leave two cords with each edge unworked. Divide the remaining cords into groups of four cords per group. Tie one Square Knot on each group. **Fig. 63.** Repeat Steps 1 and 2 for pattern. **Fig. 64.**

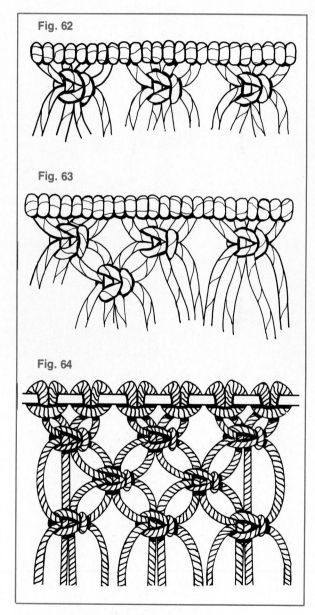

Fig. 62

Fig. 63

Fig. 64

**Square Knot Pattern**

**Step 5:** Tie a Square Knot directly below button to hold the knot in place. **Fig. 60.**

**Gathering Square Knot:** The purpose of the Gathering Square Knot is to gather a group of cords together. It can be worked with any number of tying lines and with any number of holding lines. **Fig. 61.**

Fig. 61

**Gathering Square Knot**

**Double Square Knot Pattern:** Following the directions for the Square Knot pattern above, work Step 1 twice — then Step 2 twice. **Fig. 65.**

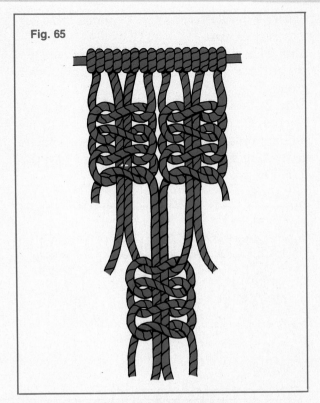

**Double Square Knot Pattern**

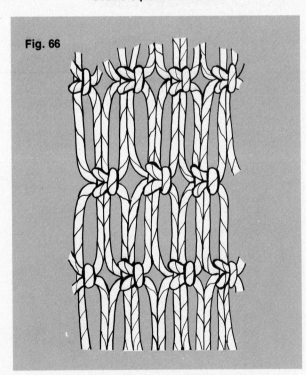

**Long Square Knot Pattern**

**Long Square Knot Pattern:** Following the directions for the Square Knot pattern, tie each row of knots about an inch below the preceding row. **Fig. 66.**

**Granny Knot:** The Granny Knot is actually the first half of the Square Knot. **Fig. 67.** When repeated several times it will twist itself around the holding line. **Fig. 68.**

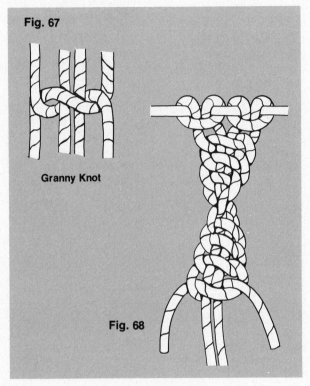

**Granny Knot Pattern**

## COMBINATIONS OF THE BASICS

Thus far the basic knots and their variations have been discussed. Included in this section are a few interesting ideas for combining the different knots.

### MOUNTING COMBINATIONS

Shown here are but a few of the alternate ways of mounting cords on the main holding line. The picot mounts look best when worked at the top of a fringe.

**Square Knot Picot:** This knot is worked with four cords.
*Step 1:* Fold two cords in half. Position the four cords next to each other.
*Step 2:* With two outside cords, tie a Square Knot over the two center cords.
*Step 3:* Tie picot to main holding line with Horizontal Clove Hitch Knots. **Fig. 69.**

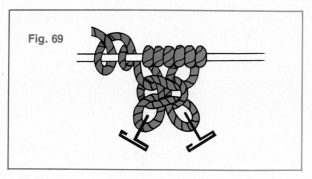

Fig. 69

**Square Knot Pattern**

**Double Square Knot Picot:** This knot is worked with six cords.
*Step 1:* Fold three cords in half, position the cords next to each other. **Fig. 70.**
*Step 2:* With one cord at each outside edge, tie two Square Knots over the four center cords. **Fig. 71.**
*Step 3:* Tie picot to main holding cord with Horizontal Clove Hitch Knots. **Fig. 72.**

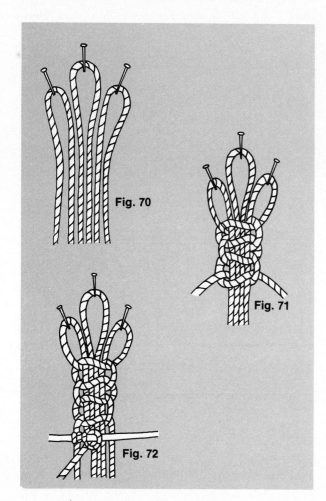

**Double Square Knot Picot**

**Half Hitch Scallop:** Mount the desired number of cords on the main holding line with Lark's Head Knots.
*Step 1:* Divide the cords into groups of eight cords per group.
*Step 2:* With the left hand cords of each group, tie Half Hitch Knots. **Fig. 73.**
*Step 3:* When nine Half Hitch Knots have been completed, tie picot to holding line with a Horizontal Clove Hitch Knot. **Fig. 74.**

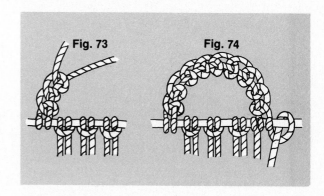

## COMBINATION BRAIDS

Braids need not be worked using only one type of knot. The simple braid can be made more interesting by combining several different types of knots.

**Square Knot/Overhand Knot Braid I:** This knot is worked with four cords.
*Step 1:* With the outside cord at each edge tie one Overhand Knot.
*Step 2:* With the outside cord at each edge, tie a Square Knot over the two center cords. Repeat Steps 1 and 2 for pattern. **Fig. 75.**

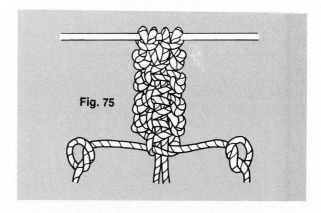

**Square Knot/Overhand Knot Braid I**

**Square Knot/Overhand Knot Braid II:** This knot is also worked with four cords. With cord at each outside edge, tie a Square Knot over the two center cords.

*Step 2:* Leave one cord with each edge unworked. Tie an Overhand Knot with the two center cords. Repeat Steps 1 and 2 for pattern. **Fig. 76.**

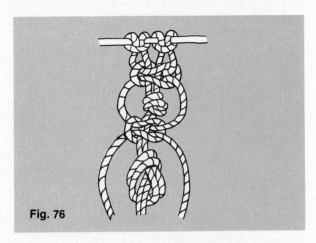

**Fig. 76**

Square Knot/Overhand Knot Braid II

## COMBINATION PATTERNS

Many times it is possible to build a whole design around one of the hundreds of combination patterns. Working many different variations of knots into one pattern adds texture and interest to the work.

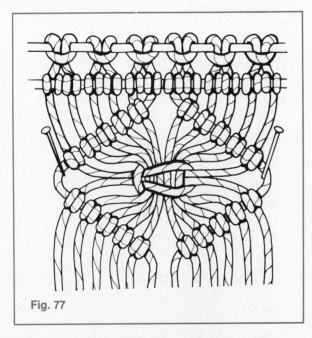

**Fig. 77**

Diagonal Clove Hitch Diamond with Gathering Knot

**Diagonal Clove Hitch Diamond with Gathering Knot:** This combination includes the basic Square Knot.

*Step 1:* Divide cords into two equal groups. Beginning at the center, tie Diagonal Clove Hitch Knots to each outside edge.

*Step 2:* Leave one cord with each edge unworked. Using the second cord from each edge, tie a Square Knot over the center cords.

*Step 3:* Beginning at each outside edge, tie Diagonal Clove Hitch Knots to the center. **Fig. 77.**

**Diagonal Clove Hitch Diamond with Square Knot Pattern:** The basic Square Knot is again used.

*Step 1:* Divide the cords into two equal groups. Beginning at the center, tie Diagonal Clove Hitch Knots to each outside edge.

*Step 2:* Using cords at the center of the diamond shape, tie Square Knots as shown in diagram.

*Step 3:* Beginning at each outside edge, tie Diagonal Clove Hitch Knots to the center. **Fig. 78.**

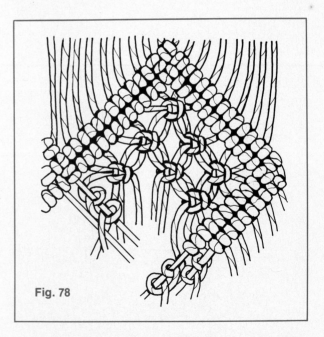

**Fig. 78**

Diagonal Clove Hitch Diamond with Square Knot Pattern

## ORNAMENTAL KNOTS

While not a part of the basic macramé knotting vocabulary, the Ornamental knots add elegance to any macramé design.

## THE JOSEPHINE KNOT

The easiest of the ornamental knots, the Josephine Knot, looks much more complicated than it actually is. This knot is worked with two cords.

*Step 1:* Make a loop with A cord as shown. **Fig. 79.**

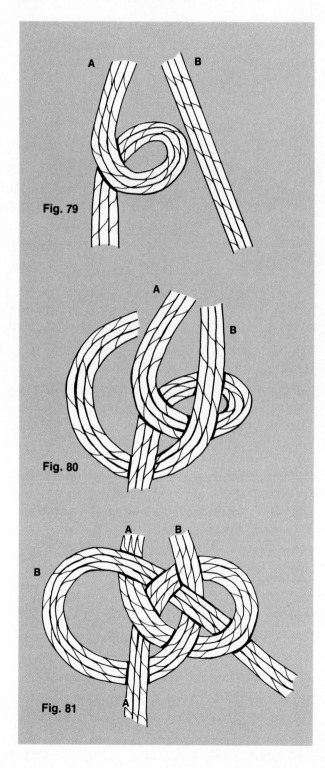

Fig. 79

Fig. 80

Fig. 81

Fig. 82

**The Josephine Knot**

*Step 2:* Lay B cord on top of the loop, under the strands of A cord at the bottom and bring it around. **Fig. 80.**

*Step 3:* Bring B cord over A cord, under the loop, over the cords, and under the next loop. **Fig. 81.**

*Step 4:* Pull knot in place, tightly or loosely, as desired. **Fig. 82.**

## ORIENTAL FROG KNOT

This knot is usually worked with more than one cord, making it larger and showing it off to a better advantage.

*Step 1:* Following the diagram, make a large Overhand Knot. **Fig. 83.**

*Step 2:* Bring the bottom cord over the top cord. **Fig. 84.**

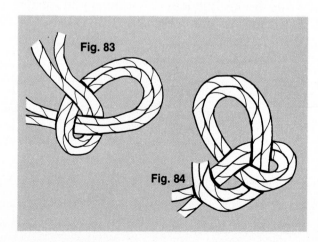

Fig. 83

Fig. 84

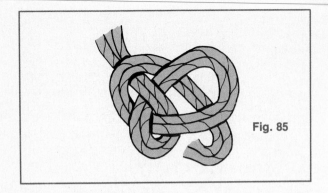

Fig. 85

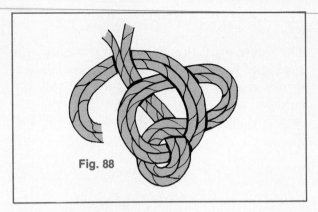

Fig. 88

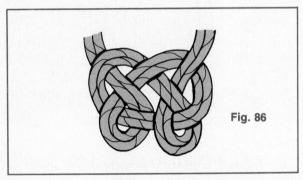

Fig. 86

**Oriental Frog Knot**

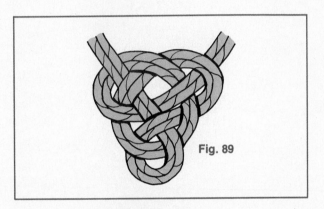

Fig. 89

**The Oriental Knot**

*Step 3:* Bring the cord under both strands of the loop, then through the loop catching the center cord. **Fig. 85.**

*Step 4:* Pull the knot into place. **Fig. 86.**

## ORIENTAL KNOT

This knot is also usually worked with more than one cord.

*Step 1:* Following the diagram make two loops with the starting end at the upper left hand side. **Fig. 87.**

*Step 2:* Following the diagram (**Fig. 88**) weave cords through the loops as shown by the arrow. Pull knot into place. **Fig. 89.**

## TURK'S HEAD KNOT

This ornamental knot can be worked in five simple steps.

*Step 1:* Following the diagram, make a loop. **Fig. 90.**

*Step 2:* Make a second loop over the first loop. Bring the cord under the starting cord. **Fig. 91.**

*Step 3:* Following the arrows work a third loop, bringing the cord over and under the center cords. **Fig. 92.**

*Step 4:* Bring the cord back around to follow the first loop. **Fig. 93.**

*Step 5:* Following the pattern exactly as set, reweave the cords through the loops as before three more times. **Fig. 94.**

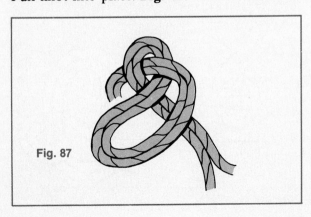

Fig. 87

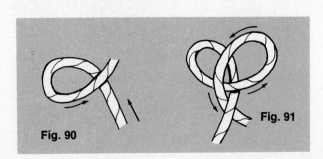

Fig. 90

Fig. 91

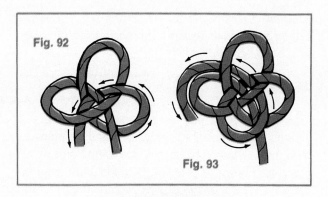

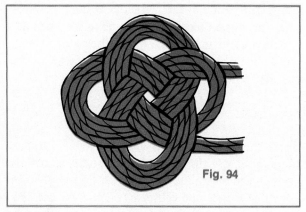

Turk's Head Knot

## INCREASING THE NUMBER OF CORDS

Adding new cords to a macramé project that is already begun can be used to introduce new color or change the shape of the design. There are several ways this can be accomplished.

*Method 1:* Add cord in the Square Knot. The new cord can be added to the holding line of the knot to make one new cord. **Fig. 95.** Looping the cord around a tying line of the knot adds two new cords. **Fig. 96.**

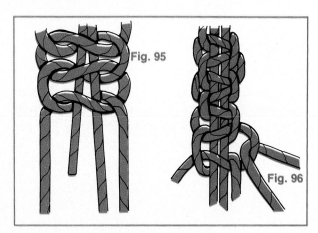

Adding New Cord in a Square Knot

*Method 2:* Add extra cord during the Clove Hitch Knot. One of the easiest techniques is to join additional holding lines in the Horizontal Clove Hitch Knot. **Fig. 97.** Each new holding line added will result in two new cords, one at each edge.

*Method 3:* Add an extra cord within the Clove Hitch Knot. **Fig. 98.** This method can be worked easily with the vertical, horizontal or diagonal Clove Hitch Knots and will supply extra working cord.

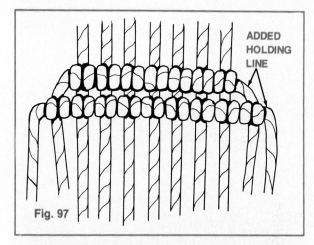

Adding Cord in a Clove Hitch Knot

*Method 4:* With the Clove Hitch Knot introduce a second dowel within the design. Tie the dowel in place with Horizontal Clove Hitch Knots. As many new cords as needed can be introduced to either side of the dowel with Lark's Head Knots.

*Method 5:* Mount an additional Lark's Head Knot at any open space during the knotting. This technique will result in two additional cords. **Fig. 99.**

## RUNNING OUT OF CORD

While it is best to cut cord lengths long enough at the beginning of a macramé project, it is difficult to prevent an occasional underestimation of the cord length needed to complete the work. When adding new cord always try to arrange the joined area within a knot.

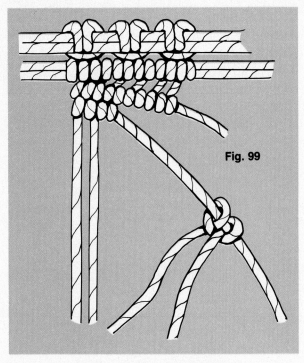

**Fig. 99**

Adding Cord with a Lark's Head Knot

## JOINING ADDITIONAL CORD

There are several ways to work the actual joining.

*Method 1:* Splice cords together as follows: Unravel the cord ends. **Fig. 100.** Dip the ends in white glue. Then twist the two cord ends together. Allow the joining to dry completely before continuing with the knotting.

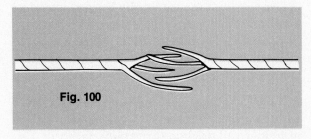

**Fig. 100**

Splicing Cord Together

*Method 2:* If working with nylon cords, melt the ends together by applying a wood burning tool or a lighted match to the two joined ends for a split second. It is wise to test this method with two pieces of extra cord before trying it on the actual macramé work.

*Method 3:* Follow the directions for adding a single cord given in the "Increasing the Number of Cords" section.

## MACRAMÉ ENDINGS

There are several ways to end macramé work. On articles such as wall hangings or hanging planters trim the cord ends to the desired length and tie an Overhand Knot to prevent the ends from fraying. This allows the cord ends to become a part of the design and adds to the attractiveness of the knotting. On some pieces of macramé work, such as a watchband, it is necessary to either glue, sew or weave the cord ends to the wrong side of the finished knotting.

### GLUING

Trim the cord ends to about 1 to 1½ inches, depending on the size of the article. Turn the ends to the back side of the work and apply a bit of white glue to the center of each cord end. Pin the ends in place with straight pins and allow the glue to dry thoroughly. Remove the pins and trim the remaining cord ends.

### SEWING

Soft, pliable cords can be sewed to the back of the macramé work with matching sewing thread. With heavier cords, such as jute or sisal, the roughness of the cord will eat through the sewing thread and the cord itself is too heavy to use for sewing. In this case dental floss serves very well as a thread. Dental floss is especially helpful when sewing the sides of a sisal or jute tote bag together.

### WEAVING

Use a crochet hook to weave cord ends under. Trim the ends to about 2 inches, and turn them to the back of the work. With the crochet hook pull the ends through the last row of knotting. For additional security, glue the cord ends with the weaving method.

## DYEING CORDS

Some macramé cords — such as cotton rug yarns, rattail cord and jute twine — can be purchased in a wide range of colors. Other cords such as sisal and nylon are available only in the natural color, and must be dyed if color is needed. It is possible to dye the cords separately, before the macramé is worked, or to dye the entire piece of macramé after the knotting has been completed. If the piece is very large, such as a wall hanging, it is best to dye the cords before beginning the knotting, since any large piece is extremely hard to dye in a pan. If the finished piece is to be exposed to a great deal of sunlight, such as a curtain, the color will probably fade.

When dyeing cord before knotting, be sure to allow a great deal of extra yardage. Many ropes and twines have a tendency to shrink in water. In any case, the ends will fray badly. It is also wise to dye extra cord, as it is nearly impossible to redye a duplicate lot of a color if the cord runs out while knitting. Natural fiber cords such as jute, cotton and linen will take dyes much easier than synthetic cords such as nylon, plastic or rayon.

Use any good commercial dye for your cords, following the instructions on the label. When dyeing cords before knotting, wrap the cord carefully and loosely in bundles and tie the bundles at both ends. Take great care that the cords do not become tangled.

## ORIGINALITY IN DESIGN

Macramé is one of the easiest crafts to individualize. Beads, shells, driftwood, mirrors, tree branches, feathers or buttons can be added to the project to make it unique.

Beads are among the most common "added touches." They can be purchased in glass, wood, plastic or ceramic, usually at the dime store jewelry counter. Many necklaces and bracelets with unusual plastic or wooden beads can be cut apart for use. Another place to try is the children's toy counter, where large colorful wooden play beads are available. When purchasing beads in a large quantity, always buy a few extras to guard against any imperfections. Be sure the holes are large enough for at least two cords to pass through. If the cord does not easily pass through the bead, it sometimes helps to dip the cord end in clear nail polish. Allow the polish to dry and harden before continuing with the knotting project. For very

stiff cord such as polished jute, use an emery board to file the end into a point.

Other extras for macramé, such as small shaped mirrors, can be purchased at stores specializing in party goods, and unique buttons can be purchased at any fabric store. Colorful plastic bracelets make unusual main holding lines and can be found in any dime store. Tree branches, acorns, driftwood and other natural products are also easily found. Using tree branches and driftwood as the main holding line provides the added beauty of three dimensional forms.

After learning the basic knots — the Square Knot and the Half Hitch — it is easy to recognize macramé knots in almost any photograph. In fact, when copying designs, it is often simpler to follow a good photograph rather than the written directions.

To develop a more personalized macramé project, here are a few helpful hints. Practice on one-yard lengths of cord to become accustomed to the knots. Next try working with five or six-foot lengths of cord to become accustomed to working with the long lengths. One of the best cords to use for practice is sisal twine. This cord is very common in hardware stores and is inexpensive. It is also large enough to see the knots while working and easy to untie in case of error.

In selecting colors for a project, red, copper, gold, tan and olive green add a rich touch to a design. Very dark colors do not show off knotting. They do, however, emphasize shape and cord movement.

When developing a project, place the emphasis on either pattern (the knots) or color. Too many knotting variations mixed with too many colors can be distracting.

Any article that is to be placed next to the skin, such as a choker or bracelet, should be made of a soft cord such as rattail or nylon twine. Rough cord used in a belt will snag any knit fabric.

Macramé pieces that will be subjected to much stress, such as a tote bag or rug, should be knotted in a much tighter pattern to allow for hard wear. Because of the additional knotting, this type of work will require much more cord.

For a macramé project that is to have a definite shape, or lay in a set position — such as a necklace — it often helps to run a very thin wire next to the main holding line.

## MACRAMÉ VEST

Interested in knotting a macramé vest? It is possible. First, find a regular clothing pattern with three finished pieces, no darts, and only the two side seams. To locate this pattern type, look in the "knits only" group of patterns produced by all major pattern companies. Select the size as if the vest were going to be sewn. Since a clothing pattern usually contains only one half of the pattern for a finished garment, trace the pattern in reverse for the second side of the vest.

Select a soft cord such as rattail, cotton rug yarn or nylon for the vest. A stiff cord will be too stiff to wear comfortably. Plan your design to be fairly open, as too much knotting will also cause stiffness.

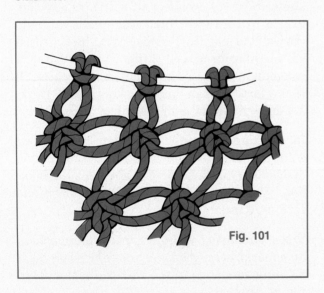

**Fig. 101**

The vest itself should be made in one piece, so that only the shoulder seams need to be sewn when finished. Lay the entire pattern out on a large knotting board. Overlap the seam areas since these areas will not be worked into the garment. Use the pattern as a guide for the size and shape of the vest. At the underarm add new cords for additional width. **Fig. 101.** This is usually done with additional Lark's Head Knots, although all of the methods listed in the "Increasing the Number of Cords" section will work.

When the vest is finished, sew the shoulder seams, and if fringe is not desired, the hem. To sew the hem in place, machine stitch blanket binding around the bottom of the vest. Cut the cords fairly close to the machine stitching, then machine stitch the same seam again for extra strength. Turn the binding to the wrong side of the vest and stitch into place.

## CAVANDOLI WORK

Cavandoli work was developed in Italy at the beginning of this century by a woman who was looking for something to occupy young school children in her care. This style of knotting is totally different from all others in that a design is developed by following a chart on graph paper. It is the easiest form of macramé to plan. Using graph paper, you can chart birds, flowers, geometric shapes or many other. Cavandoli work is solid knotting, using only the Clove Hitch Knots. It requires much more cord than the more open macramé designs. Cavandoli work is also especially strong, and is the best form of macramé to use when making rugs. The one drawback to this style is that it is very time consuming to work.

On the graph **(Fig. 102)** each square represents one knot. The blank squares represent the Horizontal Clove Hitch Knots, while the x squares represent the Vertical Clove Hitch Knots. The cords arranged from top to bottom are of one color, while the cord worked from side to side is of another color. When the Horizontal Clove Hitch Knot is tied, the top to bottom color shows. When the Vertical Clove Hitch Knot is tied, the side to side color appears. **Fig. 103.** The

same cord is used to work across the piece at all times. Since the cord worked across must be extremely long, it is usually easier to work with the whole ball of cord rather than the shorter lengths.

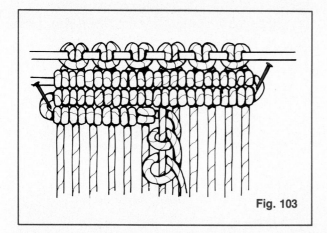

Fig. 103

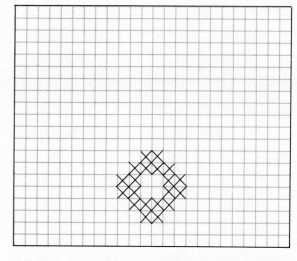

Diagrams for Second Color on Cavandoli Work, page 551.

## INDEX OF KNOTTING TECHNIQUES

# MACRAMÉ PROJECTS

Cavandoli Work as seen from both sides.

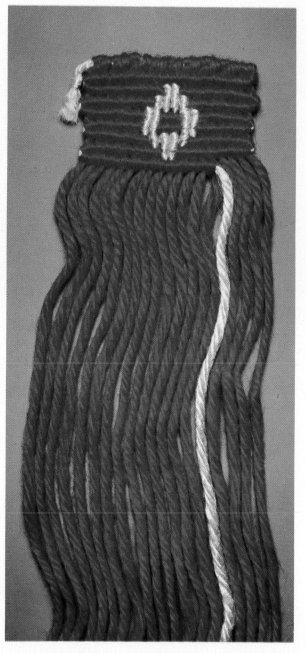

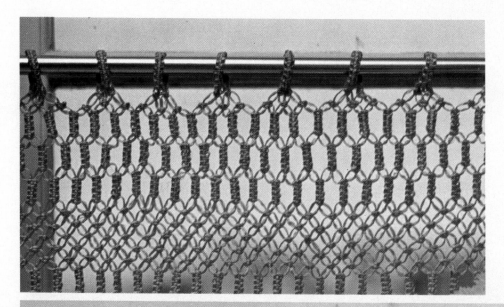

## STRAW CURTAIN

**SIZE:** About 16 inches long, including fringe.
**MATERIALS:** Straw yarn, 290 yards beige. Curtain rod. Note: If you have a hard time finding straw yarn, Lily Soft Sheen Craft Yarn can be used as a substitute.

**Note:** If working with straw yarn, tie all knots loosely. Tie each row of knots ¹/₂ inch below last row.

Cut 48 four-yard cords.

*Step 1:* Fold 4 cords in half. At exact center tie 20 Square Knots. Arrange Square Knots over top of rod as shown in photograph — 8 cords per group. Repeat this step until you have 12 groups of cords across curtain rod.
*Step 2:* With the 4 center cords of each group, tie one Square Knot.
*Step 3:* For each group, cut another cord 4 yards long. Fold the new cord in half. Using the 2 new cords, plus 2 cords from right-hand side of group, tie another Square Knot on same row with the Square Knot of Step 2.
*Step 4:* Repeat Step 3 on the left-hand side.
*Step 5:* With the 2 left-hand cords from the first group and 2 right-hand cords from the second group, tie 5 Square Knots.
*Step 6:* Divide the remaining cords into groups of 4 cords each, tie 5 Square Knots on each group.
*Step 7:* With the 2 remaining cords left unworked at each outside edge of the curtain, tie 5 Half Hitch Knots.
*Step 8:* Beginning at the outside edge, divide the cords into groups of 4 cords per group. Tie 5 Square Knots on each group.
*Step 9:* Leaving 2 cords on each edge unworked, repeat Step 8.
*Step 10:* Repeat Step 7.
*Step 11:* Beginning at the outside edge, divide the cords as in Step 8. Tie one Square Knot on each group.
*Step 12:* Leaving 2 cords on each edge unworked, repeat Step 11.
*Step 13:* Repeat Steps 11 and 12 one time more; then repeat Step 11.
*Step 14:* Repeat Step 9.
*Step 15:* Repeat Steps 8 and 9; then repeat Step 8.
*Step 16:* Tie an Overhand Knot, as shown in the photograph.

**Finishing:** Trim cord ends to 5 inches, or desired length.

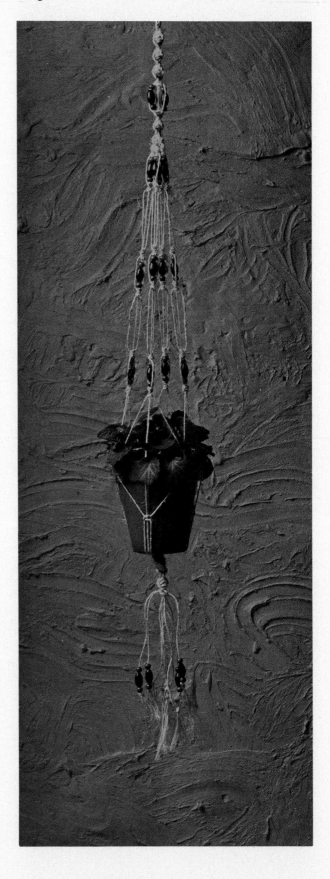

## HANGING PLANTER

**SIZE:** About 52 inches long.

**MATERIALS:** Sisal twine, one ply, 54 yards. Metal ring, 2 inches in diameter. Eighteen brown oblong wooden beads. Thirty-six red wooden beads, 1/2 inch in diameter. Clay flower pot, red paint. Rubber bands.

Cut six 9-yard cords.

*Step 1:* Fold each cord in half and tie it to the ring with a Lark's Head Knot — 12 cords. Bundle excess cord and secure with a rubber band.

*Step 2:* With the 2 outside cords at each edge, tie 20 Granny Knots over the 8 center cords.

*Step 3:* String one red, one brown, and one red bead on the second cord from each outside edge.

*Step 4:* With 2 outside cords at each edge, tie 10 Granny Knots over the 8 center cords.

*Step 5:* Divide the cords into 4 groups of 3 cords per group.

*Step 6:* On each group tie 10 Granny Knots.

*Step 7:* On the center cord of each group, string one red bead, one brown, and one red bead in place.

*Step 8:* Tie 5 Granny Knots directly under the beads.

*Step 9:* Again, working with the same groups of cords as before, and leaving 3 inches of cord unworked, tie 5 more Granny Knots.

*Step 10:* Repeat Steps 7 and 8.

*Step 11:* Repeat Steps 9 and 10.

*Step 12:* Leaving 4 inches of cord unworked, using one outside cord from one group with the outside cord of the adjoining group, tie an Overhand Knot. Working in this fashion, tie Overhand Knots around.

*Step 13:* Divide cords as they were in Step 5. Leaving 4 inches of cord unworked, tie a Square Knot with each group.

*Step 14:* About 2 inches below the last knots, gather all of the cords together and tie one large Overhand Knot.

*Step 15:* Tie 10 Granny Knots directly under the Overhand Knot.

**Finishing:** Cut cord ends to 12 inches. String beads in place as shown in photograph. Tie an Overhand Knot on all of the cord ends. Untwist the cord ends below the Overhand Knots.

## GREEN AND SILVER RING

**SIZE:** Make to desired size.

**MATERIALS:** Lily Metallic Thread, silver, 1 skein; six-strand embroidery floss, kelly green, 1 skein. Knotting board, pins, sewing needle, and white glue.

**Note:** Use all six strands embroidery floss. For each individual metallic cord, cut six strands. Work the six strands as one throughout. Cut yardage for 2 silver cords and 2 green cords, each 16 inches long.

*Step 1:* Center and pin one green cord on the knotting board. Center silver cords and tie Clove Hitch Knots over the green cord — 6 cords.

*Step 2:* Using right green cord as holding line, tie Clove Hitch Knots across.

*Step 3:* Center second green cord across directly under the last row. Using new cord as holding line, tie Clove Hitch Knots across — 8 cords.

*Step 4:* Beginning at right-hand edge, tie 2 more rows of Diagonal Clove Hitch Knots.

*Step 5:* Beginning at right edge, tie Vertical Clove Hitch Knots across.

*Step 6:* Repeat Step 5 two times more. All green cords are now at the right, all silver cords at the left.

*Step 7:* Beginning at right-hand edge, tie Diagonal Clove Hitch Knots to the opposite side.

*Step 8:* Repeat Step 7 four times more.

*Step 9:* Repeat Steps 5 through 8 to desired length.

**Finishing:** With sewing needle tack cord ends to the back of the starting row. Apply a bit of white glue to secure the cords in place.

## JUTE WALL HANGING

**SIZE:** About 20 inches long, plus fringe.

**MATERIALS:** Lily Jute-Tone, #4 Natural, 1 skein. Eighteen brown oblong wooden beads, 1 inch long; 20 brown rounded wooden beads, ½ inch in diameter. One plastic ring, 3 inches in diameter.

Cut twelve 6-yard cords. Fold the cords in half and tie Lark's Head Knots over the plastic ring — 24 cords. Fold the extra yardage in bundles and fasten at the center with a rubber band.

*Step 1:* Beginning at outer edge on each side and following the shape of the ring, tie Horizontal Clove Hitch Knots directly under Lark's Head Knots to the center. Tie Chevron Clove Hitch Knot at the center.

*Step 2:* String one oblong bead on each outer-edge cord.

*Step 3:* Beginning at the center, tie Horizontal Clove Hitch Knots to the outside edges.

*Step 4:* Repeat Step 3 two times more.

*Step 5:* Keeping cords divided into two equal groups, with 4 center cords of each group tie 10 Granny Knots.

*Step 6:* With remaining outside cords, beginning at the inner edge, tie Horizontal Clove Hitch Knots to the outside edges.

*Step 7:* Repeat Step 6 two times more.

*Step 8:* Working with the same 8 cords as in Step 7, beginning at outside edges, tie Horizontal Clove Hitch Knots to the center.

*Step 9:* Repeat Step 8 three times more.

*Step 10:* Beginning at outside edges and working to the center, tie Horizontal Clove Hitch Knots across all 12 cords on each side.

*Step 11:* Tie Chevron Clove Hitch Knot at the center.

*Step 12:* With 4 center cords tie 6 Square Knots.

*Step 13:* Bring all 4 cords of Square Knot in Step 12 around the back, through the center hole, and to the front.

*Step 14:* Leaving one cord unworked each edge, tie Vertical Clove Hitch Knots to the center.

*Step 15:* Repeat Step 14 one time more.

*Step 16:* With outer edge cord left unworked in Step 14, tie Diagonal Clove Hitch Knots to the center, molding the cord to fit the last rows of knots.

*Step 17:* With 4 outside cords at each edge, tie 15 Granny Knots.

*Step 18:* With fifth cord from each outside edge, string one oblong bead in place.

*Step 19:* Working toward the center, with the next 4 cords tie 15 Granny Knots.

*Step 20:* On tenth cord from each outside edge, string one oblong bead in place.

*Step 21:* With 4 center cords, tie 15 Granny Knots.

*Step 22:* Beginning at outside edges, tie Diagonal Clove Hitch Knots to the center. Tie Chevron Clove Hitch Knot at the center.

*Step 23:* Repeat Step 22 one time more.

*Step 24:* Beginning at the center, tie Diagonal Clove Hitch Knots to outside edges.

*Step 25:* Repeat Step 24 one time more. Steps 22 through 25 form an X.

*Step 26:* With 4 center cords tie 20 Granny Knots.

*Step 27:* Repeat Steps 22 and 23.

*Step 28:* Beginning with the first cord at each outside edge, string one rounded bead on every other cord.

*Step 29:* Beginning at the outside edge, tie Diagonal Clove Hitch Knots to the center.

*Step 30:* Repeat Step 29 one time more.

*Step 31:* Beginning at the center, tie Horizontal Clove Hitch Knots to outside edges.

*Step 32:* Repeat Step 31 two times more.

*Step 33:* String one oblong bead on each of the two center cords.

*Step 34:* Beginning at outside edges, tie Diagonal Clove Hitch Knots to the center.

*Step 35:* Repeat Step 34 one time more.

*Step 36:* Beginning at the center tie Diagonal Clove Hitch Knots to outside edges.

*Step 37:* Repeat Step 36 two times more.

*Step 38:* Repeat Steps 34 and 35.

*Step 39:* String one oblong bead in place on each outside edge cord.

*Step 40:* Beginning at outside edges, tie Horizontal Clove Hitch Knots to the center.

*Step 41:* Repeat Step 40 three times more.

*Step 42:* With 4 center cords, tie 10 Granny Knots.

*Step 43:* With 4 cords at each side of Granny Knots in Step 42, tie 8 Granny Knots.

**Finishing:** String remaining beads at random on the cord ends. Tie an Overhand Knot below each bead to hold it in place. Tie Overhand Knots on the remainder of the cords. Trim ends to desired length.

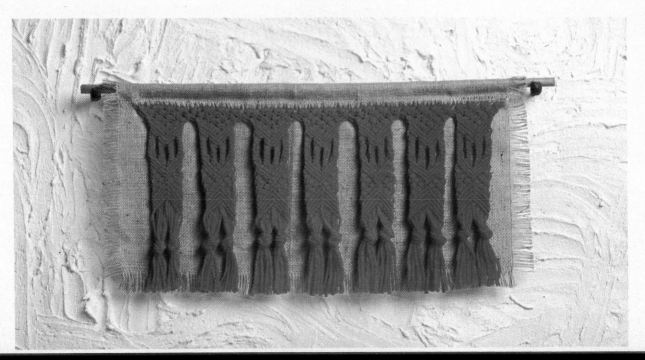

## BLUE BAG

**SIZE:** About 10 inches wide.
**MATERIALS:** Lily Soft Sheen Craft Yarn, 3 skeins #36, Turquoise. Button, matching sewing thread, white glue. Knotting board and pins.

**Note:** Bag is worked in three separate pieces — the flap and back, the front and the strap.

Cut 28 seven-yard cords.

**Step 1:** Beginning at the point of the front flap, center one cord across knotting board (main holding line). Fold 2 cords in half and tie to the main holding line with Reverse Lark's Head Knots. Allow cords of the main holding line to drop in place beside the cords just added — 6 cords across.

**Step 2:** Arrange another cord across directly under the Lark's Head Knots. Tie Horizontal Clove Hitch Knots across. Allow the cords to drop to the side as before — 8 cords.

**Step 3:** Arranging another cord across directly under the last row of knots, repeat Step 2 — 10 cords.

**Step 4:** Divide cords into 2 equal groups of 5 cords per group. Beginning with the center cord on each side, tie Horizontal Clove Hitch Knots to the outside edges.

**Step 5:** Beginning at the outside edges, tie Horizontal Clove Hitch Knots to the center.
**Step 6:** Repeat Step 4.
**Step 7:** Repeat Step 5. Buttonhole complete.
**Step 8:** Repeat Step 3 — 12 cords.
**Step 9:** Repeat Step 3 — 14 cords.
**Step 10:** Repeat Step 3 — 16 cords.
**Step 11:** Divide cords into 4 groups of 4 cords per group. Tie one Square Knot on each group.
**Step 12:** Fold a new cord in half. Pin it to the right side and just below the Square Knots of the last row. Using the 2 new cords and the 2 cords from the right hand side of the previous Square Knot, tie another Square Knot.
**Step 13:** Repeat Step 12 on left side — 20 cords.
**Step 14:** On the 12 center cords divide the cords into 3 groups of 4 cords per group. Tie a Square Knot on each group.
**Step 15:** Repeat Steps 12 and 13 — 24 cords.
**Step 16:** Following the pattern as established, tie 4 Square Knots across center cords.

**Step 17:** Continue repeating Steps 12 and 13, adding center cords into Square Knot pattern, until there are 14 Square Knots across — 56 cords.
**Step 18:** Leaving 2 cords on each edge unworked, tie 13 Square Knots across remaining cords.
**Step 19:** Beginning with the cords at the outside edge, following the pattern as established, tie 14 Square Knots across.
**Step 20:** Cut 2 cords, each 16 inches long. Using the 2 cords held together as one, place the cords across the cords of the last row of Square Knots. Tie Horizontal Clove Hitch Knots over the cords. Leave the ends of these cords unworked. They will be secured to the back of the bag when the macrame is finished.
**Step 21:** Divide the cords into groups of 4 cords per group. Tie one Square Knot with each group — 14 Square Knots across.
**Step 22:** Leaving 2 cords on each edge unworked, tie 13 Square Knots across.
**Step 23:** Repeat Steps 21 and 22 for 12 inches.
**Front:** Cut 28 four yard cords. Cut three 16 inch cords. Using the 3 short cords held together as one for a main holding line, fold the remaining cords in half and tie to the main holding line with Lark's Head Knots — 56 cords.
Repeat Steps 22 and 23 for 9 inches.
**Strap:** Cut two 6-yard cords and one 16-yard cord. Cut two 4-inch cords for main holding line. Fold 6-yard cords in half and tie to the holding line with Lark's Head Knots — four 3-yard cords. Fold the last cord so that outer edge cord is 13 yards long. Fasten the last cord with a Lark's Head Knot to the main holding line.
**Step 1:** With the long outer edge cord, tie Horizontal Clove Hitch Knots to opposite side.
**Step 2:** Leaving a small space between each row, as shown in the photograph, using the same cord as before, tie Horizontal Clove Hitch Knots to opposite side.
**Step 3:** Repeating Steps 1 and 2, continue working longer cord back and forth across the 5 cords. Work the piece until it is long enough to fit around the pieces of the bag and is of a comfortable shoulder length (about 55 inches). Sew strap ends together.
**Finishing:** Cut all cord ends to about 2 inches. Sew front piece to strap as shown in photograph. Place back/flap piece in place and sew to the

strap. Weave cord ends in on the inside of the bag; then, apply a bit of white glue to each cord to secure in place. Sew button in place on the front.

## BURLAP AND RED WALL HANGING

**SIZE:** 12 inches x 24 inches.
**MATERIALS:** Lily Soft Sheen Craft Yarn, #95 red, two 105-yard skeins. A piece of natural brown burlap, 15 inches x 24 inches. Dowel, 28 inches long. Stain for dowel.

About 5 inches from top of the burlap (top is 24-inch edge), pull out about ½ inch of the threads. Cut 56 two and one-half yard cords. Pull cords through the threaded burlap so that the lengths are even — 112 cords.

**Section 1:** All cords are used in the first section.

**Step 1:** Using 4 cords per knot, tie 28 Square Knots across.
**Step 2:** Leaving 2 cords on each edge unworked, tie 27 Square Knots across.
**Step 3:** Repeat Step 1.
**Step 4:** Repeat Step 2.

**Section 2:** Divide the cords into 7 groups of 16 cords per group. Macramé will now be worked separately on each group of cords. On each group of 16 cords, work as follows:

**Step 1:** On the 8 center cords, tie 2 Square Knots using 4 cords per knot.
**Step 2:** Tie 1 Square Knot on the 4 center cords.
**Step 3:** Beginning at the outside edge on each side, tie Diagonal Clove Hitch Knots to the center. Tie a Chevron Clove Hitch Knot at the center.
**Step 4:** Repeat Step 3 two times more.
**Step 5:** Divide the cords into 4 groups of 4 cords per group. On each group tie 5 Square Knots.
**Step 6:** Repeat Steps 3 and 4.
**Step 7:** Working at the side of the Diagonal Clove Hitch Knots, with the 4 cords at each outside edge, tie one Square Knot.
**Step 8:** Leaving 2 cords on each edge unworked, tie one Square Knot on the next 4 cords.
**Step 9:** With the 8 cords at each edge, tie 2 Square Knots using 4 cords per knot.
**Step 10:** Repeat Step 8.

**Step 11:** With the 4 cords at each edge, tie one Square Knot.
**Step 12:** Beginning at the center with a Chevron Clove Hitch Knot, tie Diagonal Clove Hitch Knots to the outside edges.
**Step 13:** Repeat Step 12 three times more.

**Finishing:** Tie 2 Overhand Knots on each section as shown in photograph. Trim cord even with the burlap. Fold the top of the burlap to the back and stitch in place. Slide the dowel through the seam. Fringe burlap about one inch at bottom and sides.

## BEIGE BELT

**SIZE:** About 26 inches, including buckle.
**MATERIALS:** Lily Soft Sheen Craft Yarn, # 90 Beige, one 105-yard skein. Belt buckle, 2 inches. Knotting board, pins, crochet hook, white glue.

**Note:** Belt is worked from the point (beginning) to the buckle (ending).

Cut eight 6½-yard cords.

**Step 1:** Beginning at the point, fold 2 cords in half and pin them side by side on the knotting board — 4 cords.
**Step 2:** Tie one Square Knot with these cords.
**Step 3:** Fold one more cord in half. Pin it to the right side and just below the Square Knot of Step 2. Using the 2 new cords and the 2 cords from the right hand side of the previous Square Knot, tie another Square Knot.
**Step 4:** Repeat Step 3 on left side — 8 cords.
**Step 5:** Fold another cord in half. Pin it to the right and just below the Square Knot of Step 3. Using the 2 new cords and the 2 right hand cords from the previous knot, tie another Square Knot.
**Step 6:** Repeat Step 5 on the left hand side — 12 cords.
**Step 7:** Following Steps 5 and 6, add another folded cord to each side of the belt — 16 cords. Following pattern, tie two Square Knots at the center.
**Step 8:** Leaving 2 cords on each edge unworked, tie 3 Square Knots across.
**Step 9:** Divide the cords into 4 groups of 4 cords per group. Tie 4 Square Knots across.
**Step 10:** Repeat Steps 8 and 9 six times more.

**Step 11:** Leaving 4 cords on each edge unworked, tie two Square Knots across.

**Step 12:** On the 4 center cords, tie one Square Knot.

**Step 13:** Beginning at each outside edge, tie Diagonal Clove Hitch Knots to the center.

**Step 14:** Tie Chevron Clove Hitch Knot at the center.

**Step 15:** Beginning at the center, tie Diagonal Clove Hitch Knots to outside edges.

**Step 16:** Repeat Step 12.

**Step 17:** Repeat Step 11.

**Step 18:** Repeat Step 8.

**Step 19:** Repeat Step 11.

**Step 20:** Repeat Step 12.

**Step 21:** Repeat Steps 13 through 20 until you have a total of 8 diamond shapes.

**Step 22:** Repeat Steps 15 through 18 for one more half diamond shape.

**Step 23:** Tie 4 Square Knots across.

**Step 24:** Leaving 2 cords on each edge unworked, tie three Square Knots across.

**Step 25:** Repeat Steps 23 and 24 from about 2 inches.

**Finishing:** Place buckle through the belt so that about 3/4 inch of the knotting will fold to the back. Trim cord ends to 2 inches. With a crochet hook, pull cords through the knotting on the back. Place a small drop of white glue on each cord end and pin the cord ends to the belt until the glue dries. Trim ends.

## GREEN BELT WITH WOODEN BEADS

**SIZE:** About 26 inches, including buckle.

**MATERIALS:** Lily Soft Sheen Craft Yarn, #62 Emerald Green, one 105-yard skein. Belt buckle, 1 3/4 inches. Seven green wooden beads about 1/2 inch in diameter. Knotting board, pins, crochet hook, white glue.

**Note:** Belt is worked from the point (beginning) to the buckle (ending).

Cut 6 seven-yard cords.

**Step 1:** Beginning at the point, fold 2 cords in half and pin them side by side on the knotting board — 4 cords.

**Step 2:** Tie one Square Knot with these cords.

**Step 3:** Fold one more cord in half. Pin it to the right side and just below the Square Knot of Step 2. Using the 2 new cords and the 2 cords from the right-hand side of the previous Square Knot, tie another Square Knot.

**Step 4:** Repeat Step 3 on left side — 8 cords.

**Step 5:** Fold another cord in half. Pin it to the right and just below the Square Knot of Step 3. Using 2 new cords and 2 right-hand cords from the previous knot, tie another Square Knot.

**Step 6:** Repeat Step 5 on left-hand side — 12 cords. Tie a Square Knot on the 4 center cords.

**Step 7:** Leaving 2 cords on each edge unworked, tie 2 Square Knots across.

**Step 8:** Divide the cords into 3 groups of 4 cords per group. Tie a Square Knot on each group of cords.

**Step 9:** Repeat Steps 7 and 8 six times more.

**Step 10:** Repeat Step 7.

**Step 11:** With 8 cords on left-hand side, work 2 Square Knots.

**Step 12:** Leaving 2 cords on left-hand side unworked, tie one Square Knot with next 4 cords.

**Step 13:** With 4 cords on left-hand side, tie one Square Knot.

**Step 14:** On right-hand side, beginning at outside edge, tie Diagonal Clove Hitch Knots to opposite side.

**Step 15:** On third cord from the left edge, string one bead in place.

**Step 16:** Beginning at left edge, tie Diagonal Clove Hitch Knots to opposite edge.

**Step 17:** Repeat Step 13.

**Step 18:** Repeat Step 12.

**Step 19:** Repeat Step 11.

**Step 20:** Leaving two cords on each edge unworked, tie 2 Square Knots across.

**Step 21:** Repeat Step 11.

**Step 22:** Repeat Step 12.

**Step 23:** Repeat Step 13.

**Step 24:** Repeat Steps 14 through 23 until seven triangles have been formed. End Step 20.

**Step 25:** Repeat Steps 7 and 8 for about 2 inches.

**Finishing:** Place buckle through belt so that about 3/4 inch of the knotting will fold to the back. Trim cord ends to 2 inches. With crochet hook, pull cord ends through knotting on the back. Place a bit of white glue on each cord end and pin ends to the belt until glue dries. Trim ends.

**Strap:** Cut 6 eight-inch cords. Using outside cord at each edge, tie Square Knots over 4 center cords. Place on belt as shown in photograph. Glue cord ends to the back of the belt.

## GOLD WATCH STRAP

**SIZE:** Each side about 2¹/₂ inches long.

**MATERIALS:** Lily Metallic Thread, gold, one skein. Watch face, watch buckle.

**Note:** Work with 6 cords held together as one throughout.

Cut enough yardage for eight 25-inch cords.

### FLAP SIDE
*Step 1:* Fold cord in half and tie to watch face with Reverse Lark's Head Knots — 16 cords.
*Step 2:* Divide cords into two groups of 8 cords per group. Beginning at the center on each side, tie Horizontal Clove Hitch Knots to the outside edges.
*Step 3:* Beginning at each outside edge, tie Diagonal Clove Hitch Knots to the center.
*Step 4:* Repeat Step 3 two times more. Tie a Chevron Clove Hitch Knot at the center.
*Step 5:* Beginning at the center, tie Diagonal Clove Hitch Knots to the outside edges.
*Step 6:* Repeat Step 5 two times more.
*Step 7:* Beginning at the outside edges, tie Horizontal Clove Hitch Knots to the center. Tie a Chevron Clove Hitch Knot at the center.
*Step 8:* Beginning at the center, tie Horizontal Clove Hitch Knots to the outside edges.
*Step 9:* Repeat Steps 3 and 4.
*Step 10:* Repeat Steps 5 and 6.
*Step 11:* Repeat Steps 7 and 8.
*Step 12:* Tying 2 less cords on each edge of each row, continue tying Horizontal Clove Hitch Knots to the center. Work until a point is formed.

### Buckle Side
*Step 13:* Cut cords and attach to watch face as before.
*Step 14:* Repeat Steps 1 through 10.
*Step 15:* Repeat Step 11 for 15 rows.
**Finishing:** Slide buckle in place. Weave excess cord through the reverse side of the watch band. Apply a bit of white glue to each cord end to secure in place.

## BLUE AND RED WATCH STRAP

**SIZE:** Each strap about 3 inches long.
**MATERIALS:** Lily Double-Quick Crochet Cotton, #98 Scarlet, 3 yards; and #28 Navy, 14 yards. Watch face, watch buckle. Knotting board, pins, crochet hook, white glue.

**Note:** Work with 2 cords held together as one throughout.

Cut yardage for one scarlet tying cord and 5 navy tying cords, each 24 inches long. Lay the remainder of the cord aside for the other half of the watch band.

*Step 1:* Tie 4 cords to watch face with Reverse Lark's Head Knots — 8 cords.
*Step 2:* Center the fifth blue cord across the cords directly under the Reverse Lark's Head Knots. Using the new cord as a holding line, tie Horizontal Clove Hitch Knots across — 10 cords.
*Step 3:* Center the scarlet cord, tie Horizontal Clove Hitch Knots as in Step 2 — 12 cords.
*Step 4:* Divide the cords into 2 equal groups of 6 cords per group.
*Step 5:* Beginning with the inside cord at each inner edge, tie Horizontal Clove Hitch Knots to the outside edges.
*Step 6:* Repeat Step 5 one time more.
*Step 7:* With the second cord from each outside edge, tie one Diagonal Clove Hitch Knot to the outside edge.
*Step 8:* With the fourth cord from each outside edge, tie Diagonal Clove Hitch Knots to the outside edges.
*Step 9:* With the inside cord of each group, tie Diagonal Clove Hitch Knots to the outside edges.
*Step 10:* Repeat Step 9 three times more.
*Step 11:* Tying Chevron Clove Hitch Knot at the center on each row, continue tying Diagonal Clove Hitch Knots until the scarlet cords meet at the center.
*Step 12:* Beginning at the center, following the shape of the last row, tie Vertical Clove Hitch Knots to the outside edges.
*Step 13:* Repeat Step 12 working one less cord at each outside edge to form a point.
*Step 14:* Side 2: Follow the same directions as for Side 1, beginning with Step 1.
**Finishing:** Trim cord ends to about 1¹/₂ inches. Pull cords around the point and through the back knots with a crochet hook. Place a bit of white glue on each cord end to secure in place.
*Buckle:* Place buckle just below the scarlet X. Finish as with opposite side, weaving the cord ends through the back of the strap.

## TABLE MAT

**SIZE:** About 16 inches x 21 inches, plus fringe.
**MATERIALS:** For one table mat: Lily Sugar-'N-Cream Cotton Yarn, two 125-yard skeins #1 white and two 125-yard skeins #17 gold. White glue. Note: For one mat you will need 160 yards white and 210 yards gold.

**Note:** All cords are to be folded in half and tied to a main holding line. If you prefer to work with a knotting board, use another cord for the main holding line; or if you prefer the "hanging free" method use a dowel. When the mat is finished the Lark's Head Knots will be cut off.

Cut 40 gold cords and 30 white cords, each 5 yards long.

**Step 1:** Fold all of the cords in half and tie them to the main holding line in the following order: Beginning with gold, 10 cords of each color alternating the white and the gold — 280 cords. You will have 4 gold stripes and 3 white stripes.
**Step 2:** Cut two 20-inch cords. Using the two cords held together as one, lay the cords across the stripes about 1 1/2 inches below the Lark's Head Knots. Using the new cord as a holding line, tie Horizontal Clove Hitch Knots across all 280 cords. This holding cord will not be used again, and the ends will be glued to the back of the mat when the macrame is finished.
**Step 3:** Divide the cords into groups of 4 cords per group. Tie one Square Knot on each group of cords — 70 Square Knots.
**Step 4:** With the 2 cords at each outside edge, tie a Half Hitch Knot. Divide the remaining cords into groups of four cords per group. Tie a Square Knot on each group — 69 Square Knots.
**Step 5:** Repeat Steps 3 and 4 one time more.
**Step 6:** Repeat Step 3.
**Step 7:** Repeat Step 2, tying the new row of Horizontal Clove Hitch Knots directly under the last row of Square Knots.
**Step 8:** Leave cords unworked for 3/4 inch. As in Step 2, tie another row of Horizontal Clove Hitch Knots across.
**Step 9:** Repeat Steps 3 and 4 for about 17 1/2 inches, end Step 3.
**Step 10:** Repeat Step 7.
**Step 11:** Repeat Step 8.
**Step 12:** Repeat Steps 3 and 4 two times more.
**Step 13:** Repeat Step 3.
**Step 14:** Repeat Step 7.

**Finishing:** Glue Horizontal Clove Hitch ends to the back with white glue. Cut fringe on both sides to one inch.

## RED, GOLD AND PURPLE CLOVE HITCH WALL HANGING

**SIZE:** About nine inches, plus fringe.

**MATERIALS:** Lily Soft Sheen Craft Yarn, #95 red, #17 gold, and #75 purple. Dowel, 12 inches long.

**Note:** Work entire hanging with two cords held together as one.

Cut enough 6 yard cord lengths for 5 red, 4 purple, and 6 gold cords. Fold cord in half and tie to the dowel with Lark's Head Knots in the following order: 3 gold, 2 purple, 5 red, 2 purple, and 3 gold — 30 cords.
**Step 1:** Beginning at the center, tie Horizontal Clove Hitch Knots to each outside edge.
**Step 2:** Repeat Step 1 four times more — five red cords at each outside edge.
**Step 3:** Leaving center purple cords unworked, tie Horizontal Clove Hitch Knots to the outside edges.
**Step 4:** Repeat Step 3 until all gold cords are at the outside edges.
**Step 5:** Beginning with the inside red cord on each side, tie Vertical Clove Hitch Knots to the outside edges.
**Step 6:** Following Step 5, tie 9 Vertical Clove Hitch Knots across.
**Step 7:** Following pattern as established, tying one less Vertical Clove Hitch Knot each row, work until all red cords are at the outside edges. Trim the red cords to 4 inches for fringe.
**Step 8:** Beginning with the inner purple cord on each side, working toward the outside edges, tie Diagonal Clove Hitch Knots over the next 3 cords.
**Step 9:** Working with purple cords only, repeat Step 8 eleven times more.
**Step 10:** Working with only the gold cords, beginning at the outside edges, tie Horizontal Clove Hitch Knots across.

*Step 11:* Repeat Step 10 five times more.

*Step 12:* Beginning at the center, with the purple cords, tie Vertical Clove Hitch Knots to the outside edges.

*Step 13:* Repeat Step 12 three times more — 4 purple cords at each outside edge.

*Step 14:* Working on purple cords only, using fourth cord from each outside edge as a holding line, the Horizontal Clove Hitch Knots to outside edges.

*Step 15:* Repeat Step 14 three times more.

*Step 16:* Working on purple cords only, beginning with the inside cord, tie Vertical Clove Hitch Knots across 3 cords.

*Step 17:* Repeat Step 16, tying knots across 2 cords.

*Step 18:* Repeat Step 16, tying knot over one cord. Trim purple cords to 4 inches for fringe.

*Step 19:* Working with gold cords only, beginning with outside edge cords and working toward the center, tie Horizontal Clove Hitch Knots across.

*Step 20:* Repeat Step 19 two times more. Trim gold cords to 3 inches.

## RED, BROWN AND GOLD TOTE BAG

**SIZE:** About eight inches long.

**MATERIALS:** Lily Jute-Tone, 2 skeins each red and gold, 1 skein brown. Red cotton fabric, 12 inches x 18 inches. Matching thread. Rubber bands to bundle the cords.

Cut 16 gold cords, 12 red cords, and 6 brown cords each 5 yards long. Cut three 12-inch cords. Using the 3 shorter cords held together as one for the main holding line, fold the longer cords in half and tie to the main holding line in the following order: 8 gold cords, 6 red, 6 brown, 6 red, and 8 gold — 68 cords. Wrap excess cord in bundles and secure with a rubber band.

*Step 1:* Divide the cords into groups of 4 cords per group. Tie 2 square knots with each group.

*Step 2:* Leaving 2 cords on each edge unworked, repeat Step 1.

*Step 3:* Leaving 4 cords on each edge unworked, repeat Step 1.

*Step 4:* Leaving 6 cords on each edge unworked, repeat Step 1.

*Step 5:* Following the pattern as established, continue working 2 less cords each edge on each row until a point is formed at the center.

*Step 6:* Beginning at each outside edge, tie Diagonal Clove Hitch Knots to the center. Tie a Chevron Clove Hitch Knot at the center.

*Step 7:* Repeat Step 6 five times more — 12 gold cords at the center.

*Step 8:* With the 4 cords at each outside edge, tie one Square Knot.

*Step 9:* Working again at the outside edges, leaving 2 cords on each edge unworked, tie a Square Knot with the next 4 cords.

*Step 10:* Beginning at the outside edge, tie 2 Square Knots across.

*Step 11:* Leaving 2 cords on each edge unworked, tie 2 Square Knots across.

*Step 12:* Beginning at the outside edge, tie 3 Square Knots across.

*Step 13:* Leaving 2 cords on each edge unworked, tie 3 Square Knots across.

*Step 14:* Following the pattern as established, continue tying the Square Knot pattern until the last row of knots is even with the point of the Diagonal Clove Hitch Knots.

*Step 15:* Repeat Steps 1 and 2 for 8 inches.

*Step 16:* Cut 3 gold cords, each 12 inches long. Working with these 3 cords held together as one, arrange the cords directly under the last row of Square Knots. Tie Horizontal Clove Hitch Knots over the cord.

**Finishing:** Trim cord ends to 2 inches. Sew to wrong side of the tote bag. Fold the bag, weave the sides together.

**Strap:** Cut 2 three-yard red cords and 2 six-yard red cords. Fold all cords in half — 8 cords. Using the 6-yard cords as tying cords, tie Square Knots over the 4 center cords for 28 inches. Sew strap in place as shown in photograph.

**Lining:** Cut fabric for lining. Sew sides, stitch in place around the top of the bag.

## GREEN RATTAIL BELT

**SIZE:** About 26 inches, plus ties.

**MATERIALS:** Medium-weight rattail cord, light green, 81 yards. 122 green plastic beads, about $1/4$ inch in diameter.

**Note:** Slightly larger or smaller beads will work if two cords can pass easily through the hole. Metal ring, 1½ inches in diameter.

Cut 10 four-yard cords. Lay remainder of cord aside for the second half of the belt.

**Step 1:** Fold the 10 cords in half and tie to the ring with Lark's Head Knots — 20 cords.

**Step 2:** Beginning at outside edges, tie Clove Hitch Knots to the center curving the row of knots to form around the ring.

**Step 3:** Repeat Step 2 one time more.

**Step 4:** Divide cords into 5 groups of 4 cords per group. Work outside edge and center groups of cords as follows: * String one bead on the 2 center cords, tie one Square Knot. Repeat from * until you have 3 beads and 3 Square Knots for each group.

**Step 5:** On the 2 remaining groups of cords tie 6 Square Knots per group.

**Step 6:** Beginning at the outside edges, tie Diagonal Clove Hitch Knots to the center.

**Step 7:** Repeat Step 6 one time more.

**Step 8:** On the 6 outside cords at each edge work as follows: With the first 4 cords tie one Square Knot; then, leaving 2 outside cords unworked, tie another Square Knot.

**Step 9:** Repeat Step 8 four times more.

**Step 10:** With the center 8 cords, between the Square Knot pattern formed in Steps 8 and 9, work as follows: Divide cords into 2 groups of 4 cords per group. ** On the 2 center cords of each group string one bead in place and tie a Square Knot directly below. Repeat from ** one time more. On the four center cords tie one Square Knot. Repeat from * one time more.

**Step 11:** Repeat Steps 6 and 7.

**Step 12:** Repeat Steps 4 and 5.

**Step 13:** Repeat Steps 6 and 7.

**Step 14:** With the 4 outside cords at each edge, tie one Square Knot.

**Step 15:** Leaving 2 cords on each edge unworked, tie a Square Knot with the next 4 cords.

**Step 16:** On each of the next two 4 cord groups, tie a Square Knot.

**Step 17:** Leaving 2 cords on each edge unworked, tie one Square Knot on each of the next two groups of 4 cords.

**Step 18:** Repeat Step 16.

**Step 19:** Repeat Step 15.

**Step 20:** Repeat Step 14.

**Step 21:** Beginning at the center, tie Diagonal Clove Hitch Knots to the outside edges.

**Step 22:** Repeat Step 21.

**Step 23:** On the 4 center cords work as follows: * String one bead on the 2 center cords, tie a Square Knot below the bead. Repeat from * 3 times more.

**Step 24:** With 4 cords at each side of the knots of Step 23, work as follows: * String one bead on the 2 center cords, tie a Square Knot below the bead. Repeat from * one time more.

**Step 25:** Repeat Steps 6 and 7.

**Step 26:** Repeat Steps 14 through 22.

**Step 27:** On the 4 center cords work as follows: * String one bead on the 2 center cords, tie 4 Square Knots below. Repeat from * one time more. String one bead on the 2 center cords, tie one more Square Knot.

**Step 28:** On the 4 cords at each side of Step 27, work as follows: Tie one Square Knot, string one bead in place; then, tie 2 Square Knots, string another bead in place, tie one Square Knot.

**Step 29:** Repeat Steps 6 and 7.

**Step 30:** Turn the belt around to the other side of the ring. Cut the cords as before, begin with Step 1, and tie the second half of the belt the same as the first.

**Finishing:** Trim cords to long random lengths. String one bead on each cord end, tie an Overhand Knot to hold the bead in place.

## RED, BLACK AND ORANGE WALL HANGING

**SIZE:** About 22 inches long, plus fringe.

**MATERIALS:** Lily Soft Sheen Craft Yarn, #20 orange, #95 red and #2 black; one 105-yard skein each. Two dowels, 11 inches and 12 inches. Stain for dowels, if desired.

**Note:** Entire hanging is worked in Horizontal and Diagonal Clove Hitch Knots.

Cut 10 red cords, 8 orange cords and 5 black cords each 6 yards long. Lay extra yarn aside to cut additional cords later. Fold cords in half and tie Lark's Head Knots over 11 inch dowel in the following order: 2 red, 1 black, 4 orange, 3 red, 2 black, 3 red, 4 orange, 1 black, 2 red — 44 cords.

*Step 1:* Center the extra black cord across the top of the hanging, directly under the Lark's Head Knots. Using the black cord as a holding line, tie Horizontal Clove Hitch Knots across the entire hanging — 44 cords. You now have one black cord at each edge.

*Step 2:* Divide the cords at the center into two groups of 23 cords each. Beginning at the center, tie Diagonal Clove Hitch Knots to the outside edges.

*Step 3:* Repeat Step 2 two times more. You will now have 3 black cords at each outside edge.

*Step 4:* Beginning at the center, tie Diagonal Clove Hitch Knots working toward outside edges over the next 5 cords (red cords only).

*Step 5:* Repeat Step 4 four times more.

*Step 6:* Beginning at the center, tie Diagonal Clove Hitch Knots to the outside edges.

*Step 7:* Repeat Step 6 five times more. Six red cords are now at each outside edge.

*Step 8:* Count over 10 cords from the center on each side. Beginning with the eleventh cord (inside red cord) tie Diagonal Clove Hitch Knots to each outside edge.

*Step 9:* Repeat Step 8 until all red cords are at the outside edges.

*Step 10:* Count over 8 cords from the center. With the ninth cord (inside black cord) at each edge work Diagonal Clove Hitch Knots to the center.

*Step 11:* Repeat Step 10 once more.

*Step 12:* Leaving cords unworked for about ³/₄ inch below Step 11, repeat Step 10 three times more. All black cords are now at the center.

*Step 13:* Count over 10 cords from each outside edge. Beginning with the eleventh cord (outside orange cord) tie Diagonal Clove Hitch Knots to the outside edges.

*Step 14:* Repeat Step 13 seven times more. You now have 8 orange cords at each outside edge.

*Step 15:* Place 12-inch dowel across hanging. Using the dowel as a holding line, tie Horizontal Clove Hitch Knots across.

*Step 16:* Cut 8 more red cords and 4 more black cords, each 4 yards long. Fold the cords in half. With Lark's Head Knots add new cords to the second dowel as follows: 4 red each edge; then, 2 black each edge — 70 cords across.

*Step 17:* Divide the cords at the center into two equal groups of 35 cords each. Beginning at the center, tie Diagonal Clove Hitch Knots to the outside edges. Tie a Chevron Clove Hitch Knot at the center.

*Step 18:* Repeat Step 17 four times more. All black cords are now at the outside edges.

*Step 19:* Count over 16 cords from each outside edge. With the seventeenth cord, moving toward the center, tie Diagonal Clove Hitch Knots over the next 8 cords.

*Step 20:* Count over 15 cords from each outside edge. With sixteenth cord, moving toward center, tie Diagonal Clove Hitch Knots over the next 9 cords.

*Step 21:* Count over 14 cords from each outside edge. With the fifteenth cord, moving toward the center, tie Diagonal Clove Hitch Knots over the next 10 cords.

*Step 22:* Continue tying Diagonal Clove Hitch Knots as in Steps 19, 20 and 21 until all red cords are in the center.

*Step 23:* Count over 18 cords from each outside edge. With the nineteenth cord tie Diagonal Clove Hitch Knots to the center. (On this step you will be working with red cords only.) Tie a Chevron Clove Hitch Knot at the center.

*Step 24:* Repeat Step 23 two times more.

*Step 25:* Count over 9 cords from each outside edge. With the tenth cord, tie Diagonal Clove Hitch Knots to the outside edge.

*Step 26:* Count over 10 cords from each outside edge. With the eleventh cord tie Diagonal Clove Hitch Knots to the outside edges.

*Step 27:* Counting over one more cord each row, continue with Steps 25 and 26 until all orange cords are at the outside edges.

*Step 28:* Tie an Overhand Knot with each group of orange cords.

*Step 29:* Excluding orange cords at the edges, count over 9 cords. With the tenth cord, tie Diagonal Clove Hitch Knots to the outside edges. Note: The knots of Step 29 will be about ¹/₄ inch below the last row of black Diagonal Clove Hitch Knots.

*Step 30:* Continue with Step 29 until all black cords are at the center.

**Finishing:** Tie an Overhand Knot with each group of red cords and each group of black cords. Trim the orange and red cords to about 9 inches below the Overhand Knot. Trim black cords to about 14 inches below the Overhand Knot.